Parenting With OCPD

The Complete Guide to Raising Kids Without
Passing on Perfectionism

Willard Mario Nixon

Table of Contents

Chapter 1: Recognizing OCPD in yourself and your parenting

You know that feeling when you watch your child struggle with something, and every fiber of your being wants to jump in and fix it? When their messy room makes your skin crawl? When you find yourself correcting their homework even though they got the answer right, just because their handwriting isn't neat enough?

If you're nodding along, you might be dealing with something deeper than typical parental concern. You might be looking at Obsessive-Compulsive Personality Disorder (OCPD) - and how it shows up in your daily life as a parent.

Here's what's important to understand right away: OCPD isn't about being a caring, involved parent. It's about control becoming so central to your parenting that it actually gets in the way of connecting with your kids. And the tricky part? It often comes from a place of genuine love and wanting the best for your children.

The perfectionist parent profile

DSM-5-TR diagnostic criteria translated into everyday parenting behaviors

Let's start with the clinical picture, but in language that makes sense for real life. According to the DSM-5-TR, OCPD involves a pattern of preoccupation with orderliness, perfectionism, and mental and interpersonal control (American Psychiatric Association, 2022). That sounds pretty dry, but when you translate it into parenting behaviors, it becomes much more recognizable.

Preoccupation with details, lists, rules, and organization might look like spending thirty minutes making your child's lunch because the sandwich has to be cut just right, or creating elaborate chore charts that are more complex than your work spreadsheets. Maybe you find yourself remaking your teenager's bed because they didn't get the corners tight enough.

Perfectionism that interferes with task completion shows up when you redo your child's school project because their work isn't "good enough," or when you spend hours helping with homework that should take twenty minutes. You want everything to be perfect, but ironically, this often means nothing gets finished on time.

Being excessively devoted to work and productivity might mean you schedule your family's free time, turning even fun activities into structured learning opportunities. Family game night becomes a lesson in strategy and following rules exactly.

Being inflexible about matters of morality and values could look like having very rigid ideas about how children should behave, with little room for age-appropriate mistakes or different personality types. There's a "right way" to do everything, and deviation from that way feels morally wrong to you.

Reluctance to delegate shows up when you can't let other people (including your partner or the children themselves) handle tasks because "they won't do it right." You end up doing everything yourself and then feeling resentful about the workload.

Research from the National Institute of Mental Health suggests that OCPD affects approximately 2.4% of adults, but the impact on families is much broader (Grant et al., 2008). When you're parenting with OCPD traits, everyone in the household feels the effects.

How OCPD differs from OCD and why this matters for families

This distinction is crucial, and it's one of the most misunderstood aspects of OCPD. Obsessive-Compulsive Disorder (OCD) involves unwanted, intrusive thoughts (obsessions) and repetitive behaviors (compulsions) that feel distressing to the person experiencing them (Pinto et al., 2022). People with OCD typically know their thoughts and behaviors don't make sense, but they feel compelled to do them anyway to reduce anxiety.

OCPD is different. The perfectionist thoughts and controlling behaviors don't feel unwanted or distressing - they feel *right*. They feel like the only sensible way to live. This is called being *ego-syntonic* - the symptoms align with your sense of self and values.

Why does this matter for families? Because when you have OCD traits, you might say to your child, "I know this seems silly, but I need to check the door locks three times." You recognize it as a quirk or problem. But with OCPD traits, you're more likely to say, "Why can't you put your backpack in the designated spot? That's where it belongs." You genuinely believe your way is the right way, and you expect others to follow it.

This creates a fundamentally different family dynamic. Children of parents with OCD often learn to accommodate their parent's anxiety with understanding and compassion. Children of parents with OCPD often feel like they can never measure up to impossible standards, because the parent truly believes those standards are reasonable and necessary.

Dr. Anthony Pinto and colleagues found that OCPD significantly impacts interpersonal functioning, particularly in close relationships like marriage and parenting (Pinto et al., 2022). The rigidity that might serve someone well in certain work environments can become a source of chronic stress in family life.

Self-assessment: identifying your OCPD traits and triggers

Before we go further, let's get honest about what OCPD looks like in your daily parenting. This isn't about shame or blame - it's about awareness. You can't change what you don't recognize.

Morning routine reality check: How do mornings go in your house? If your child's routine gets disrupted - they can't find their favorite shirt, or they want to eat cereal instead of the breakfast you planned - what happens inside you? Do you feel that familiar spike of anxiety, that sense that the whole day is now "ruined"? Do you find yourself snapping at them for "being difficult" when they're just being kids?

Homework and school projects: When your child has an assignment, who really does the work? Are you "helping" in ways that mean you're essentially completing the project yourself? Do you feel physically uncomfortable when they turn in work that you know could be "better"? Do you find yourself staying up late fixing their projects after they've gone to bed?

Social situations and playdates: How do you handle the chaos that comes with kids being kids? When your house gets messy during a playdate, or when children don't follow the rules exactly as you've explained them, what happens to your stress level? Do you find yourself constantly redirecting and correcting instead of letting kids just play?

Emotional expression: This one's big. When your children express big emotions - anger, sadness, frustration - how comfortable are you just letting them feel those feelings? Do you immediately jump into problem-solving mode or try to get them to "calm down" quickly? Do you struggle with your own emotional expression, finding anger easier to access than vulnerability?

Here's a key trigger pattern to watch for: **When something doesn't go according to your plan or expectations, how intense is your internal response?** OCPD traits often show up as a disproportionate stress response to minor deviations from what you think should happen.

Case study: Sarah's morning routine meltdowns

Sarah is a single mom with two kids, ages 7 and 10. She works full-time and prides herself on being organized and prepared. But mornings in her house had become a battlefield, and she couldn't understand why her children were so "difficult."

Here's what a typical morning looked like: Sarah would wake up at 5:30 AM to prepare everything perfectly. Clothes laid out just so, breakfast planned and partially prepared, backpacks organized with everything in the right compartments. She had a detailed timeline - kids needed to be up by 6:45, dressed by 7:00, eating breakfast by 7:15, teeth brushed and ready to go by 7:45.

But kids, being kids, rarely followed the timeline perfectly. Maybe Emma couldn't find her favorite hair tie and wanted to wear her hair differently. Maybe Jake decided he wasn't hungry for the breakfast Sarah had prepared. Maybe someone spilled juice on their carefully selected outfit.

Each deviation from the plan sent Sarah into a spiral of stress and frustration. She'd find herself yelling about things that, deep down, she knew weren't that important. "Why can't you just put on the clothes I picked out? We don't have time for this! You're making us late!"

The kids started dreading mornings. Emma developed stomachaches before school. Jake began having meltdowns that seemed to come out of nowhere. Sarah felt like a terrible mother, but she also felt like she was the only one who cared about getting things done properly.

The turning point came when Emma, in tears after a particularly difficult morning, said, "Mommy, why are you always mad at us? We're trying to be good." Sarah realized that her need for control was hurting the people she loved most.

Sarah's story illustrates something crucial: OCPD traits in parenting often masquerade as being responsible, organized, and caring. Sarah genuinely believed she was helping her children by having everything perfectly planned. She couldn't see that her inflexibility was creating more stress than it was preventing.

When control becomes overcontrol

The line between healthy structure and harmful overcontrol isn't always obvious. All children need routines, boundaries, and guidance. The difference lies in the rigidity and the emotional intensity behind your need for control.

The eight faces of OCPD in parenting: from rigidity to emotional withholding

OCPD shows up differently in different parents, but research has identified several common patterns. Understanding these patterns can help you recognize where your own tendencies might be creating problems.

1. The Micromanager: Every detail of your child's life needs to be supervised and corrected. You find yourself hovering over homework, redoing chores they've already completed, and giving step-by-step instructions for tasks they could figure out themselves. You genuinely believe you're being helpful, but you're actually preventing your children from developing independence and confidence.

2. The Rule Enforcer: Rules exist for good reasons, and exceptions feel dangerous or wrong. If bedtime is 8:00 PM, then it's 8:00 PM every single night, regardless of circumstances. You might find yourself enforcing rules even when they don't make sense in the moment, because flexibility feels like chaos.

3. The Performance Monitor: Your child's achievements feel like a reflection of your worth as a parent. You find yourself more invested in their grades, sports performance, or social success than they are. You might coach from the sidelines, critique their efforts, or feel genuinely distressed when they don't live up to their potential.

4. The Efficiency Expert: Everything should be done the most efficient, logical way. You get frustrated when your children take longer routes, try things in different orders, or want to do something just for fun rather than productivity. Play time needs to have educational value. Messes need to be cleaned up immediately.

5. The Moral Authority: You have strong ideas about right and wrong, and you expect your children to share those values completely. Grey areas make you uncomfortable. You might find yourself lecturing about character and values in situations where empathy and understanding would be more helpful.

6. The Emotional Regulator: Big emotions - both your children's and your own - feel threatening or unacceptable. You might find yourself saying things like "calm down" or "don't be dramatic" when your children express strong feelings. You pride yourself on being rational and might see emotional expression as weakness or manipulation.

7. The Time Manager: Schedules are sacred. You plan family time, structure free time, and feel anxious when things run over or get off track. Spontaneity feels irresponsible. You might find yourself rushing your children through experiences because you're worried about staying on schedule.

8. The Quality Controller: "Good enough" isn't good enough. Whether it's school projects, room cleanliness, or thank-you notes, you find yourself redoing things to meet your standards. You might stay up late "fixing" things your children have done, or insist they redo tasks until they meet your expectations.

Here's what's important to understand: these behaviors often come from genuine love and care. You want your children to succeed, to be responsible, to develop good character. The problem isn't your intentions - it's that the intensity and rigidity of these approaches often backfire.

Research from the International OCPD Foundation shows that children of parents with strong OCPD traits often struggle with anxiety, perfectionism, and difficulty making decisions independently (IOCPDF, 2023). They may become either rebellious against all structure or overly compliant and anxious about making mistakes.

How perfectionism manifests differently with infants, children, and teens

Your OCPD traits don't show up the same way at every stage of your child's development. Understanding how perfectionism adapts to different ages can help you recognize patterns you might not have noticed.

With infants and toddlers: You might find yourself obsessing over feeding schedules, sleep routines, and developmental milestones. Every crying episode needs to be solved immediately. You might keep detailed logs of everything - feeding times, diaper changes, sleep patterns - and feel anxious when things don't go according to plan.

You might also struggle with the natural chaos that comes with small children. Toddlers are supposed to be messy, impulsive, and unpredictable, but this feels intolerable to you. You might find yourself constantly cleaning up after them, preventing normal exploratory behavior, or feeling genuinely distressed by the disorder they create.

With school-age children: This is often when OCPD traits in parenting become most obvious. There are concrete things to measure - grades, behavior reports, extracurricular performance. You might find yourself heavily involved in homework, school projects, and organizational systems.

You might create elaborate reward and consequence systems, trying to motivate your children to meet your standards. You probably have strong opinions about their friendships, their teachers, and their activities. You want them to develop good habits, but you're doing most of the work of maintaining those habits yourself.

With teenagers: This is typically the most challenging stage for parents with OCPD traits. Teenagers are supposed to be developing independence, questioning authority, and making some mistakes as they figure out who they are. Everything about normal adolescent development can trigger your need for control.

You might find yourself in constant battles about curfews, room cleanliness, academic effort, or future planning. Your teenager's natural push for autonomy feels like rejection or disrespect. You might have elaborate plans for their college and career path that they're not interested in following.

The tragedy is that your intense involvement often pushes your children away during the very stage when they most need your emotional support and guidance.

The paradox of loving too much through controlling too much

Here's the heartbreaking irony of OCPD in parenting: the more you love your children, the more you want to protect them from failure, disappointment, and mistakes. But your efforts to control their experiences often prevent them from developing the very skills they need to handle life's challenges.

When you constantly monitor and correct their homework, they don't learn to be responsible for their own academic success. When you solve all their social problems, they don't develop conflict resolution skills. When you prevent them from experiencing natural consequences, they don't learn to make better choices.

Dr. Madeline Levine's research on overparenting shows that children who are heavily managed and controlled often struggle with anxiety, depression, and poor self-regulation in young adulthood (Levine, 2012). They may perform well in structured environments but fall apart when they have to navigate independence.

The love is real. The concern is genuine. But the method - trying to control outcomes through micromanagement - creates the very problems you're trying to prevent.

Exercise: Mapping your control patterns throughout the day

Take a moment to honestly assess where control shows up in your parenting. For the next three days, keep a simple log. You don't need to write essays - just quick notes about moments when you felt that familiar spike of stress or frustration with your children.

Morning observations: What specific behaviors or situations trigger your control responses? Is it when routines get disrupted? When things take longer than expected? When children express preferences different from your plans?

During homework/activities: Notice when you step in to "help." Are you genuinely helping them learn, or are you taking over to make sure things are done correctly? How comfortable are you with their work being imperfect?

Evening and bedtime: How rigid are your routines? What happens when children resist or want to do things differently? How do you handle the transition from day to night?

Weekend and free time: This is often when control patterns become most obvious. How structured is your family's free time? How comfortable are you with boredom, mess, or unproductive activities?

Look for patterns. Are there certain times of day, certain types of activities, or certain behaviors from your children that consistently trigger your need to control?

Also notice your internal experience. What does it feel like in your body when things aren't going according to your expectations? Do you feel anxious, angry, frustrated, or physically uncomfortable? Understanding your internal signals can help you recognize when you're moving from healthy parenting into overcontrol.

The cost of perfection on family dynamics

The effects of perfectionist parenting ripple out through the entire family system. Understanding these impacts isn't meant to create guilt - it's meant to provide motivation for change and help you understand what your children might be experiencing.

Impact on children's emotional and social development

Children who grow up with perfectionist parents often develop what researchers call "maladaptive perfectionism" - a pattern of setting impossibly high standards for themselves and feeling devastated when they fall short (Choosingtherapy.com, 2023). This isn't the healthy desire to do well; it's a paralyzing fear of not being good enough.

Academic and performance anxiety: When your love and approval seem conditional on performance, children learn that their worth is tied to their achievements. They might become high achievers, but at the cost of chronic anxiety and fear of failure. They might also become underachievers, giving up entirely rather than risk not meeting expectations.

Difficulty with emotional regulation: Children need to learn that all emotions are acceptable, even if all behaviors aren't. When parents consistently shut down or redirect strong emotions, children don't learn how to process and cope with feelings like anger, sadness, or frustration. They might become emotionally shut down or prone to explosive outbursts.

Problems with independence and decision-making: When parents make most decisions for their children in the name of ensuring good outcomes, children don't develop confidence in their own judgment. They might become overly dependent on others for guidance, or they might rebel completely against any structure or authority.

Social difficulties: Children who are heavily managed at home often struggle in peer relationships. They might have trouble with the give-and-take of friendship, be inflexible in group situations, or struggle with situations that don't have clear rules and expectations.

Research from the Choose Therapy organization shows that children of parents with OCPD traits are at higher risk for developing anxiety disorders, depression, and their own perfectionist patterns (Choosingtherapy.com, 2023). They may also struggle with self-esteem and have difficulty forming secure relationships in adulthood.

Effects on partner relationships and co-parenting

OCPD traits don't just affect your relationship with your children - they also create significant stress in partnerships and co-parenting relationships. Your need for control and your certainty that your way is the right way can leave partners feeling criticized, undermined, or shut out of parenting decisions.

Constant criticism and correction: If you find yourself frequently correcting your partner's parenting choices, suggesting better ways to handle situations, or redoing things they've done with the children, you're probably creating resentment and distance. Your partner may start withdrawing from parenting activities to avoid your feedback.

Difficulty with compromise: Healthy co-parenting requires flexibility and the ability to discuss different approaches. When you're convinced that your way is objectively better, compromise feels like accepting a worse outcome for your children. This can lead to ongoing conflicts and power struggles.

Emotional disconnection: If you tend to focus on tasks, schedules, and performance rather than emotions and relationships, your partner might feel like you're more interested in running an efficient household than in connecting as a family. This can create loneliness and distance in your relationship.

Division of labor issues: Your reluctance to delegate, combined with your high standards, often means you take on more than your share of household and childcare tasks. This can lead to burnout and resentment, even though you're the one insisting on doing everything yourself.

Many partnerships struggle under the weight of one partner's perfectionist expectations. The non-OCPD partner may feel like they can never do anything right, while the OCPD partner feels like they're carrying all the responsibility for the family's well-being.

Sibling dynamics in OCPD households

When one or both parents have OCPD traits, it creates unique challenges for sibling relationships. Children in these families often develop different coping strategies, which can create tension and competition between them.

The "perfect" child and the "problem" child: Often, one child will try to meet all of the parents' expectations, becoming the "good" kid who follows rules and performs well. Another child might rebel against the rigid expectations, becoming the "difficult" one who gets in trouble frequently. Both children are struggling with the same underlying issue - the pressure to be perfect - but they're handling it in opposite ways.

Competition for approval: When love and attention seem conditional on performance, siblings often compete with each other rather than supporting each other. They might tattle, try to make each other look bad, or feel threatened by each other's successes.

Different treatment based on compliance: Parents with OCPD traits often favor the child who is more compliant and less challenging. This creates resentment and can damage sibling relationships for years to come. The favored child might feel guilty about their position, while the less favored child might feel rejected and angry.

Parentification: Sometimes the "perfect" child takes on adult responsibilities, trying to help manage the household or even taking care of younger siblings. This robs them of their childhood and places them in an inappropriate role within the family system.

Personal narrative: A child's perspective on growing up with an OCPD parent

The following is a composite narrative based on common experiences shared by adult children of parents with OCPD traits. While this represents a real pattern, individual experiences vary widely.

"I learned very early that there was a right way to do everything, and it was my job to figure out what that way was. My mom wasn't mean or abusive - she was actually very loving in her own way. But her love always came with conditions and corrections.

I remember being six years old and trying to help her make dinner. She'd given me the job of setting the table, and I was proud to be helping. But when I put the forks on the right side of the plates instead of the left, she sighed and redid the whole table. 'This is how we set a proper table,' she said, not unkindly, but firmly. The message was clear: my way was wrong.

School projects were torture. I'd work really hard on something, and then my mom would 'help' me make it better. Her help usually meant completely redoing whatever I'd done. I started to feel like nothing I did was ever good enough on its own. I'd get good grades, but they never felt like my accomplishments because she'd been so involved in the process.

The hardest part was never knowing when I was going to disappoint her. She'd be fine with something one day and upset about it the next, depending on her stress level or what else was going on. I became hypervigilant, constantly scanning for signs that I was doing something wrong.

By high school, I was exhausted. I was getting good grades and staying out of trouble, but I felt empty inside. I didn't know who I was apart from what my mother wanted me to be. When I went to college, I fell apart. Without her constant structure and direction, I had no idea how to make decisions or take care of myself.

It took me years of therapy to understand that my mother's perfectionism was about her anxiety and need for control, not about my inadequacies. She genuinely thought she was helping me become successful and responsible. But what I actually learned was that I couldn't trust my own judgment and that love was something you had to earn through performance.

I love my mother, and I know she loves me. But I wish she had been able to love me imperfectly, to let me make mistakes and figure things out on my own. I wish she had valued connection over correction."

This narrative illustrates the long-term impact that perfectionist parenting can have on children's sense of self, their ability to form relationships, and their confidence in their own capabilities.

Chapter 2: The science of intergenerational transmission

The question that haunts many parents with OCPD traits is this: "Am I going to mess up my kids the way I was messed up?" It's a painful question because it cuts to the heart of your deepest fear - that despite your best intentions, you might be recreating the same patterns that caused you pain in your own childhood.

Here's what the research tells us: yes, OCPD traits can be passed from parents to children. But - and this is crucial - it's not inevitable. Understanding how this transmission happens gives you power to interrupt the cycle.

The science of intergenerational transmission shows us that perfectionism travels through families via multiple pathways. Some are genetic, some are environmental, and some are about the complex dance of relationships and attachment. The good news is that awareness and intentional change can break these patterns, even if you've been parenting with OCPD traits for years.

Nature and nurture: How OCPD travels through families

The 27-78% heritability factor: what genetics really means

Let's start with the numbers, because they're both sobering and hopeful. Twin studies and family research suggest that OCPD has a heritability factor somewhere between 27% and 78%, depending on which specific traits researchers are measuring (Van Grootheest et al. 2007). That sounds like a huge range, but it reflects the complexity of how personality disorders develop.

Here's what these numbers actually mean in real life: if you have significant OCPD traits, your children have a higher likelihood of developing similar patterns than children whose parents don't have these traits. But genetics isn't destiny. Even with the highest heritability estimates, environmental factors still account for at least 22% of the variance - and that's where your parenting choices matter enormously.

Think about it this way: genetics might give your child a temperamental tendency toward rigidity, anxiety about disorder, or sensitivity to criticism. But whether those tendencies develop into problematic patterns depends largely on their environment - specifically, how you respond to and shape those tendencies.

Dr. Svenn Torgersen's research on personality disorders in Norwegian twins found that genetic factors create vulnerabilities, but environmental factors determine whether those vulnerabilities become disorders (Torgersen et al., 2008). This is actually encouraging news for parents, because it means your awareness and effort to change your parenting patterns can make a real difference in your children's outcomes.

Some children seem to inherit what researchers call "behavioral inhibition" - a tendency to be cautious, to prefer routine, and to feel anxious in new or chaotic situations. If you parent this child with rigid control and high expectations, you might amplify their natural tendencies into problematic perfectionism. But if you parent them with warm structure and flexibility, you can help them channel their natural tendencies into positive traits like reliability and thoughtfulness.

Environmental transmission through modeling and expectations

While genetics loads the gun, environment pulls the trigger. The way perfectionism gets passed from parent to child through daily interactions is both subtle and powerful. Children are constantly learning not just from what you tell them, but from what you model, what you pay attention to, and what seems to matter to you.

Modeling perfectionist behaviors: Your children watch how you handle mistakes, how you respond to disorder, how you approach

16

tasks, and how you treat yourself when things don't go according to plan. If they see you staying up late to perfect a work presentation, criticizing yourself for small errors, or redoing household tasks because they weren't done "right" the first time, they're learning that this is how responsible adults behave.

Research by Hewitt and Flett shows that children often internalize their parents' perfectionist standards without any direct instruction (Hewitt & Flett, 1991). They simply absorb the message that excellence is expected and anything less is disappointing.

Conditional approval and social expectations: This is perhaps the most damaging pathway. When children learn that love, attention, and approval are tied to performance, they develop what psychologists call "contingent self-worth." Their value as people becomes dependent on meeting external standards.

This doesn't mean you consciously withhold love from your children when they struggle. It might be as subtle as showing more enthusiasm for their successes than empathy for their struggles, or giving more attention to their achievements than to their emotional needs. Children are incredibly attuned to what gets their parents' positive attention, and they'll shape themselves accordingly.

A meta-analysis by Curran and Hill found that socially prescribed perfectionism - the belief that others expect perfection from you - has increased significantly over the past 30 years (Curran & Hill, 2019). This cultural shift affects all families, but it hits hardest in households where parents already have perfectionist tendencies.

Information transfer and explicit teaching: Sometimes perfectionist patterns are passed down through direct instruction. You might find yourself teaching your children elaborate organizational systems, giving detailed instructions for tasks they could figure out themselves, or explicitly teaching them that "there's a right way to do everything."

You might also pass on perfectionist thinking patterns through the way you talk about problems, setbacks, and other people. Comments like "I can't believe she turned that project in looking like that" or "If you're going to do something, you might as well do it right" teach children that your approval depends on meeting high standards.

The role of attachment in passing on perfectionist patterns

Attachment theory gives us crucial insights into how perfectionism travels through families. The quality of the emotional bond between parent and child shapes not just their relationship, but the child's entire approach to relationships and self-worth.

Research from Frontiers in Psychology shows that children who develop secure attachment relationships - characterized by consistent emotional availability, responsiveness to their needs, and comfort with their full range of emotions - are significantly less likely to develop problematic perfectionism, even if they have genetic vulnerabilities (Rodgers et al., 2013).

But here's where OCPD traits can interfere with secure attachment: when you're focused on performance, behavior, and outcomes, you might miss opportunities for emotional connection. Your children might learn that they get your attention and approval when they're achieving or complying, but not when they're struggling, making mistakes, or just needing comfort.

Anxious attachment and perfectionism: Children who develop anxious attachment often become what researchers call "adaptive perfectionists" - they work extremely hard to please others and avoid abandonment, but they never feel secure in their relationships. They might excel in school and activities but struggle with anxiety and self-criticism.

Avoidant attachment and perfectionism: Some children respond to perfectionist parenting by becoming emotionally distant and self-reliant. They might develop what looks like independence but is actually a protective strategy to avoid disappointment and criticism.

They may become high achievers but struggle with intimacy and emotional expression.

The most hopeful finding from attachment research is that attachment patterns can change. Even if you've been parenting in ways that create insecure attachment, you can repair and strengthen your bond with your children at any stage of their development.

Research spotlight: Norwegian Twin Study findings

The Norwegian Twin Study, led by Dr. Svenn Torgersen, provides some of the most comprehensive data we have about how personality traits are transmitted through families. This study followed twins over multiple decades, allowing researchers to separate genetic influences from environmental ones in ways that smaller studies can't.

Key findings relevant to OCPD transmission include:

Genetic factors account for approximately 60% of perfectionist traits, but this varies significantly based on which specific aspects of perfectionism researchers measure (Torgersen et al., 2008). Some traits, like orderliness and attention to detail, show higher heritability, while others, like emotional expression and flexibility, are more influenced by environment.

Environmental factors have the strongest influence during critical periods of development, particularly early childhood (ages 2-6) and adolescence (ages 12-18). This suggests that changing your parenting patterns can have maximum impact during these developmental windows.

The presence of one secure, flexible caregiver serves as a protective factor, even when the other parent has significant OCPD traits. Children who have at least one parent who provides emotional warmth and flexibility are significantly less likely to develop problematic perfectionism.

Trauma and significant stress can activate genetic vulnerabilities for perfectionism and other personality disorders. Children with genetic predispositions who experience high stress, family conflict, or traumatic events are more likely to develop OCPD traits.

These findings suggest that while you can't change your child's genetic makeup, you have enormous influence over the environmental factors that determine whether genetic vulnerabilities become actual problems.

Four pathways of perfectionist transmission

Understanding the specific ways that perfectionism travels from parent to child can help you identify where you might be inadvertently passing on patterns you'd rather interrupt.

Direct modeling: when children mirror what they see

Children are natural mimics, especially of their parents. They absorb not just your obvious behaviors, but your emotional reactions, your problem-solving approaches, and your relationship with yourself and others.

How you handle your own mistakes becomes a template for how your children will handle theirs. If you catastrophize errors, criticize yourself harshly, or try to hide or fix everything before anyone notices, your children learn that mistakes are shameful and must be avoided at all costs.

Sarah, whom we met in Chapter 1, realized she was modeling perfectionist stress when her 7-year-old daughter started having meltdowns over minor mistakes in her artwork. Emma would crumple up drawings and declare them "stupid," using the same frustrated tone Sarah used when something went wrong in the kitchen.

Your relationship with time and productivity also gets modeled. If you're constantly rushing, scheduling every moment, or expressing frustration when things take longer than expected, your children learn that time is scarce and productivity is paramount. They might develop anxiety about "wasting time" or struggle to enjoy unstructured activities.

The way you talk about other people teaches your children your standards and values. Comments about other people's houses, appearances, parenting choices, or performance communicate what you consider acceptable and unacceptable. Children internalize these standards and apply them to themselves.

Research by Bandura on social learning theory shows that children are particularly likely to model behaviors that seem important to their parents and behaviors that get positive attention (Bandura, 2001). If perfectionist behaviors get your attention and approval, children will naturally gravitate toward them.

Social expectations: the pressure of conditional love

This pathway is often the most painful for parents to recognize because it challenges the fundamental belief that you love your children unconditionally. The reality is that most parents do love their children unconditionally, but children don't always experience that love as unconditional.

Performance-based attention: If your children get significantly more positive attention for achievements than for just being themselves, they learn that their worth is tied to performance. This doesn't mean you shouldn't celebrate their successes, but it does mean you need to balance achievement-focused attention with relationship-focused attention.

Criticism and correction patterns: The ratio of criticism to praise in your daily interactions shapes your child's sense of self-worth. Research suggests that children need at least 5 positive interactions for every negative one to maintain emotional well-being (Gottman, 2021). If your interactions are heavily focused on correction and improvement, children may feel like they're constantly disappointing you.

Emotional availability during struggles: How you respond when your children are having difficulties - struggling with homework, dealing with social problems, or going through emotional challenges

- teaches them whether they can count on your support during tough times. If you become anxious, critical, or controlling during these moments, children learn to hide their struggles to maintain your approval.

A study by Flett and colleagues found that children who perceive their parents' love as conditional on their performance are more likely to develop depression, anxiety, and perfectionist patterns that persist into adulthood (Flett et al., 2002).

Information transfer: explicit teaching of rigid standards

Sometimes perfectionist patterns are passed down through direct instruction and explicit teaching about "the right way" to do things. This pathway often feels the most justified to parents because you're genuinely trying to teach your children important skills and values.

Elaborate systems and detailed instructions: When you provide extremely detailed instructions for tasks your children could figure out themselves, you're teaching them that there's one correct way to do everything and that they can't be trusted to find good solutions on their own.

Corrections and improvements: The habit of automatically correcting and improving your children's work - even when it's adequate for their age and developmental stage - teaches them that their efforts are never quite good enough. They might stop trying to do things independently because they know you'll redo it anyway.

Teaching anxiety about imperfection: Comments like "Let's make sure this is perfect before we turn it in" or "What will people think if your room looks like this?" explicitly teach children that imperfection is dangerous and that others' opinions should drive their behavior.

Research shows that children who receive excessive instruction and correction often develop what psychologists call "learned helplessness" - they become dependent on external guidance and lose confidence in their own problem-solving abilities (Peterson et al., 2022).

Family system dynamics: how perfectionism shapes the entire household

The fourth pathway is about how perfectionist patterns create family cultures that reinforce and perpetuate themselves. Everyone in the family adapts to the perfectionist parent's needs and expectations, creating a system where perfectionism feels normal and necessary.

Family roles and dynamics: In perfectionist families, family members often take on rigid roles - the responsible one, the problem one, the peacekeeper, the achiever. These roles become part of each person's identity and are difficult to change even when they're no longer serving the family well.

Communication patterns: Perfectionist families often develop communication patterns that avoid conflict, focus on tasks rather than emotions, and prioritize problem-solving over understanding. Children learn to suppress their authentic thoughts and feelings to maintain family harmony.

Stress and crisis management: How your family handles stress, unexpected events, and crises becomes a template for how your children will handle difficulties throughout their lives. If your family's approach is to increase control and structure during stressful times, children learn that flexibility is dangerous and control is safety.

Fun and spontaneity: The way your family approaches leisure time, play, and spontaneous activities shapes your children's ability to enjoy life and tolerate uncertainty. If family fun is heavily structured or if there's always an underlying agenda (learning opportunities, skill development, character building), children might struggle to simply enjoy themselves.

Interactive assessment: Identifying your family's transmission patterns

Take some time to honestly assess which pathways might be active in your family. This isn't about shame or blame - it's about awareness and the possibility of change.

Modeling assessment: What do your children see you do when things don't go according to plan? How do you handle your own mistakes, stress, and imperfections? What messages about perfectionism do you model through your daily behaviors?

Social expectations review: What gets your positive attention in your family? What do you praise, celebrate, and focus on? How do you respond when your children struggle, fail, or make mistakes? Do they experience your love as conditional or unconditional?

Information transfer evaluation: What explicit messages do you give your children about standards, expectations, and the "right way" to do things? How much instruction and correction do you provide? Do you allow them to develop their own systems and solutions?

Family dynamics analysis: What roles have family members taken on? How does your family handle stress, conflict, and challenges? What is the emotional climate of your household? Is there room for imperfection, spontaneity, and authentic expression?

Understanding these patterns is the first step toward changing them. In the next section, we'll explore what can protect children from developing problematic perfectionism, even in families where these patterns are present.

Breaking the chain: Understanding protective factors

The most hopeful aspect of research on intergenerational transmission is the identification of factors that can protect children from developing problematic perfectionism, even when they have genetic vulnerabilities and even when they're exposed to perfectionist parenting patterns.

What prevents some children from developing OCPD traits

Not all children who grow up with perfectionist parents develop perfectionist patterns themselves. Researchers have identified several factors that seem to provide protection:

Temperamental resilience: Some children seem naturally more resilient to perfectionist pressures. They might be more emotionally expressive, more socially oriented, or more naturally flexible. These temperamental qualities can serve as a buffer against perfectionist family dynamics.

Early secure attachment: Children who develop secure attachment relationships in their first few years of life seem to have more resilience to later perfectionist pressures. Even if family dynamics become more controlling as children get older, that early foundation of security provides protection.

Exposure to alternative perspectives: Children who have regular contact with other adults who have different approaches - grandparents, teachers, coaches, family friends - get exposure to alternative ways of thinking and being. This exposure can help them realize that their family's standards aren't universal truths.

Natural areas of competence: Children who find areas where they feel naturally skilled and confident - whether in sports, arts, academics, or social situations - develop a sense of self-worth that's independent from their performance in other areas. This can provide protection against global perfectionist pressures.

Peer relationships: Strong friendships can provide children with experiences of unconditional acceptance and opportunities to see that they're valued for who they are, not just what they achieve.

The power of one flexible parent or caregiver

Perhaps the most powerful protective factor is the presence of at least one adult who provides warmth, acceptance, and flexibility. This doesn't have to be a parent - it could be a grandparent, teacher, coach, or family friend. But when it is one of the parents, the protection is particularly strong.

Research consistently shows that children can develop secure attachment and healthy self-esteem even when one parent has significant mental health challenges, as long as the other parent provides emotional stability and responsiveness (Masten, 2001).

If you're recognizing perfectionist patterns in your own parenting, but your partner has a different approach, this is actually excellent news for your children. Your partner's flexibility and emotional availability can serve as a buffer against your perfectionist tendencies.

If you're a single parent or if both you and your partner struggle with perfectionist patterns, you can still provide this protective factor by developing awareness and working to change your approach. Even imperfect change in the direction of greater flexibility and emotional availability can make a significant difference.

Building resilience through secure attachment

The good news about attachment is that it's never too late to strengthen your bond with your children. Even if you've been parenting in ways that create distance or anxiety, you can repair and rebuild your relationship.

Emotional availability over task focus: Start paying attention to your children's emotional needs, not just their behavioral compliance or academic performance. This means being present when they want to talk, showing interest in their inner world, and providing comfort when they're struggling.

Validation before correction: When your children make mistakes or struggle with something, try offering understanding and empathy before jumping into problem-solving or correction mode. "That sounds frustrating" or "I can see why you're upset" can be more helpful than immediately trying to fix the situation.

Unconditional positive regard: Find ways to express love and appreciation for your children that aren't tied to their performance or behavior. "I love spending time with you," "You have such a kind heart," or "I'm grateful you're my child" communicate unconditional love.

Repair and reconnection: When you handle a situation in a perfectionist way that creates distance or hurt, repair the relationship quickly. Apologize genuinely, acknowledge the impact of your behavior, and recommit to doing better. Children are remarkably forgiving when they feel heard and valued.

Research shows that parents who can acknowledge their mistakes and repair relationship ruptures actually strengthen their bond with their children and model important life skills like emotional regulation and accountability (Siegel & Hartzell, 2020).

Case study: Two siblings, different outcomes

Let me tell you about the Martinez family - Maria and Carlos, and their two sons, Diego and Alex. Maria had significant OCPD traits that showed up in highly structured household routines, detailed expectations for the boys' academic and social performance, and difficulty tolerating disorder or spontaneity.

Diego, the older son, seemed to absorb his mother's perfectionist patterns completely. By age 10, he was organizing his room obsessively, getting upset when his homework wasn't perfect, and becoming anxious when family plans changed. He was a high achiever but struggled with anxiety and had few close friendships.

Alex, two years younger, seemed largely unaffected by the same family dynamics. He was naturally more social and emotionally expressive. While he sometimes got in trouble for being messy or not following routines exactly, he didn't internalize his mother's anxiety about these things. He maintained close friendships, could laugh off mistakes, and seemed genuinely happy most of the time.

What made the difference? Several factors seemed to protect Alex:

Different temperament: Alex was naturally more extroverted and less sensitive to his mother's stress. Diego was more introverted and seemed to absorb the family's emotional climate more intensely.

Birth order effects: As the younger child, Alex had more opportunities to see his older brother navigate the family's expectations. He learned from watching Diego's struggles and seemed to develop strategies to avoid the same pitfalls.

Different relationship with father: Carlos was naturally more flexible and emotionally expressive than Maria. Diego seemed to model his mother's approach, while Alex connected more with his father's laid-back style.

Peer influences: Alex was involved in sports and had a large friend group from an early age. These relationships provided him with alternative perspectives and experiences of unconditional acceptance.

Natural areas of strength: Alex was a natural athlete and artist, areas where his mother's perfectionist concerns were less intense. This gave him domains where he could feel successful and confident without triggering family stress.

The most important insight from families like the Martinez's is that the same parenting approach can have very different effects on different children. This suggests that adaptation and flexibility in your parenting approach - responding to each child's unique needs and temperament - may be one of the most important skills you can develop.

What this means for you

Understanding the science of intergenerational transmission is both sobering and empowering. Yes, perfectionist patterns can be passed from parent to child through multiple pathways. But awareness of these pathways gives you the power to interrupt them.

The research clearly shows that change is possible at any stage of your children's development. Whether your children are toddlers or teenagers, your efforts to become more flexible, emotionally available, and accepting can make a real difference in their outcomes.

The goal isn't to become a perfect parent - that would be just another version of the same problem. The goal is to become a more aware, flexible, and emotionally connected parent. Your children don't need you to be perfect. They need you to be real, to be present, and to love them for who they are, not just for what they achieve.

In the next chapter, we'll explore practical strategies for developing the awareness needed to recognize and interrupt perfectionist patterns as they happen in daily life. Because understanding how perfectionism is transmitted is only the first step - the real work begins with learning to catch yourself in the moment and choose a different response.

What to remember from these insights

The science of intergenerational transmission teaches us several crucial lessons about perfectionism in families. First, genetics creates tendencies, not destinies - while children may inherit vulnerabilities to perfectionist thinking, environmental factors largely determine whether these tendencies become problematic patterns.

The four pathways of transmission - direct modeling, social expectations, information transfer, and family system dynamics - show us exactly where intervention can be most effective. When you change how you model mistake-making, provide unconditional love, reduce excessive instruction, and create more flexible family cultures, you disrupt the transmission process.

Most importantly, protective factors like secure attachment, alternative perspectives, and natural areas of competence can shield children from perfectionist pressures even in high-expectation families. This means that your efforts to become more emotionally available and flexible can provide genuine protection for your children's mental health and development.

The research offers genuine hope: change is possible at any stage, one flexible parent can make a tremendous difference, and awareness combined with intentional effort can break intergenerational cycles that may have persisted for generations.

Chapter 3: Developing mindful awareness of OCPD patterns

That moment when you catch yourself redoing your teenager's "sloppy" homework for the third time this week, or when you realize you've been lecturing your 8-year-old about proper sock-folding techniques for ten minutes - these are the moments when awareness begins. They're also the moments when you have the most power to change.

The tricky thing about OCPD patterns is that they feel so *right* in the moment. Your internal voice says, "Of course I should fix this essay - it's full of mistakes," or "Obviously the dishes need to be done properly." The urgency feels completely justified. But here's what you might not realize: that sense of urgency, that feeling that everything depends on getting this one thing right, is often your OCPD talking, not your wisdom.

Developing mindful awareness doesn't mean becoming a passive parent who doesn't care about standards or structure. It means learning to recognize when your need for control is driving your parenting decisions instead of your love for your children. It means creating space between the trigger and your response - space where you can choose how to act instead of just reacting automatically.

The good news? You don't need to meditate for hours or completely transform your personality. You just need to start noticing patterns and practicing small moments of pause. These tiny changes in awareness can create enormous shifts in your family dynamics.

The pause that changes everything

Recognizing triggers before they control you

Think about your last big parenting meltdown - you know, the one where you ended up yelling about something that wasn't really that important, or where you spent two hours "helping" with homework that should have taken twenty minutes. What happened right before you lost it?

Most OCPD parents can trace their reactive moments back to specific triggers. The problem is, by the time you're in full control mode, it's really hard to step back and choose a different response. The key is learning to recognize your triggers before they take over your nervous system.

Common OCPD parenting triggers include:

- Plans changing unexpectedly (the school calls about early dismissal, weekend plans get canceled, your child forgets their lunch)

- Children moving too slowly or inefficiently (taking forever to get dressed, dawdling during homework, not following your step-by-step instructions)

- Mistakes that feel preventable (your teenager leaves their backpack at school, your child spills something on their clean shirt, someone forgets an important deadline)

- Disorder or messes (toys scattered around, backpacks dumped in the hallway, bedrooms that look like disaster zones)

- Children expressing big emotions (crying, anger, frustration, disappointment - especially when these feelings seem "unreasonable" to you)

- Other people doing things differently than you would (your partner using different discipline strategies, teachers not following through on expectations, other parents having different rules)

The physical experience of being triggered is usually pretty obvious once you start paying attention. Your heart rate increases. Your breathing gets shallow. Your muscles tense up, especially in your jaw, shoulders, or stomach. You might feel hot or flushed. Your thinking becomes more rigid and focused on what's "wrong" and how to fix it immediately.

But here's the thing - those physical sensations happen *before* you say or do anything. They're your early warning system. If you can learn to recognize them, you can use them as a cue to pause instead of a cue to control.

Research from Focus on the Family shows that parents who learn to identify their trigger patterns and physical responses are significantly more likely to respond thoughtfully rather than reactively in challenging situations (Focus on the Family, 2023). The awareness itself becomes a protective factor.

The 30-second pause technique for reactive moments

This is stupidly simple, which is why it works. When you notice those early warning signs - the tight chest, the mental urgency, the immediate impulse to fix or correct something - you stop and count to thirty. That's it.

Thirty seconds is long enough for your nervous system to settle slightly but short enough that you won't forget to do it. During those thirty seconds, you're not trying to solve the problem or figure out the perfect response. You're just breathing and letting your body calm down.

Here's exactly how to do it:

1. **Notice the trigger response** - that feeling of urgency or frustration rising in your body

2. **Say to yourself** (silently): "I'm having a strong reaction to this. I'm going to pause."

3. **Take three slow, deep breaths** - in through your nose, out through your mouth

4. **Count slowly to thirty** - you can do this silently or even out loud if the situation allows

5. **Ask yourself**: "What does my child need from me right now?" (not "What needs to be fixed?" but "What does my child need?")

Sometimes, after thirty seconds, you'll realize the situation isn't actually urgent. Your child's messy room can wait another day. The homework that isn't perfect is still adequate. The schedule disruption is annoying but not catastrophic.

Other times, you'll still need to address the situation, but you'll be able to do it from a calmer, more connected place. Instead of snapping, "Why can't you ever remember to put your backpack away?" you might say, "I notice your backpack is on the floor. Let's figure out a system that works better for you."

The magic isn't in the thirty seconds themselves - it's in breaking the automatic pattern of trigger-to-reaction. You're training your brain to pause and choose instead of just responding on autopilot.

Body awareness: physical signs of control urges

Your body knows you're moving into control mode before your mind does. Learning to read these physical signals gives you earlier and earlier opportunities to pause and choose a different response.

Tension patterns: Where do you hold stress in your body when things feel out of control? Many OCPD parents notice tension in their jaw (from clenching their teeth), shoulders (from bracing against stress), or stomach (from anxiety about outcomes). Some people get headaches or feel pressure in their chest.

Breathing changes: When you're moving into control mode, your breathing typically becomes more shallow and rapid. You might even find yourself holding your breath when you're concentrating intensely on a problem or feeling frustrated with your child's behavior.

Energy shifts: Some parents notice they feel suddenly energized and urgent when triggered - like they need to fix everything right now. Others feel heavy and exhausted, especially if they've been in control mode for a while.

Temperature changes: Getting hot, flushed, or sweaty when frustrated is common. Some people get cold or feel shaky when their nervous system is activated.

The goal isn't to eliminate these physical responses - they're natural reactions to stress. The goal is to use them as information. When you notice your shoulders tensing up while watching your child struggle with homework, that's your cue to ask yourself: "Am I about to take over here? What would be most helpful right now?"

Daily practice: Morning mindfulness for OCPD parents

You don't need to become a meditation expert to benefit from mindfulness practice. For OCPD parents, even five minutes of intentional awareness in the morning can make a huge difference in how reactive you are throughout the day.

The OCPD morning practice (5 minutes total):

Minute 1: Body check-in - Before you get out of bed, notice how your body feels. Are you already thinking about your to-do list? Are you feeling anxious about the day ahead? Just notice without trying to change anything.

Minutes 2-3: Breathing space - Take ten slow, deep breaths. As you breathe, remind yourself: "I don't have to be perfect today. My children don't have to be perfect today. We just need to connect and do our best."

Minute 4: Intention setting - Think about one thing you want to focus on in your parenting today. Maybe it's being more patient during morning routines, or asking your children about their feelings instead of jumping straight to problem-solving, or letting them handle their own homework struggles.

Minute 5: Compassion practice - Think about yourself as a parent who's trying hard and learning as you go. Send yourself the same kindness you'd send a good friend who's struggling. "I'm doing the best I can with what I know right now."

This isn't about becoming zen or never feeling frustrated. It's about starting your day with awareness instead of automatically shifting into productivity mode. Research shows that even brief mindfulness practices can significantly reduce parental stress and improve emotional regulation throughout the day (Chaplin et al. 2018).

Cognitive patterns that trap OCPD parents

Your thinking patterns have a huge impact on your emotional reactions and parenting behaviors. OCPD tends to create very specific cognitive traps - ways of thinking that feel logical and reasonable but actually make parenting harder and family life more stressful.

All-or-nothing thinking in daily parenting

This is probably the most common cognitive trap for perfectionist parents. In your mind, things are either done right or they're done wrong. There's no middle ground, no "good enough," no room for learning curves or individual differences.

All-or-nothing thinking shows up in statements like:

- "If you're going to do something, you might as well do it right"
- "There's no point in turning in sloppy work"
- "Either you follow the rules or you don't - there are no exceptions"
- "If we don't stay on schedule, the whole day will be ruined"

Research from The Recovery Village shows that all-or-nothing thinking is one of the strongest predictors of parental stress and child behavioral problems (The Recovery Village, 2023). When parents think in extremes, children feel like they can never measure up, which often leads to either anxious perfectionism or rebellious giving up.

Here's what all-or-nothing thinking looks like in real parenting situations:

Homework time: Your child's math homework has several small errors. Instead of seeing this as a normal part of learning, you think, "This is completely unacceptable. If she's going to do homework, it needs to be done correctly." You end up sitting with her for two hours, correcting every mistake and re-explaining every concept until it's perfect.

Morning routines: Your teenager is moving slowly and you're running five minutes behind schedule. Instead of thinking, "We're a little late, but it's not the end of the world," you think, "If we can't even get out the door on time, how is he going to succeed at anything?" You end up yelling about responsibility and time management while rushing around trying to make up the lost time.

Room cleaning: Your child's room is messy but not unsanitary - clothes on the floor, unmade bed, some books scattered around. Instead of seeing this as typical kid behavior, you think, "This room is a disaster. If I don't make him clean it properly, he'll never learn to take care of his things." You end up supervising a three-hour deep clean that leaves everyone frustrated.

The National Center for Biotechnology Information research shows that parents who can tolerate "good enough" outcomes have children with better emotional regulation and higher self-esteem (NCBI, 2022). The children learn that mistakes are normal, progress matters more than perfection, and they can handle challenges without everything falling apart.

Challenging all-or-nothing thinking:

- Instead of "right" or "wrong," try thinking in terms of "learning" and "improving"

- Ask yourself: "What's good enough for this situation and this child's developmental stage?"

- Practice saying: "This isn't perfect, but it's adequate" or "We're making progress"
- Remind yourself that children learn from mistakes, not from having everything done correctly the first time

The "right way" fallacy and its impact on children

OCPD parents often operate under the belief that there's one correct way to do most things - and that it's their job to teach children this "right way." This feels responsible and loving, but it can actually interfere with children's ability to develop problem-solving skills, creativity, and confidence.

The "right way" fallacy shows up when you:

- Give detailed, step-by-step instructions for tasks children could figure out themselves
- Correct methods that work fine but aren't the way you would do them
- Feel anxious or frustrated when children want to try different approaches
- Redo or "improve" things that were adequate as they were

Here's what this looks like in daily life: Your 10-year-old wants to organize her backpack. You watch her put her folders in first, then her textbooks, then her pencil case. This isn't how you would do it - you'd put the heavy books on the bottom, folders in the middle, supplies on top. So you say, "Let me show you a better way to pack that."

Your intention is good - you want to help her be more organized and efficient. But what she learns is that her natural problem-solving isn't trustworthy, that there's always a better way she should have thought of, and that her efforts aren't quite good enough on their own.

The impact on children's development:

- **Reduced self-confidence**: Children start doubting their own judgment and waiting for adult approval before making decisions

- **Decreased problem-solving skills**: When adults consistently provide the "right" way, children don't get practice figuring things out themselves

- **Performance anxiety**: Children become afraid to try new approaches because they might not be doing it "correctly"

- **Resentment and rebellion**: Some children push back against constant correction by refusing help or doing things deliberately differently

Moving beyond the "right way" fallacy:

- Ask yourself: "Is their way working? Is it safe? Is it helping them learn something?"

- Practice saying: "That's an interesting approach" or "I can see that's working for you"

- Offer your method as one option: "Would you like to try the way I usually do it, or do you want to stick with your system?"

- Focus on outcomes rather than methods: "The important thing is that your backpack is organized in a way that helps you find what you need"

Catastrophizing normal childhood behavior

OCPD parents often have a hard time distinguishing between normal developmental challenges and serious problems that need immediate intervention. This leads to catastrophizing - imagining worst-case scenarios and feeling like every small issue is a sign of bigger problems to come.

Catastrophizing sounds like:

- "If she can't remember to turn in her homework now, how is she going to handle college?"

- "If he keeps losing his temper like this, he's going to have problems with relationships his whole life"

- "If they can't follow simple rules, they're going to end up in trouble with authority figures"

- "If I don't fix this behavior now, it's just going to get worse and worse"

This type of thinking creates enormous pressure for both you and your children. Every normal childhood struggle becomes loaded with significance about your child's future and your success as a parent.

Common areas where parents catastrophize normal behavior:

- **Academic struggles**: A bad grade or missing assignment becomes evidence that your child doesn't care about education or won't succeed in life

- **Social conflicts**: Normal friend drama gets interpreted as signs that your child has poor social skills or will struggle with relationships

- **Emotional outbursts**: Age-appropriate big feelings (tantrums in toddlers, dramatic reactions in teens) get seen as signs of serious behavioral or emotional problems

- **Responsibility lapses**: Forgetting chores or losing items gets interpreted as evidence of poor character or lack of respect

Reality check for catastrophic thinking:

- Most childhood behaviors are temporary and developmental, not permanent personality traits

- Children's brains are still developing impulse control, emotional regulation, and executive functioning well into their twenties

- Normal childhood includes lots of mistakes, struggles, and less-than-perfect behaviors

- Your job as a parent is to guide and support, not to prevent all struggles or fix all problems immediately

Worksheet: Challenging your automatic thoughts

When you notice yourself feeling triggered or moving into control mode, try working through these questions. You don't need to do this perfectly - just honestly.

Step 1: Identify the situation What exactly happened that triggered your response? Try to stick to facts, not interpretations. Example: "My daughter left her science project materials scattered on the kitchen table after working on it"

Step 2: Notice your automatic thoughts What went through your mind immediately when this happened? Example: "She never cleans up after herself. This kitchen is a disaster. If I don't make her clean this up right now, she'll never learn to be responsible."

Step 3: Identify the thinking traps Which cognitive patterns do you recognize?

- All-or-nothing thinking ("never/always," "disaster/perfect")

- "Right way" thinking ("She should have...")

- Catastrophizing ("She'll never learn...")

- Mind reading ("She doesn't care about...")

Step 4: Challenge the thoughts

- What evidence supports this thought? What evidence contradicts it?

- Is this thought helpful for my relationship with my child?

- What would I tell a friend who was having this thought about their child?

- Is there a more balanced way to think about this situation?

Step 5: Choose a response Based on your more balanced thinking, what would be most helpful here? Example: "She's learning to manage multiple projects and sometimes forgets to clean up. I can ask her to clean up the kitchen and help her think about systems for keeping track of her materials."

Emotional awareness for the overcontrolled parent

One of the hallmarks of OCPD is being "overcontrolled" - which means your natural tendency is to manage emotions (both yours and others') rather than experience and express them fully. This creates problems in parenting because children need emotional connection, not just behavioral management.

Why OCPD parents struggle with emotional expression

According to research from Choosing Therapy, people with OCPD traits often have difficulty accessing and expressing their full range of emotions (Choosing Therapy, 2024). This isn't because you don't have feelings - you have the same emotional capacity as anyone else. It's because you've learned to prioritize thinking over feeling, control over vulnerability, and solutions over connection.

Common emotional struggles for OCPD parents:

- **Anger feels safer than sadness or fear**: When your child is struggling, you might feel frustrated or annoyed rather than worried or heartbroken. Anger feels more actionable and less vulnerable.

- **Anxiety gets channeled into control**: Instead of recognizing and expressing anxiety directly, you might find yourself micromanaging or trying to prevent all possible problems.

- **Joy feels conditional**: You might notice you feel happiest when things are going smoothly and according to plan, but struggle to feel joyful during messy or chaotic moments.

- **Guilt gets converted into justification**: When you've been too controlling or critical, you might find yourself explaining why your response was necessary rather than simply acknowledging that you made a mistake.

Why this matters for your children: Children need to see their parents experience and express the full range of human emotions in healthy ways. When you consistently suppress or convert your emotions, your children learn that:

- Some feelings are acceptable and others aren't
- Emotions should be fixed or solved rather than experienced
- Vulnerability is dangerous or weak
- Love is conditional on maintaining emotional control

Research shows that children of emotionally expressive parents develop better emotional intelligence, stronger relationships, and greater resilience to stress (Emotion Research Institute, 2023).

Identifying suppressed feelings before they explode

OCPD parents often experience what therapists call "emotional buildup" - suppressed feelings that accumulate over time until they come out in explosive or disproportionate ways. Learning to identify emotions earlier in the process helps prevent these explosions and allows for more authentic connection with your children.

Physical signs of suppressed emotions:

- Tension that doesn't go away even when the stressful situation is resolved
- Feeling emotionally "numb" or disconnected from your body
- Sleep problems, especially difficulty falling asleep because your mind won't stop racing

- Irritability that seems out of proportion to current circumstances
- Feeling like you're constantly on the verge of losing it, even during normal daily activities

Emotional warning signs:

- Finding yourself frequently annoyed with your children for normal kid behavior
- Feeling resentful about household responsibilities or parenting tasks
- Criticizing yourself harshly for small mistakes or imperfections
- Feeling disconnected from joy, even during activities you used to enjoy
- Having trouble empathizing with your children's emotions because you're so focused on their behavior

The suppression-explosion cycle: This is a common pattern for OCPD parents. You suppress frustration, sadness, anxiety, or overwhelm for days or weeks, trying to maintain control and keep everything running smoothly. Then something small happens - your child spills juice, forgets their homework, or pushes back on a rule - and you react with intensity that's way out of proportion to the actual situation.

Your child experiences this as unpredictable and confusing. They can't understand why leaving socks on the floor suddenly triggered a lecture about responsibility and respect. What they don't see is all the suppressed emotion that was already building up.

The connection between control and anxiety

For many OCPD parents, the drive to control outcomes is actually an attempt to manage underlying anxiety. You might not even recognize the anxiety because it gets channeled immediately into action and problem-solving. But understanding this connection can help you address the root cause instead of just managing the symptoms.

Common anxiety triggers for OCPD parents:

- **Future-focused worry**: "What if my child doesn't develop good habits? What if they struggle in college? What if I'm not preparing them properly for adult life?"

- **Judgment anxiety**: "What will other parents think if my child's behavior is inappropriate? What will teachers think if his project isn't good enough?"

- **Control anxiety**: "What if something goes wrong and I can't fix it? What if there's a problem I haven't anticipated?"

- **Performance anxiety**: "What if I'm not being a good enough parent? What if I'm making mistakes that will hurt my children?"

Instead of experiencing these anxieties as emotions to be felt and processed, you might immediately shift into control mode - managing your child's behavior, environment, or outcomes to reduce the anxiety-provoking uncertainty.

The problem with using control to manage anxiety: It works temporarily, but it doesn't actually resolve the underlying anxiety, and it often creates new problems. When you control your child's homework, you temporarily reduce your anxiety about their academic performance, but you also prevent them from developing self-regulation skills, which creates more anxiety in the long run.

Healthy alternatives to control-based anxiety management:

- **Recognize and name the anxiety**: "I'm feeling worried about how this will turn out"

- **Practice tolerating uncertainty**: "I don't know how this will go, but I trust that we can handle whatever happens"

- **Focus on your sphere of influence**: "I can't control the outcome, but I can provide support and guidance"

- **Use emotional regulation techniques**: Deep breathing, physical exercise, talking to a friend, or other anxiety-management strategies that don't involve controlling other people

Guided exercise: Emotion mapping throughout your day

For the next week, try this simple emotion-mapping exercise. It will help you become more aware of your emotional patterns and identify opportunities for greater authenticity with your children.

Set three random alarms on your phone for different times during your typical day - maybe 10 AM, 3 PM, and 8 PM.

When each alarm goes off, pause and ask yourself:

1. **What am I feeling right now?** (Use specific emotion words: frustrated, worried, overwhelmed, content, excited, tired, etc.)

2. **Where do I feel this emotion in my body?** (Tight chest, clenched jaw, relaxed shoulders, etc.)

3. **What was I thinking about just before the alarm went off?**

4. **Have I expressed this emotion to anyone, or am I keeping it internal?**

5. **What does my child need to know about how I'm feeling right now?** (Not everything, but maybe something)

At the end of each day, look for patterns:

- Do you experience certain emotions at certain times of day?

- Are there emotions you consistently suppress or avoid?

- How often are your emotions connected to your child's behavior versus other factors in your life?

- When do you feel most and least emotionally available to your children?

Example of what this might look like:

10 AM alarm: "I'm feeling frustrated and a little anxious. My chest feels tight and my shoulders are tense. I was thinking about how my son didn't finish his chores before school and wondering if I should text him a reminder or just let him face the consequences. I haven't expressed these feelings - I just kept busy with other tasks. Maybe I should tell him when he gets home that I felt worried about him, not just angry about the chores."

The goal isn't to express every emotion to your children - they don't need to manage your feelings. The goal is to become more aware of your inner emotional life so you can respond from a place of authentic connection rather than suppressed stress.

Chapter 4: The growth mindset revolution for perfectionist families

Something magical happens when families move from "Am I smart enough?" to "How can I get better at this?" It's the difference between children who are paralyzed by challenges and children who see challenges as interesting puzzles to solve. For perfectionist families, this shift from a fixed mindset to a growth mindset isn't just helpful - it's revolutionary.

If you're parenting with OCPD traits, you probably have some mixed feelings about the idea of focusing on growth over outcomes. Part of you knows that learning and effort matter more than natural talent, but another part of you still gets that familiar anxiety when your child's work isn't as good as it could be. You want them to develop resilience, but you also want them to succeed. You want them to be okay with mistakes, but you also want them to learn from those mistakes and do better next time.

Here's what's beautiful about growth mindset for perfectionist families: it gives you a way to maintain high standards while reducing the anxiety and pressure that make those standards feel impossible to reach. Your children can still strive for excellence, but they can do it from a place of curiosity and confidence rather than fear and desperation.

From fixed to growth: Rewiring perfectionist beliefs

Understanding Dweck's mindset theory for OCPD parents

Dr. Carol Dweck's research on mindset provides a powerful framework for understanding why some children thrive under challenge while others crumble. According to Psychology Today, people with a *fixed mindset* believe that abilities are static traits -

you're either smart or you're not, either talented or you're not, either good at something or you're not (Psychology Today, 2023). People with a *growth mindset* believe that abilities can be developed through effort, practice, and learning from mistakes.

For OCPD parents, this distinction is crucial because perfectionism naturally creates fixed mindset thinking. When you focus intensely on outcomes and correct answers, children learn that their worth depends on being right, being smart, or being naturally good at things. They become afraid of challenges because challenges might reveal that they're not as capable as everyone thinks they are.

Fixed mindset in perfectionist families sounds like:

- "You're so smart!" (praising the person rather than the effort)

- "This should be easy for you" (implying that struggle means inadequacy)

- "Let me show you the right way" (suggesting there's one correct approach)

- "I can't believe you made such a careless mistake" (treating mistakes as character flaws)

- "If you just try harder, you'll get it" (implying that current effort is insufficient)

Growth mindset in perfectionist families sounds like:

- "You worked really hard on this problem" (praising effort and strategy)

- "This is challenging - what can we learn from it?" (normalizing difficulty)

- "I'm curious about your approach" (valuing process over outcome)

- "Mistakes help our brains grow - what did this one teach you?" (reframing mistakes as learning opportunities)

- "What strategy do you want to try next?" (focusing on problem-solving)

Research shows that children who develop growth mindsets are more resilient, more willing to take on challenges, and ultimately more successful academically and socially (Dweck, 2023). But here's what's particularly relevant for OCPD parents: children with growth mindsets also experience significantly less anxiety and perfectionist stress.

How perfectionism creates a fixed mindset trap

Perfectionist parenting, despite good intentions, often reinforces fixed mindset beliefs. When you focus heavily on correct outcomes, high grades, and proper behavior, children naturally conclude that their worth depends on achieving these things consistently. The pressure to maintain high performance makes them avoid risks and challenges that might threaten their image of competence.

The perfectionist fixed mindset trap works like this:

1. **High standards communicate that excellence is expected,** not that learning and growth are valued

2. **Mistakes feel like failures** rather than information about how to improve

3. **Struggling becomes evidence of inadequacy** rather than a normal part of learning

4. **Children avoid challenges** that might reveal they're not as capable as everyone thinks

5. **Performance anxiety increases** because so much seems to depend on being right the first time

Take homework, for example. In a perfectionist household, homework often becomes about getting the right answers rather than practicing skills and learning from mistakes. Children learn to ask for help immediately when something is difficult (to avoid making mistakes) or to give up when they can't figure something out quickly (to avoid the discomfort of struggle).

According to research from Relationships.ca, children who grow up with perfectionist expectations often develop what psychologists call "performance goals" rather than "learning goals" (Relationships.ca, 2024). They focus on looking smart rather than getting smarter, on avoiding failure rather than embracing challenge.

Signs your family might be stuck in fixed mindset:

- Your children frequently say "I'm not good at this" or "I can't do this"

- They get upset or give up quickly when something is challenging

- They're reluctant to try new activities or take on difficult tasks

- They focus more on grades and outcomes than on what they're learning

- They hide mistakes or try to fix them before you notice

- They seem to think that needing to practice or get help means they're not smart

Teaching children that abilities develop through practice

One of the most powerful shifts you can make as a perfectionist parent is helping your children understand that abilities are like muscles - they get stronger with exercise, including the exercise of making mistakes and figuring out how to do better.

This doesn't mean lowering your standards or accepting poor effort. It means helping your children see that current performance doesn't predict future potential, and that the process of learning is just as important as the end result.

Practical ways to reinforce growth mindset:

Focus on effort and strategy: Instead of praising intelligence ("You're so smart!"), praise the work they put in ("You kept trying different approaches until you found one that worked"). Instead of praising natural talent ("You're a natural at math"), praise their developing skills ("Your math skills are really improving with all this practice").

Normalize struggle: When your child is finding something difficult, resist the urge to immediately help or simplify the task. Instead, try saying things like, "This is hard work for your brain right now - that means you're learning something new" or "I can see you're really thinking about this."

Make mistakes part of the process: When your child makes an error, try responding with curiosity instead of correction: "That's interesting - what do you think happened there?" or "What would you try differently next time?" This helps them see mistakes as information rather than failures.

Share your own learning process: Talk about things you're working to improve, strategies you're trying, and mistakes you've made. "I'm still learning how to use this new computer program - I made three mistakes today, but I figured out something new each time."

Psychology Today research shows that when parents consistently focus on growth and learning over performance and outcomes, children develop greater resilience, creativity, and intrinsic motivation (Psychology Today, 2024). They also experience less anxiety and are more likely to seek help when they need it.

Family activity: Creating a growth mindset wall

This is a simple but powerful way to make growth mindset visible and concrete in your household. You'll create a space where the whole family can celebrate learning, effort, and progress rather than just achievements and perfect outcomes.

What you'll need:

- A wall space or large bulletin board

- Index cards or sticky notes

- Markers or pens

- Maybe some fun decorations (completely optional)

How to set it up: Create sections for each family member, including parents. Each week, everyone adds cards about:

- Something challenging they tried (whether they succeeded or not)

- A mistake they made and what they learned from it

- A skill they're working to improve

- Someone who helped them learn something new

- A strategy they tried that worked (or didn't work)

Example cards might say:

- "Tried cooking dinner by myself - burned the chicken but learned to set a timer!"

- "Asked for help with math instead of pretending I understood"

- "Practiced piano even though it was frustrating"

- "Made a mistake on my presentation but figured out how to improve it for next time"

Family growth mindset conversations: Once a week, spend a few minutes looking at the wall together. Ask questions like:

- "What's something new you learned this week?"

- "What's something you're getting better at?"

- "What mistake taught you the most?"

- "What do you want to practice more of?"

The goal isn't to eliminate all focus on outcomes and achievements - it's to balance outcome focus with process focus, so your children learn that their worth isn't dependent on being perfect.

Embracing "good enough" parenting

This might be the hardest concept for OCPD parents to accept, but it's also the most liberating: you don't have to be a perfect parent for your children to thrive. In fact, trying to be perfect often gets in the way of what your children actually need from you.

Winnicott's 30% rule and why it works

British pediatrician and psychoanalyst Donald Winnicott introduced the concept of the "good enough mother" - a parent who meets their child's needs most of the time but not all of the time. According to Forest Psychology, Winnicott argued that children actually benefit from having parents who are imperfect, because this teaches them resilience and helps them develop their own coping skills (Forest Psychology, 2024).

Winnicott suggested that parents need to be attuned and responsive to their children's needs about 70% of the time. The other 30% - when you're tired, distracted, stressed, or just human - provides valuable learning opportunities for children. They learn that relationships can survive disappointment, that people can make mistakes and repair them, and that they have their own inner resources for handling challenges.

What this means in practical terms:

- You don't have to respond perfectly to every emotional outburst or crisis

- You don't have to have the right answer or solution for every problem your child faces

- You don't have to prevent all struggles, disappointments, or mistakes

- You don't have to be emotionally available and patient every single moment

- You don't have to create perfect learning opportunities or flawless family experiences

What "good enough" parenting provides:

- **Realistic expectations**: Children learn that perfection isn't required for love and connection

- **Resilience building**: Children develop coping skills when they have to handle some challenges on their own

- **Authentic relationships**: Children learn that people can love each other even when they're not perfect

- **Self-reliance**: Children develop confidence in their ability to handle difficulties

- **Emotional regulation**: Children learn to tolerate disappointment and imperfection

The paradox of better outcomes with lower standards

Here's something that might sound counterintuitive: research consistently shows that children of "good enough" parents often have better outcomes than children of parents who try to be perfect. When you lower your standards from perfection to adequacy, several positive things happen.

Children develop internal motivation: When they're not constantly trying to meet your high expectations, they have space to discover what they actually care about and want to work toward.

Children take appropriate risks: When failure isn't catastrophic, children are more willing to try challenging things, which leads to greater learning and growth.

Children develop problem-solving skills: When you don't rescue them from every difficulty or provide perfect solutions to every problem, they learn to figure things out for themselves.

Family relationships improve: When there's less pressure to be perfect, everyone can relax and actually enjoy each other's company.

Children develop realistic self-expectations: When they see that you can make mistakes and still be loveable, they learn to treat themselves with similar compassion.

This doesn't mean you stop caring about your children's development or success. It means you create space for imperfection, learning, and authentic connection alongside your expectations for growth and effort.

Redefining success in parenting

For OCPD parents, success often gets defined in terms of outcomes: good grades, well-behaved children, smooth-running households, children who meet developmental milestones on schedule. But research on child development suggests that these external markers may be less important than internal qualities like resilience, emotional intelligence, and secure relationships.

Traditional perfectionist measures of parenting success:

- Children who excel academically
- Children who follow rules and meet expectations consistently
- Organized households and efficient family systems
- Children who represent the family well in public
- Prevention of major problems or failures

Growth mindset measures of parenting success:

- Children who can handle challenges and setbacks
- Children who have secure, authentic relationships

- Children who can identify and express their emotions
- Children who are curious and motivated to learn
- Children who treat themselves and others with kindness
- Children who can ask for help when they need it
- Children who bounce back from disappointments

Questions to ask yourself about your definition of success:

- What do I want my children to remember about their childhood?
- What qualities do I hope they'll have as adults?
- What kind of relationship do I want to have with them when they're grown?
- How do I want them to handle challenges and mistakes?
- What do I want them to believe about their own worth and capabilities?

Personal experiment: One week of "good enough"

This is a practical experiment in lowering your standards just enough to create space for connection and authentic relationship. For one week, try consciously aiming for "good enough" instead of perfect in your parenting.

Choose three areas where you typically have high standards: Maybe it's homework supervision, household organization, and behavior management. For this week, you're going to intentionally dial down your involvement and expectations in these areas.

Homework experiment: Instead of checking every problem and ensuring everything is correct, try saying, "This looks like good effort - I trust you to turn it in as it is." Let your child experience the natural consequences of incomplete or incorrect work.

Household experiment: Instead of having everything organized perfectly, let some mess and disorder exist. See what happens when you don't immediately clean up after everyone or insist that everything be put away properly.

Behavior experiment: Instead of addressing every small behavioral issue or imperfection, choose to let some things go. Focus only on behaviors that are genuinely harmful or disrespectful.

What to pay attention to during your experiment:

- How does it feel to let go of some control?
- How do your children respond to the decreased pressure?
- What do you learn about your children's capabilities when you step back?
- What happens to your stress level and your relationships?
- Are the outcomes actually worse, or just different from what you expected?

Common discoveries from the "good enough" experiment:

- Children are often more capable than you thought when you're not doing things for them
- Relationships feel warmer and more connected when there's less focus on perfection
- Your anxiety about lowered standards is usually worse than the actual outcomes
- Children often rise to meet appropriate expectations when they're not overwhelmed by perfectionist pressure
- Everyone in the family feels more relaxed and authentic

Modeling mistakes and learning

One of the most powerful things you can do as a perfectionist parent is to let your children see you struggle, make mistakes, and learn from those mistakes. This teaches them that mistakes are part of life, not evidence of failure, and that growth comes from embracing challenges rather than avoiding them.

Why sharing your failures is crucial for OCPD parents

OCPD parents often work very hard to appear competent and in control, especially in front of their children. You might think you're modeling responsibility and high standards, but what your children might actually be learning is that adults are supposed to have everything figured out and that struggling or making mistakes is shameful.

According to research from Big Life Journal, children need to see their parents make mistakes and handle them gracefully in order to develop healthy relationships with failure and learning (Big Life Journal, 2023). When parents hide their struggles and mistakes, children can develop unrealistic expectations for themselves and intense shame when they inevitably struggle with something.

What happens when you hide mistakes from your children:

- They develop unrealistic expectations about what adult competence looks like

- They feel ashamed and alone when they struggle, because they don't see struggle as normal

- They don't learn strategies for recovering from mistakes and setbacks

- They may become afraid to take risks or try challenging things

- They miss opportunities to see that you value learning and growth over perfection

What happens when you share your struggles appropriately:

- They learn that everyone makes mistakes and faces challenges

- They develop realistic expectations about the learning process

- They see concrete examples of how to bounce back from setbacks

- They feel permission to be imperfect and still loveable

- They learn that asking for help and trying new strategies is normal and healthy

The key word here is "appropriately": You don't want to burden your children with adult problems or use them as emotional support for serious struggles. But you can share age-appropriate challenges, mistakes, and learning experiences that help them see you as human.

Creating family "failure celebrations"

This might sound weird at first, but celebrating failures and mistakes can completely transform your family's relationship with learning and growth. The idea isn't to celebrate mediocrity or carelessness - it's to celebrate the courage to try difficult things and the wisdom that comes from learning what doesn't work.

How family failure celebrations work:

Weekly failure sharing: At dinner once a week, everyone shares something they "failed" at or struggled with during the week, and what they learned from it. The rule is that everyone celebrates each person's willingness to share and learn.

The mistake jar: Create a family jar where people can write down mistakes they made and what they learned. Once a month, read some of them together and celebrate the learning that happened.

Famous failure stories: Research and share stories of famous people who failed before they succeeded. Talk about how their failures led to their eventual achievements.

Failure awards: Create silly certificates for different types of valuable failures: "Most Creative Mistake," "Best Learning from a Disaster," "Bravest Attempt at Something Difficult."

Example of what this might sound like: "I failed at making dinner tonight - I completely burned the chicken and we ended up ordering pizza. But I learned that I need to set a timer when I'm cooking and not try to multitask with work calls. What did everyone else fail at this week?"

This approach helps normalize struggle and makes your family culture one where people can be honest about challenges instead of hiding them.

Teaching children to see mistakes as data

One of the most important shifts you can help your children make is moving from "I made a mistake, I'm stupid" to "I made a mistake, what can I learn from this?" This reframing turns mistakes from sources of shame into sources of information.

Language that reframes mistakes as learning:

- Instead of "You should have known better," try "What would you do differently next time?"

- Instead of "That was careless," try "What do you think happened there?"

- Instead of "Let me fix this," try "What's your plan for handling this?"

- Instead of "You need to be more careful," try "What did this mistake teach you?"

Research from Healthy Children shows that children who learn to view mistakes as information develop greater resilience, creativity, and problem-solving skills (Healthy Children, 2023). They also experience less anxiety and are more willing to take on challenges.

The scientist approach to mistakes: Teach your children to approach mistakes like scientists approach experiments. Scientists don't get upset when experiments don't work out as expected - they get curious about what the results can teach them. They ask questions like:

- What happened?

- Why do I think it happened?

- What could I try differently?

- What did I learn that I can use next time?

Script library: How to talk about your mistakes with children

Having actual scripts can help you practice sharing your own mistakes and struggles in ways that are helpful rather than overwhelming for your children.

Age 3-6: "I made a mistake when I was cooking dinner - I forgot to watch the timer and the cookies got too brown. Next time I'll set the timer where I can see it better. Everyone makes mistakes sometimes, and that's okay."

Age 7-11: "I'm really frustrated with myself - I scheduled two meetings for the same time and now I have to call people and reschedule. I learned that I need to check my calendar more carefully before I agree to meetings. It's embarrassing, but everyone makes mistakes like this sometimes."

Age 12-18: "I handled that conversation with your teacher poorly - I got defensive instead of listening to her concerns. I think I was so worried about you getting in trouble that I didn't really hear what she was trying to tell us. I'm going to call her back and apologize, and ask if we can start over with the conversation."

Key elements of helpful mistake-sharing:

- Take responsibility for the mistake without excessive shame or self-criticism

- Share what you learned or what you plan to do differently

- Normalize the experience of making mistakes

- Model how to recover and move forward

- Keep the focus on learning rather than self-punishment

Moving forward with growth mindset

Shifting from perfectionist parenting to growth mindset parenting isn't about lowering your expectations or caring less about your children's success. It's about creating an environment where your children can develop genuine confidence, resilience, and love of learning.

The beautiful thing about growth mindset is that it actually supports higher achievement in the long run, while reducing the anxiety and pressure that make perfectionist households so stressful. When children believe they can improve through effort and learning, they're more willing to take on challenges, more resilient in the face of setbacks, and more intrinsically motivated to keep growing.

Your journey from fixed mindset to growth mindset won't happen overnight, and it doesn't need to be perfect. The goal is progress, not perfection - which is exactly the message you want your children to internalize about their own learning and development.

Essential insights for lasting change

The shift from perfectionist parenting to growth mindset parenting represents a fundamental change in how families approach learning, mistakes, and success. This transformation requires patience with yourself as much as with your children, since you're rewiring deeply ingrained patterns of thinking and responding.

Growth mindset isn't about abandoning standards or accepting mediocrity - it's about creating conditions where children can meet high expectations from a place of curiosity and confidence rather than fear and anxiety. When families embrace "good enough" parenting and celebrate learning from mistakes, children develop the resilience and intrinsic motivation that actually lead to higher achievement over time.

The most powerful tool in this transformation is your willingness to model imperfection and learning. When your children see you struggle, make mistakes, and bounce back with curiosity rather than shame, they learn that their worth isn't dependent on being perfect. This single shift can break generational cycles of perfectionist anxiety and create space for authentic connection and genuine growth.

Chapter 5: Infancy through toddlerhood (0-3 years)

The first three years of your child's life can feel like the ultimate test of your perfectionist tendencies. Here's this tiny human who doesn't follow schedules, makes incredible messes, and seems to have no regard whatsoever for your carefully planned routines. They cry when you're not sure why, refuse to sleep when they're obviously tired, and turn mealtimes into abstract art projects involving flying food.

If you're parenting with OCPD traits, these early years might feel particularly challenging because everything about infant and toddler development seems designed to trigger your need for control and predictability. But here's what's fascinating: the very things that make your perfectionist brain uncomfortable - the unpredictability, the messiness, the trial-and-error nature of early development - are exactly what your child's developing brain needs to grow optimally.

This doesn't mean you have to abandon structure entirely or let chaos rule your household. It means learning to dance between providing the security and routine that young children need while staying flexible enough to follow their developmental lead. It means accepting that "good enough" parenting during these early years actually produces better long-term outcomes than trying to control every aspect of their experience.

Responding vs. controlling in early development

Following infant cues vs. imposing schedules

New parents get a lot of conflicting advice about schedules. Some experts say babies need strict routines from day one. Others say you should follow your baby's lead completely. For OCPD parents, this dilemma can feel particularly intense because schedules feel safe and manageable, while "following baby's lead" can feel like giving up all control.

The research on infant development suggests that the healthiest approach falls somewhere in the middle. Babies do benefit from predictable routines, but they also need you to be responsive to their individual rhythms and changing needs. The goal isn't to impose an adult schedule on an infant, but to gradually help them develop their own natural rhythms while providing the structure they need to feel secure.

What following infant cues looks like:

- Watching for early signs of hunger (rooting, sucking motions) rather than feeding strictly by the clock

- Recognizing tired cues (rubbing eyes, yawning, becoming fussy) rather than enforcing rigid nap times

- Paying attention to your baby's social cues (making eye contact when they want interaction, looking away when they need a break)

- Adjusting routines when your baby goes through growth spurts or developmental changes

- Trusting your baby's appetite and sleep needs rather than comparing to charts or other babies

What this doesn't mean:

- Having no routine or structure at all

- Never trying to guide your baby toward healthy patterns

- Abandoning all attempts at scheduling

- Letting your baby's needs completely take over your household

- Ignoring your own needs as a parent

The key is learning to read your individual baby's signals and building routines around their natural patterns rather than trying to force them into predetermined schedules. This actually creates more predictability in the long run because you're working with your baby's biology rather than against it.

The developmental need for messy exploration

Toddlers are supposed to be messy. This isn't a character flaw or poor parenting - it's how their brains learn about the world. Every time your toddler dumps out a container of toys, they're learning about cause and effect. When they finger-paint with their food, they're exploring textures and developing fine motor skills. When they empty your kitchen cabinets, they're practicing problem-solving and spatial relationships.

For OCPD parents, this developmental need for mess and chaos can feel genuinely distressing. Your brain sees the scattered toys and thinks "disorder," but your toddler's brain sees "learning laboratory." Understanding this difference can help you tolerate the messiness that's necessary for healthy development.

Why mess matters for toddler development:

- **Sensory integration**: Toddlers need to touch, squeeze, pour, and manipulate different textures to develop their sensory processing abilities

- **Cause and effect learning**: Dropping things, knocking things over, and taking things apart teaches them how the physical world works

- **Fine and gross motor development**: Messy play activities help develop the small and large muscle control they'll need for writing, sports, and daily life skills

- **Creative thinking**: Unstructured, messy exploration encourages creativity and flexible thinking

- **Problem-solving skills**: When toddlers encounter obstacles during play (lid won't come off, blocks won't stack), they develop persistence and problem-solving strategies

Strategies for OCPD parents to handle developmental messiness:

- Create designated mess zones where exploration is encouraged

- Set up contained activities (finger painting in the high chair, water play in the bathtub)

- Have realistic expectations about cleanup time built into activities

- Focus on the learning happening rather than the mess being created

- Take before and after photos to see that cleanup is possible and the mess is temporary

Managing OCPD anxiety during the "terrible twos"

The toddler years are often when OCPD traits in parenting become most problematic. Toddlers are developmentally programmed to test boundaries, assert independence, and express big emotions - all of which can trigger intense anxiety in perfectionist parents.

The term "terrible twos" is actually misleading because it suggests that oppositional behavior is a problem to be solved rather than a normal developmental stage. Toddlers aren't being difficult on purpose - they're learning about autonomy, practicing new skills, and developing their sense of self. But when your toddler has a meltdown in the grocery store or refuses to follow simple instructions, your OCPD brain might interpret this as failure in your parenting or signs of future behavioral problems.

Common OCPD triggers during the toddler years:

- Tantrums and big emotional expressions that feel out of proportion

- Refusal to follow instructions or cooperate with routines

- Inconsistent behavior (cooperating one day, resisting the next)

- Mess and disorder that seems constant and overwhelming

- Slow progress in areas like potty training or learning new skills

- Public behavior that feels embarrassing or reflects poorly on your parenting

Reframing toddler behavior for OCPD parents: Instead of seeing oppositional behavior as defiance, try thinking of it as your toddler practicing important life skills:

- Saying "no" is practicing boundary-setting and self-advocacy

- Testing limits is learning about safety and social expectations

- Emotional outbursts are practicing emotional expression and regulation

- Wanting to do things themselves is developing independence and self-confidence

- Making messes is exploring and learning about their environment

Managing your anxiety during challenging toddler moments:

- Take deep breaths and remind yourself that this behavior is normal and temporary

- Focus on connection before correction - make sure your toddler feels understood before trying to change their behavior

- Lower your expectations during stressful times (transitions, illness, developmental leaps)

- Have realistic timelines for activities and transitions

- Build in extra time for everything because toddlers move at their own pace

Practical guide: Flexible routines that still provide structure

The goal is creating routines that provide the security and predictability that both you and your toddler need, while maintaining enough flexibility to accommodate their changing needs and developmental stages.

Morning routine framework: Instead of rigid timelines, create a predictable sequence of activities that can flex based on your toddler's mood and pace:

1. Wake up and snuggle time (5-15 minutes depending on your toddler's needs)
2. Diaper change/potty time
3. Get dressed (with choices when possible)
4. Breakfast
5. Brush teeth
6. Outside time or structured activity

Flexible scheduling principles:

- **Use sequence instead of time**: "After breakfast, we brush teeth" is more flexible than "We brush teeth at 8:15 AM"

- **Build in buffer time**: If you need to leave at 9:00, start getting ready at 8:30 instead of 8:55

- **Have backup plans**: If your toddler refuses to get dressed, have simple alternatives ready

- **Allow for individual rhythms**: Some toddlers are naturally slow in the morning, others are ready to go immediately

- **Adjust expectations based on developmental phases**: During sleep regressions or growth spurts, routines might need to be looser

Creating structure within flexibility:

- Use visual cues like picture schedules that show the sequence of activities

- Create predictable transitions with songs or special phrases

- Maintain consistent bedtime and mealtime routines even when other parts of the day are flexible

- Have designated spaces for different activities (quiet time corner, play area, art space)

Building secure attachment despite OCPD tendencies

Secure attachment - the deep emotional bond between parent and child - is one of the most important factors in healthy child development. Research shows that securely attached children have better emotional regulation, stronger relationships, and greater resilience throughout their lives. But OCPD traits can sometimes interfere with the emotional availability and responsiveness that secure attachment requires.

The challenge of emotional availability for OCPD parents

According to research from Choosing Therapy, parents with OCPD traits sometimes struggle with emotional availability because they tend to focus on tasks and outcomes rather than emotional connection (Choosing Therapy, 2023). This doesn't mean you love your children any less, but it might mean that your love gets expressed more through doing things for them than through emotional presence and attunement.

Common emotional availability challenges for OCPD parents:

- **Task focus over relationship focus**: Getting caught up in the logistics of childcare (feeding, changing, scheduling) while missing opportunities for emotional connection

- **Discomfort with big emotions**: Feeling anxious or overwhelmed when your child expresses intense feelings like anger, sadness, or frustration

- **Problem-solving instead of empathizing**: Immediately trying to fix or solve your child's problems instead of first validating their emotions

- **Perfectionist pressure**: Feeling like you need to be the "perfect" parent instead of just being present and responsive

- **Difficulty with unstructured time**: Feeling uncomfortable during open-ended play or cuddle time that doesn't have a specific purpose or outcome

Signs that you might need to work on emotional availability:

- Your child seeks comfort from other caregivers more often than from you

- Your child has frequent meltdowns that you struggle to soothe

- Your child seems anxious or clingy in ways that feel excessive

- You feel more confident about the practical aspects of parenting (feeding, diaper changing) than the emotional aspects (comforting, playing)

- Your interactions with your child focus mostly on instruction and correction rather than connection and enjoyment

Techniques for increasing warmth and responsiveness

The good news is that emotional availability is a skill that can be developed with practice and intention. Even if it doesn't come naturally to you, you can learn to be more emotionally present and responsive to your child's needs.

The PACE approach to emotional availability:

- **Playfulness**: Find joy and humor in your interactions with your child

- **Acceptance**: Accept your child's emotions without trying to change or fix them immediately

- **Curiosity**: Be genuinely interested in your child's inner world and experiences

- **Empathy**: Try to understand what your child might be feeling from their perspective

Practical techniques for building emotional connection:

Follow your child's lead in play: Instead of directing every activity, spend time each day letting your child choose what to do and how to do it. Get down on their level and enter their world without trying to turn it into a learning experience.

Practice emotional reflection: When your child expresses feelings, reflect back what you see and hear: "You seem really frustrated that the tower fell down," or "I can see you're excited about going to the park."

Use physical affection intentionally: Regular hugs, snuggles, and gentle touches help build emotional connection. Even a hand on the shoulder during difficult moments can communicate support and love.

Create special one-on-one time: Set aside time each day for focused attention on your child without distractions from phones, household tasks, or other children.

Validate emotions before addressing behavior: When your child is upset, acknowledge their feelings before trying to change their behavior: "You're angry that it's time to clean up. You were having so much fun playing."

Managing perfectionist anxiety about developmental milestones

The first few years of your child's life are filled with developmental milestones - first smiles, first words, first steps, potty training, and countless others. For OCPD parents, these milestones can become sources of intense anxiety and comparison rather than celebration and joy.

Research from Cleveland Clinic and the CDC shows that children develop at widely different rates, and the ranges for "normal" development are much broader than many parents realize (Cleveland Clinic, 2023; CDC, 2023). A child who walks at 9 months and a child who walks at 15 months are both developing normally, but perfectionist parents often worry if their child isn't on the earlier end of every developmental range.

Common perfectionist anxieties about development:

- Comparing your child's progress to other children or to milestone charts

- Worrying that delays in one area indicate broader developmental problems

- Feeling like you need to actively teach every new skill instead of allowing natural development

- Interpreting normal variations in development as signs of your inadequacy as a parent

- Focusing more on when milestones are reached than on celebrating your child's individual growth

Strategies for managing milestone anxiety:

Focus on your individual child's progress: Instead of comparing to other children, pay attention to your child's own growth and development over time. Are they making progress in their own way and at their own pace?

Use milestone ranges, not specific ages: Most developmental milestones have wide ranges for normal development. Focus on the range rather than the average age.

Celebrate small steps: Instead of waiting for major milestones, notice and celebrate the small improvements and attempts your child makes every day.

Trust your child's natural development: Most skills develop naturally through play and exploration rather than through direct instruction. Your job is to provide opportunities and encouragement, not to teach every skill directly.

Consult professionals for genuine concerns: If you have real worries about your child's development, talk to your pediatrician rather than researching online or comparing to other children.

Case study: Tom's journey from rigid scheduling to responsive parenting

Tom was a first-time father who approached parenting the same way he approached his career as an engineer - with detailed planning, careful research, and systematic implementation. Before his daughter Lily was born, he had created elaborate spreadsheets tracking feeding schedules, sleep patterns, and developmental milestones. He had researched the "best" methods for everything from sleep training to introducing solid foods.

The first few months were a struggle. Lily didn't seem to follow any of the schedules Tom had researched. She would be hungry before her designated feeding times, sleepy when she was supposed to be awake, and alert when she was supposed to be napping. Tom found himself becoming increasingly anxious and frustrated, feeling like he was failing as a parent because he couldn't get his daughter to follow the "optimal" routines.

The turning point came when Lily was about four months old and going through a growth spurt. She was cluster feeding, wanting to eat every hour or two, which completely disrupted Tom's carefully planned schedule. His wife Sarah suggested they just follow Lily's lead and feed her when she seemed hungry, but Tom was convinced this would create bad habits and make everything worse.

After three days of fighting with Lily's natural rhythms and feeling like a complete failure as a father, Tom finally decided to try a different approach. He put away his schedules and spent a week just observing Lily - when she naturally got hungry, when she seemed tired, when she was most alert and social.

What he discovered surprised him. Lily did have natural patterns, just not the ones from the books. She was naturally an early riser who liked to cluster feed in the mornings and have her longest awake period in the early evening. She slept better with shorter morning naps and one longer afternoon nap.

Once Tom started working with Lily's natural rhythms instead of against them, everything became easier. Lily was happier and more settled, which made Tom feel more confident and relaxed. He still maintained structure and routines, but they were based on Lily's needs and patterns rather than external recommendations.

What Tom learned from this experience:

- Individual children have their own natural rhythms that may not match general recommendations

- Fighting against a child's biology creates stress for everyone

- Flexibility doesn't mean chaos - it means adapting structure to fit your child's needs

- Being responsive to your child's cues actually creates more predictability in the long run

- "Good enough" parenting based on your individual child is better than "perfect" parenting based on external standards

How Tom's approach changed over time: Instead of rigid schedules, Tom learned to create flexible frameworks. Instead of precise feeding times, he watched for hunger cues. Instead of forcing nap times, he created calm environments when Lily showed signs of tiredness. Instead of following every expert recommendation, he trusted his observations of his own child.

This shift not only made daily life easier but also strengthened Tom's bond with Lily. When he stopped focusing so intensely on schedules and outcomes, he was able to enjoy her personality and respond to her individual needs. Lily developed secure attachment and grew into a confident, well-regulated toddler.

Early warning signs and prevention

While most toddler behaviors that concern OCPD parents are actually normal and temporary, there are some early signs that might indicate a child is developing their own perfectionist or rigid patterns. Learning to distinguish between normal developmental phases and concerning patterns can help you provide early support when needed.

Normal toddler rigidity vs. concerning patterns

All toddlers go through phases of rigidity and inflexibility - this is actually a normal part of cognitive development. Toddlers' brains are working hard to understand patterns and rules, which can lead to very black-and-white thinking and resistance to changes in routine. The question isn't whether your toddler shows rigid behaviors, but whether these behaviors are interfering with their development and well-being.

According to Lerner Child Development, normal toddler rigidity typically includes preferences for routine, resistance to changes, and strong reactions when things don't go as expected (Lerner Child Development, n d). This is different from concerning rigidity, which might interfere with a child's ability to adapt, learn, and form relationships.

Normal toddler rigidity:

- Wanting the same bedtime routine every night

- Preferring foods prepared or presented in specific ways

- Having strong reactions to changes in plans or routines

- Insisting on doing certain tasks themselves in their own way

- Going through phases of being very particular about clothes, toys, or arrangements

- Developing strong preferences for certain activities or objects

Potentially concerning patterns:

- Extreme distress that lasts for extended periods when routines change

- Rigidity that interferes with basic daily activities (eating, sleeping, playing)

- Inability to adapt to new situations even with support and time

- Aggressive or self-harming behaviors when things don't go as expected

- Social isolation due to inflexibility in play or interactions

- Developmental regression in areas like language, social skills, or self-care

Key differences:

- **Intensity**: Normal rigidity involves strong preferences; concerning rigidity involves extreme distress

- **Duration**: Normal phases last weeks or months; concerning patterns persist without improvement

- **Flexibility**: Normal rigidity can be negotiated or adapted; concerning rigidity is completely inflexible

- **Impact**: Normal rigidity doesn't interfere with overall development; concerning rigidity limits learning and growth

Supporting flexibility from the start

Rather than waiting to see if problematic patterns develop, OCPD parents can actively support flexibility and adaptability from early toddlerhood. This doesn't mean avoiding all routines or structure, but rather helping your child develop the skills to handle changes and uncertainty.

Ways to build flexibility in toddlers:

Practice small changes regularly: Instead of keeping everything exactly the same all the time, introduce small, manageable changes to help your toddler practice adapting. Maybe take a different route to the park sometimes, or let them choose between two breakfast options.

Use transitional language: Help your toddler understand that changes can happen by using phrases like "Usually we do this, but today we're going to try something different" or "Our plan changed, so now we're going to..."

Model flexibility yourself: Let your toddler see you adapt to changes and handle unexpected situations. Talk about your own flexibility: "I was planning to make pasta for dinner, but we're out of pasta, so I'm going to make rice instead."

Offer choices within structure: Give your toddler opportunities to make decisions and have control over some aspects of their day, which builds confidence in their ability to handle different situations.

Validate feelings while supporting adaptation: When your toddler struggles with changes, acknowledge their feelings while helping them move forward: "You're disappointed that we can't go to the park because it's raining. It's hard when plans change. Let's think of something fun to do inside instead."

Creating an environment that encourages exploration

The physical and emotional environment you create has a huge impact on your toddler's willingness to explore, take risks, and develop flexibility. OCPD parents sometimes create environments that are so controlled and organized that children don't get opportunities to practice problem-solving and adaptation.

Physical environment considerations:

Child-proofed exploration spaces: Create areas where your toddler can explore freely without constant "no" or redirection. This might mean having one room or area where most things are safe to touch and investigate.

Accessible materials: Keep some toys, books, and materials at your child's level so they can independently choose what to engage with rather than always needing to ask for things.

Mess-friendly zones: Designate areas where messier activities are welcome - maybe a kitchen corner for play-dough, a bathroom space for water play, or an outdoor area for digging and exploring.

Variety of textures and materials: Provide opportunities for sensory exploration with different textures, temperatures, and materials, even if this creates some mess and unpredictability.

Emotional environment considerations:

Curiosity over criticism: When your toddler makes mistakes or creates messes, respond with curiosity about what they were trying to do rather than immediate correction or cleanup.

Process over outcome: Focus more on what your child is learning and experiencing than on the end result of their activities.

Acceptance of noise and chaos: Recognize that learning and exploration often involve noise, movement, and disorder - this is the sound of healthy development.

Patience with repetition: Toddlers learn through repetition, which might mean doing the same "messy" activity many times before they master new skills.

Checkpoint: Monthly development tracking without obsessing

It's natural and healthy to pay attention to your child's development, but OCPD parents can sometimes turn developmental tracking into an anxiety-provoking obsession. The goal is to stay aware of your child's progress while maintaining perspective and joy in their growth.

Monthly check-in framework:

Growth celebration: Each month, take note of new skills, behaviors, or interests your child has developed. Focus on celebrating progress rather than identifying gaps or delays.

Photo documentation: Take photos or videos that capture your child's current abilities and interests. This creates a visual record of growth that you can look back on during times when progress seems slow.

Milestone awareness without anxiety: Stay generally aware of developmental milestones for your child's age, but focus on ranges rather than specific timelines, and remember that every child develops differently.

Professional guidance when needed: If you have genuine concerns about your child's development, consult with your pediatrician rather than trying to diagnose or fix things yourself.

Questions for monthly reflection:

- What new skills has my child developed this month?
- What brings them joy and excitement right now?
- How has their personality or interests changed?
- What challenges are they working on?
- How is our relationship and connection?
- What do I want to focus on supporting next month?

Red flags that warrant professional consultation:

- Loss of previously acquired skills

- Significant delays in multiple developmental areas

- Extreme rigidity that interferes with daily activities

- Social withdrawal or lack of interest in interaction

- Persistent eating or sleeping difficulties

- Your own anxiety about development that interferes with enjoying your child

Chapter 6: Preschool years (3-5 years)

The preschool years bring a fascinating paradox for perfectionist parents: your child is becoming more capable and independent, which should make things easier, but they're also becoming more opinionated, creative, and interested in doing things their own way, which can trigger every OCPD tendency you have.

This is the age when children start to have real conversations, express complex ideas, and demonstrate genuine problem-solving abilities. But it's also when they want to dress themselves in completely impractical outfits, spend twenty minutes arranging their toys "just right," and have strong opinions about everything from which cup they drink from to the exact way their sandwich should be cut.

For OCPD parents, these years can feel like a constant negotiation between wanting to guide your child toward efficient, practical choices and recognizing that their growing independence is exactly what you want to encourage. The key is learning to offer structure and guidance while leaving room for your child's emerging sense of self and personal preferences.

Fostering autonomy while maintaining structure

The art of offering controlled choices

One of the most effective strategies for preschool-age children is offering choices within acceptable parameters. This gives them the autonomy they're craving while maintaining the structure you need as a parent. The key is offering real choices that you can live with, rather than fake choices that will frustrate both of you.

According to research from Substack and Upshur Bren, offering children appropriate choices helps them develop decision-making skills, builds their confidence, and reduces power struggles (Substack, 2023; Upshur Bren, 2023). For OCPD parents, this approach can feel challenging because it requires giving up some control, but it actually creates more cooperation in the long run.

Examples of effective controlled choices:

Getting dressed: Instead of laying out one specific outfit, offer two or three weather-appropriate options and let your child choose. You might also let them choose between getting dressed before or after breakfast, as long as they're dressed before you need to leave.

Meals: Rather than making one meal and insisting your child eat it, offer choices within healthy parameters: "Would you like carrots or broccoli with dinner?" or "Do you want your sandwich cut into triangles or rectangles?"

Activities: Instead of planning every moment of your child's day, offer choices about how to spend free time: "Would you like to read books or do a puzzle during quiet time?" or "Should we go to the park or work in the garden this afternoon?"

Routines: Let your child have some control over the order of routine activities: "Do you want to brush your teeth first or put on pajamas first?" or "Should we read one long book or two short books at bedtime?"

What makes choices work for OCPD parents:

- You maintain control over the acceptable options
- Your child gets to exercise independence and decision-making
- Power struggles are reduced because your child feels they have some control
- You can still ensure that practical needs are met
- Your child learns to work within reasonable boundaries

Common mistakes with choices:

- Offering choices you can't actually live with ("What do you want for dinner?" when you're only prepared to make two specific things)

- Too many options, which can overwhelm preschoolers

- Fake choices that aren't really optional ("Do you want to clean up your toys now?" when cleanup isn't actually negotiable)

- Taking back choices when your child doesn't choose what you prefer

Age-appropriate expectations vs. perfectionist standards

Preschoolers are capable of much more than toddlers, but they're still developing basic skills like impulse control, emotional regulation, and logical thinking. OCPD parents sometimes have expectations that are technically appropriate for a child's age but don't account for the normal variability in how these skills develop.

Research from Wikipedia on age appropriateness shows that developmental milestones have wide ranges, and expecting children to perform at the top of these ranges consistently can create unnecessary stress and pressure (Wikipedia, 2023). The goal is having expectations that challenge your child appropriately without setting them up for failure.

Age-appropriate expectations for preschoolers (3-5 years):

Self-care skills: Can dress themselves with minimal help, use the bathroom independently most of the time, brush teeth with supervision, help with simple meal preparation

Social and emotional skills: Can express basic emotions in words, show empathy for others, play cooperatively for short periods, follow simple rules in group settings

Cognitive skills: Can follow multi-step instructions, engage in pretend play, show interest in letters and numbers, ask lots of questions about how things work

Physical skills: Can run, jump, climb stairs alternating feet, use scissors and crayons with increasing control, catch a large ball

Perfectionist expectations that might be too high:

- Never having accidents after potty training is "complete"
- Always sharing and playing cooperatively without conflicts
- Remembering and following all household rules consistently
- Completing tasks the first time they're asked without reminders
- Having neat handwriting or perfect cutting skills
- Never losing or forgetting belongings
- Always choosing practical, weather-appropriate clothing

Signs your expectations might be too high:

- Your child frequently seems stressed or anxious about meeting your standards
- You find yourself constantly correcting or redirecting your child
- Your child has stopped trying things independently because they're afraid of making mistakes
- You feel frustrated with your child's performance most days
- Your child's behavior is significantly different at home versus other settings

Supporting emotional regulation without suppression

Preschoolers are still learning to manage big emotions, and they need support in developing these skills rather than simply being told to "calm down" or "control themselves." For OCPD parents, children's emotional outbursts can feel particularly challenging because they disrupt order and feel unpredictable.

According to research from WebMD and the Illinois Early Learning Project, preschoolers' emotional regulation skills are still developing, and they need patient, consistent support to learn these complex abilities (WebMD, 2023; Illinois Early Learning Project, 2023). Suppressing emotions or rushing children through emotional experiences actually slows down this developmental process.

Healthy emotional regulation support:

Validate emotions before addressing behavior: "You're really angry that your tower fell down. It's frustrating when something you worked hard on gets wrecked. Let's take some deep breaths together and then figure out what to do next."

Teach emotional vocabulary: Help your child learn words for different emotions and the physical sensations that go with them: "It looks like you're feeling disappointed. Sometimes disappointment feels heavy in our chest."

Model regulation strategies: Show your child how you handle your own big emotions: "I'm feeling really frustrated right now because the computer isn't working. I'm going to take three deep breaths and count to ten."

Create calm-down strategies together: Work with your child to develop their own toolbox of regulation strategies: deep breathing, counting, squeezing a stress ball, looking at a favorite book.

Problem-solving approach to emotions: Rather than seeing emotions as problems to be fixed, help your child understand what their emotions are telling them and how to respond appropriately.

What emotional suppression looks like (and why it's problematic):

- Immediately redirecting attention away from emotions ("Don't cry, let's go play")

- Dismissing emotions as unimportant ("You're fine, it's not a big deal")

- Using distraction to avoid dealing with emotions ("Here, have a snack")

- Punishing emotional expression ("If you keep crying, you'll go to your room")

- Comparing emotions unfavorably ("Your sister doesn't cry about things like this")

Tool kit: Visual schedules with built-in flexibility

Visual schedules can be incredibly helpful for preschoolers because they provide predictability while still allowing for some flexibility. For OCPD parents, they offer structure and organization, while for children, they provide independence and security.

Creating flexible visual schedules:

Use pictures or symbols to represent different activities rather than specific times. This allows you to maintain the sequence of activities while being flexible about timing.

Include choice points in your schedule where your child can select from acceptable options. Maybe there's a "choice time" slot where they can pick between three activities.

Build in transition warnings by including "warning" pictures before major transitions. This might be a picture of a timer or clock that signals "almost time to clean up."

Use moveable pieces so you can adjust the schedule when needed without completely disrupting the structure. Velcro or magnets work well for this.

Include both must-do and choice activities so your child learns to distinguish between non-negotiable parts of the day and areas where they have more control.

Sample flexible morning routine visual schedule:

1. Wake up/snuggle time

2. Use bathroom

3. Get dressed (picture showing choice between two outfits)

4. Breakfast

5. Brush teeth

6. Choice time (pictures of 3-4 possible activities)

7. Get ready to go (shoes, jacket, backpack)

Benefits of visual schedules for OCPD parents:

- Reduces the need to constantly give verbal reminders
- Allows your child to be more independent in following routines
- Provides structure without rigidity
- Makes changes visible and manageable
- Reduces power struggles about daily activities

Managing OCPD triggers in daily routines

Daily routines with preschoolers can be particularly challenging for OCPD parents because children this age are capable enough that their resistance or inefficiency feels more frustrating, but they still lack the impulse control and planning abilities to consistently meet adult expectations.

Morning chaos: strategies for letting go of perfection

Mornings with preschoolers can feel like chaos, especially when you're trying to get everyone out the door on time. The combination of a child who might be tired, grumpy, or distracted with a parent who needs things to go smoothly can create daily stress and conflict.

Common morning challenges for OCPD parents:

- Getting dressed takes forever because your child wants to do it themselves but lacks efficiency

- Breakfast becomes a negotiation about what to eat and how much

- Finding lost items that should have been put in designated places

- Children moving slowly when you feel pressed for time

- Resistance to necessary tasks like tooth brushing or putting on shoes

- Meltdowns over minor issues that derail the entire routine

Strategies for more flexible morning routines:

Prepare the night before: Set out clothes, pack backpacks, and prepare breakfast items so there are fewer decisions and tasks in the morning rush.

Build in extra time: If you need to leave at 8:00, start getting ready at 7:15 instead of 7:45. Having buffer time reduces the pressure on everyone.

Create morning choice points: Let your child choose between two breakfast options or two outfits so they feel some control over their morning.

Use timers as helpers, not pressure: "Let's see if we can get dressed before this song ends" feels more playful than "Hurry up, we're going to be late."

Have backup plans: Know what you'll do if your child has a meltdown, if you can't find something important, or if you're running behind schedule.

Focus on connection first: A few minutes of positive interaction at the beginning of the morning can prevent bigger problems later.

Mealtime battles: when control meets picky eating

Mealtimes can become major battlegrounds between OCPD parents who want their children to eat nutritious, properly prepared meals and preschoolers who are naturally picky and want to assert independence around food choices.

Why mealtime battles escalate for OCPD parents:

- You've put effort into preparing nutritious meals and feel frustrated when they're rejected
- Picky eating feels like a reflection of your parenting or meal planning abilities
- Wasted food triggers anxiety about efficiency and resource management
- Irregular eating patterns feel unpredictable and concerning
- Messy eating triggers discomfort with disorder

Strategies for reducing mealtime stress:

Division of responsibility: You decide what foods to offer and when to serve them; your child decides how much to eat and whether to eat. This reduces battles while ensuring your child gets adequate nutrition over time.

Family-style serving: Put foods in serving bowls and let your child serve themselves. This gives them control while exposing them to variety.

Include one preferred food: Make sure each meal includes at least one food you know your child will eat, along with other options they can try or ignore.

Minimize mealtime negotiations: Avoid bargaining, bribing, or negotiating about food during meals. Offer what you've prepared and let your child make their choices.

Keep meals social and pleasant: Focus on family connection and conversation rather than monitoring what and how much your child is eating.

Trust your child's appetite: Preschoolers are generally good at self-regulating their food intake over time, even if individual meals seem inadequate to adults.

Bedtime resistance: flexibility within boundaries

Bedtime routines are often very important to OCPD parents because they provide structure and ensure children get adequate sleep. But preschoolers often resist bedtime, want to negotiate routines, or have difficulty settling down, which can trigger control battles.

Common bedtime challenges:

- Requests for "one more" story, drink, or trip to the bathroom
- Difficulty settling down and falling asleep
- Resistance to parts of the bedtime routine
- Variations in sleep needs that don't match your schedule
- Fear or anxiety that makes bedtime more complex

Flexible bedtime strategies:

Consistent routine with small choices: Maintain the same basic sequence (bath, pajamas, teeth, stories, bed) but allow choices about details like which pajamas or which books.

Gradual wind-down time: Build in a calm transition period before the actual bedtime routine starts so your child can mentally prepare for the day to end.

Address needs proactively: Offer water, bathroom trips, and comfort items before the final "good night" to reduce requests for delays.

Set clear expectations with empathy: "I know you don't want the day to end, and it's hard to stop playing. Our bodies need sleep to grow and feel good tomorrow. After this story, it's time for lights out."

Plan for variations: Some nights will go smoothly, others won't. Having strategies for difficult nights reduces stress when they happen.

Real-life scripts: Responding to common preschooler challenges

Having prepared responses can help you stay calm and consistent when challenging situations arise. Here are scripts for common preschooler behaviors that often trigger OCPD parents:

When your child refuses to get dressed: Instead of: "You have to get dressed right now! We're going to be late and this is ridiculous!" Try: "Getting dressed is hard sometimes. Would you like to choose your shirt first or your pants first? I can help if you need me to."

When your child makes a mess during an activity: Instead of: "Look at this mess! You need to be more careful and clean this up immediately!" Try: "Wow, you were really focused on your project. I can see you were experimenting with the paints. Let's clean this up together and then you can tell me about what you were making."

When your child has a meltdown over something minor: Instead of: "You're overreacting. This is not a big deal and you need to calm down right now." Try: "You have big feelings about this. It's really important to you. I'm going to sit with you while you feel upset, and then we can figure out what to do together."

When your child doesn't follow instructions: Instead of: "I already told you to clean up your toys. Why don't you listen to me?" Try: "I notice the toys are still out. What's your plan for cleaning them up? Do you need help getting started or do you want to do it yourself?"

When your child is moving too slowly: Instead of: "Hurry up! You're taking forever and we're going to be late!" Try: "I notice you're taking your time today. We need to leave in five minutes. What do you still need to do to get ready?"

Social development and play

Preschoolers are developing complex social skills and engaging in increasingly sophisticated play. For OCPD parents, this can create anxiety because social situations are unpredictable and play often involves mess, noise, and activities that don't have clear productive outcomes.

Overcoming discomfort with messy, unstructured play

Play is how preschoolers learn about the world, practice social skills, develop creativity, and process their experiences. But the type of play that's most beneficial for development - open-ended, child-directed, sometimes messy exploration - can be difficult for OCPD parents to tolerate.

Why unstructured play is important for preschoolers:

- **Creativity development**: Open-ended play allows children to use their imagination and come up with novel solutions to problems

- **Social skill practice**: Unstructured play with peers requires negotiation, compromise, and cooperation

- **Emotional processing**: Through play, children work through experiences, fears, and concerns

- **Self-direction skills**: When adults don't structure every activity, children learn to entertain themselves and make their own choices

- **Problem-solving abilities**: Unstructured play presents natural problems and challenges that children must figure out on their own

Strategies for OCPD parents to support messy play:

Designate mess-friendly spaces: Create areas where messy play is welcome and expected. This might be an art corner, an outdoor play area, or a specific room where different rules apply.

Set time boundaries: Knowing that messy play has a defined start and end time can make it more tolerable. "We're going to do art projects for thirty minutes, and then we'll clean up together."

Focus on the process, not the product: Instead of evaluating what your child creates, pay attention to what they're learning and experiencing during the activity.

Join in occasionally: Playing alongside your child can help you understand the value of their activities and reduce your anxiety about the mess and apparent lack of productivity.

Prepare for cleanup: Having cleanup supplies ready and involving your child in the cleanup process makes the mess feel more manageable and temporary.

Supporting peer interactions without micromanaging

Preschoolers are learning how to navigate friendships, share, take turns, and handle conflicts with peers. These social skills develop through practice and experience, but OCPD parents sometimes intervene too quickly or frequently, preventing children from learning to handle social situations independently.

Common social challenges for preschoolers:

- Difficulty sharing toys or materials
- Conflicts over rules in games or activities
- Exclusion or being left out of play
- Different play styles or interests leading to disagreements
- Big emotions when social interactions don't go as expected

How to support without micromanaging:

Stay nearby but don't hover: Position yourself where you can observe and intervene if necessary, but allow children to interact without constant adult direction.

Wait before intervening: Give children a chance to work through minor conflicts on their own before stepping in to help. Many social problems resolve naturally if adults don't jump in too quickly.

Teach problem-solving skills: When you do need to intervene, help children generate their own solutions rather than imposing adult solutions: "You both want to use the swings. What are some ideas for solving this problem?"

Model social skills: Show children how to handle social situations through your own behavior and by coaching them through difficulties rather than solving problems for them.

Validate emotions while supporting growth: "You're disappointed that Sarah doesn't want to play the game your way. That's hard. What could you do when friends want to play differently than you do?"

Allowing natural consequences in social situations

Natural consequences are powerful teachers for preschoolers, but OCPD parents sometimes try to prevent or fix these consequences instead of allowing children to learn from their experiences.

Examples of natural social consequences:

- If your child is bossy or controlling with friends, peers might not want to play with them

- If your child doesn't take turns, others might not include them in games

- If your child has meltdowns during playdates, friends might feel uncomfortable and want to leave

- If your child is rough or aggressive, others might avoid physical play with them

Supporting learning from natural consequences:

Resist the urge to rescue: When your child experiences social disappointment, avoid immediately trying to fix the situation or explain away the other child's behavior.

Help process the experience: Talk with your child about what happened and what they might do differently next time, but avoid lecturing or over-explaining.

Trust the learning process: Children are motivated to improve their social skills when they experience natural feedback from peers. Your job is to support them through disappointments, not prevent all social challenges.

Focus on skill development: Use social difficulties as opportunities to practice skills like compromise, empathy, and flexibility rather than trying to control social outcomes.

Activity guide: Structured play that builds flexibility

You can create play activities that satisfy your need for some structure while still promoting the flexibility and creativity your child needs. These activities have loose frameworks but allow for individual expression and adaptation.

Art exploration stations: Set up different art materials at stations around a room - watercolors at one table, clay at another, collage materials at a third. Children can move between stations and combine materials in their own ways.

Building challenges: Provide blocks or other construction materials with loose prompts like "build something that can hold water" or "create a structure that's taller than you are." Children can interpret these challenges in their own ways.

Story creation activities: Start a story with one sentence and let your child add to it, or provide story prompts like picture cards that children can arrange and narrate in different ways.

Science experiments: Simple experiments like mixing colors, growing plants, or exploring magnets provide structure while allowing for discovery and individual exploration.

Dramatic play themes: Set up dramatic play areas with themes like "restaurant," "doctor's office," or "space station," but let children decide how to play within these frameworks.

Benefits of structured flexibility in play:

- Provides enough structure to feel manageable for OCPD parents
- Allows children to express creativity and make choices within boundaries
- Builds problem-solving and adaptive thinking skills
- Creates opportunities for social interaction and cooperation
- Develops confidence in handling open-ended situations

Chapter 7: School-age children (6-11 years)

The elementary school years bring a whole new set of challenges for perfectionist parents. Your child now has homework, grades, extracurricular activities, and social relationships that extend far beyond your direct control. They're developing their own opinions, interests, and ways of doing things that might not match your preferences. And for the first time, their performance is being evaluated by outside authorities - teachers, coaches, other parents - in ways that can feel like reflections of your parenting.

This is often when OCPD traits in parenting become most visible and problematic. The stakes feel higher because academic and social foundations are being established. There are concrete measures of success and failure. Other parents are watching and comparing. Your child's struggles feel more significant because they're happening in "real" settings with lasting consequences.

But here's what research consistently shows: children who are allowed to take age-appropriate responsibility for their own learning and social relationships develop stronger skills and greater confidence than children whose parents manage these areas for them. The goal during these years isn't to control your child's outcomes, but to teach them the skills they need to manage challenges independently.

Academic achievement without perfectionist pressure

Separating your worth from your child's grades

One of the biggest traps for OCPD parents is tying their sense of success as a parent to their child's academic performance. When your child brings home a poor grade or struggles with a concept, it can feel like a direct reflection of your adequacy as a parent. This emotional fusion makes it almost impossible to support your child effectively because you're managing your own anxiety rather than responding to their needs.

Signs that you might be too emotionally invested in your child's grades:

- You feel more upset about poor grades than your child does
- You find yourself doing homework assignments or projects to ensure they're "good enough"
- You check your child's grades online more frequently than they do
- You feel embarrassed or defensive when teachers mention areas where your child is struggling
- You compare your child's performance to their siblings or peers and feel anxious when they don't measure up
- You find yourself arguing with teachers about grades or assignments
- Your mood is significantly affected by your child's academic ups and downs

Strategies for emotional separation:

Focus on your child's relationship with learning: Instead of asking "How can I make sure they get good grades?" ask "How can I help them develop a positive relationship with learning and challenge?"

Trust the process of education: One poor grade or struggling semester doesn't predict future academic failure. Children learn and develop at different paces and in different ways.

Define your role clearly: Your job is to provide support, resources, and encouragement. Your child's job is to engage with their education and take age-appropriate responsibility for their learning.

Practice perspective-taking: Ask yourself how you want your child to remember their elementary school years. Do you want them to remember stress and pressure about grades, or curiosity and joy about learning?

Address your own academic history: If you struggled academically as a child or felt pressure from your own parents about grades, you might be unconsciously recreating those patterns. Consider how your own school experiences might be affecting your reactions to your child's education.

Supporting homework without controlling it

Homework can become a major battleground between OCPD parents and school-age children. You want to ensure your child is learning and completing assignments properly, but your child needs to develop independent study skills and take ownership of their academic responsibilities.

According to research from Lynn Lyons, children who are over-supported with homework often fail to develop the executive functioning skills they need for academic independence (Lyons, 2023). They learn to depend on adult management rather than developing their own systems for managing time, organizing materials, and persisting through challenges.

The homework challenge for OCPD parents:

- You can see exactly what needs to be improved or corrected
- Incomplete or incorrect work triggers your anxiety about your child's learning
- You worry that poor homework habits will create long-term academic problems
- You have strong opinions about the "right" way to approach assignments

- You feel responsible for ensuring your child meets teacher expectations

Guidelines for healthy homework support:

Create a consistent homework environment: Provide a designated space, necessary supplies, and a regular time for homework, but let your child manage the actual work.

Be available for help, not management: Position yourself as a resource your child can access when they're stuck, rather than as a supervisor monitoring every moment of their work.

Focus on effort and process: Instead of checking every answer, ask questions about your child's approach: "How did you figure out this problem?" or "What was challenging about this assignment?"

Allow natural consequences: If your child forgets an assignment or doesn't complete work to their capability, let them experience the consequences at school rather than rushing to rescue them.

Teach organizational systems: Help your child develop their own systems for tracking assignments, organizing materials, and managing their time, but let them implement and modify these systems.

Resist the urge to perfect: If your child's work is adequate for their age and ability level, resist the temptation to suggest improvements or corrections that would make it "better."

Managing your anxiety about their performance

School-age children go through natural ups and downs in their academic performance. They might excel in some subjects while struggling in others, have good semesters followed by challenging ones, or show inconsistent effort and engagement. For OCPD parents, this variability can create significant anxiety and impulses to intervene.

Common performance anxieties for OCPD parents:

- Worrying that current struggles predict future academic failure

- Feeling like you need to fix or solve every academic challenge immediately

- Comparing your child's performance to siblings, peers, or your own childhood achievements

- Catastrophizing normal learning difficulties into serious problems

- Feeling responsible for preventing all academic disappointments or setbacks

Strategies for managing performance anxiety:

Normalize learning variability: All children have subjects that come easily and others that require more effort. All children go through periods of high engagement and times when they're less motivated.

Focus on long-term patterns: Instead of reacting to individual grades or assignments, look at overall trends in your child's learning and engagement over months and semesters.

Trust your child's natural development: Most academic skills develop naturally through practice and maturation. Your child doesn't need to master every concept immediately or perform at the top of their class in every subject.

Communicate with teachers regularly: Instead of worrying alone about your child's performance, maintain regular communication with teachers to understand their perspective and get guidance about when concerns are warranted.

Separate temporary struggles from permanent problems: A child who's having difficulty with multiplication isn't destined for mathematical failure. A poor grade on a science project doesn't indicate a lack of intelligence or future academic problems.

Framework: The collaborative homework approach

This approach balances your desire to ensure your child is learning with their need to develop independence and ownership of their academic work. The key is shifting from manager to consultant - available for support but not responsible for outcomes.

Phase 1: Setup and environment (your responsibility)

- Provide a consistent homework space with necessary supplies
- Establish a regular homework time that works for your family
- Ensure your child has eaten, used the bathroom, and is ready to focus
- Remove distractions and create a calm environment

Phase 2: Planning and organization (collaborative)

- Help your child look at their assignments and estimate time needed
- Support them in prioritizing tasks and making a plan
- Ask questions that help them think through their approach
- Teach planning skills but let them make decisions about their homework order and timing

Phase 3: Work time (child's responsibility with available support)

- Allow your child to work independently while you remain available for questions
- Respond to requests for help with guidance rather than answers
- Encourage your child to try strategies before asking for assistance
- Resist the urge to monitor their progress or correct mistakes in real-time

Phase 4: Review and completion (collaborative with limits)

- If your child asks, you can review their work and ask questions that help them identify areas to double-check

- Focus on the process they used rather than the accuracy of every answer

- Help them organize completed work and pack it in their backpack

- Avoid doing final checks or corrections that they should be responsible for

Questions that support learning without controlling:

- "What's your plan for tackling this assignment?"

- "What part seems most challenging to you?"

- "How did you figure out that problem?"

- "What would you do differently if you were starting this assignment over?"

- "Is there anything you want to double-check before you put this away?"

Developing independence through scaffolded support

The elementary school years are when children begin taking on real responsibilities and developing the skills they'll need for increasing independence. OCPD parents sometimes struggle with this process because it requires gradually letting go of control while trusting that your child can handle more than you might feel comfortable with.

The gradual release of control model

This educational framework can be adapted for parenting to help you support your child's growing independence in age-appropriate ways. The idea is that you start with high support and structure, then gradually transfer more responsibility to your child as they demonstrate readiness.

Level 1: I do, you watch (High parent control) This is appropriate for new skills or during times when your child needs extensive support. You model the skill or behavior while your child observes and learns.

Level 2: I do, you help (Moderate parent control) Your child begins participating in the activity but you're still providing most of the direction and structure. They're learning by doing with significant support.

Level 3: You do, I help (Moderate child control) Your child takes the lead but you're available to provide guidance, encouragement, and assistance when needed. This is where many school-age activities should fall.

Level 4: You do, I watch (High child independence) Your child handles the responsibility independently while you remain available for support if needed. You're observing to ensure safety and provide encouragement but not actively managing the process.

Examples of gradual release in daily life:

Morning routine: Start by helping your child get ready each morning, then gradually transfer responsibility for different tasks (choosing clothes, packing backpack, preparing breakfast) until they can manage their entire morning routine independently.

Chores and responsibilities: Begin by doing household tasks together, then let your child take the lead while you provide guidance, and eventually let them handle age-appropriate chores completely on their own.

Social problem-solving: Initially, you might help your child navigate peer conflicts by providing specific scripts and strategies. Over time, you help them brainstorm their own solutions, and eventually they handle most social challenges independently.

Age-appropriate responsibilities and natural consequences

School-age children can handle significantly more responsibility than many parents realize. Giving children appropriate responsibilities not only helps with household functioning but also builds their confidence, competence, and sense of contribution to the family.

Age-appropriate responsibilities for elementary school children:

Ages 6-7: Simple daily self-care (getting dressed, brushing teeth), basic household tasks (setting the table, feeding pets), organizing their own belongings (putting away toys, hanging up backpacks)

Ages 8-9: More complex self-care (packing lunch, organizing homework materials), regular chores (loading dishwasher, folding laundry), managing their own social plans with guidance (calling friends, remembering playdates)

Ages 10-11: Increased independence in self-care (choosing weather-appropriate clothes, managing personal hygiene), significant household contributions (preparing simple meals, managing their own laundry), greater responsibility for academic and social life (tracking assignments, resolving peer conflicts)

The role of natural consequences in building responsibility:

Natural consequences are the automatic results of choices and behaviors. They're powerful teachers because they're directly connected to the child's actions rather than imposed by parents.

Examples of natural consequences:

- If your child forgets their lunch, they experience hunger or have to eat school lunch

- If they don't put their bike away, it might get wet in the rain or be harder to find next time

- If they don't complete homework, they face teacher consequences and might need to use free time to catch up

- If they're careless with belongings, they might lose things they care about

Supporting learning from natural consequences:

- Allow consequences to happen instead of rescuing your child

- Show empathy for their disappointment without fixing the situation

- Help them problem-solve ways to prevent similar problems in the future

- Resist the urge to lecture or say "I told you so"

Allowing children to fail safely

This might be the hardest concept for OCPD parents to accept: children need to experience failure and disappointment in age-appropriate ways to develop resilience and problem-solving skills. According to research from Lynn Lyons and the Child Mind Institute, children who are protected from all failure often struggle more as adults when they inevitably encounter challenges they can't handle (Lyons, 2023; Child Mind Institute, 2023).

Safe failures for school-age children:

- Getting a poor grade on an assignment they didn't put effort into

- Losing a privilege because they didn't follow family rules

- Having a friendship conflict because of their own poor choices

- Facing consequences for forgetting responsibilities or materials

- Not making a team or getting a part in a play they wanted

Supporting children through failures:

Validate their disappointment: "You're really disappointed that you didn't make the soccer team. That's hard when something you wanted doesn't work out."

Help them process the experience: "What do you think happened? Is there anything you would do differently next time?"

Focus on learning and growth: "What did this experience teach you about yourself or about how things work?"

Avoid immediate fixing: Resist the urge to call the school, intervene with other parents, or solve the problem for your child unless there are genuine safety or fairness concerns.

Rebuild confidence through action: "What would you like to try next? How can you use what you learned from this experience?"

Case study: Maria's journey from helicopter to lighthouse parent

Maria was a successful professional who approached her daughter Carmen's education with the same intensity and attention to detail she brought to her career. She checked the school website daily for new assignments, maintained detailed charts of Carmen's progress in different subjects, and spent hours each evening supervising homework to ensure it met her standards.

Initially, this approach seemed to work well. Carmen's grades were excellent, her projects were always completed on time, and teachers praised her organized approach to learning. But by fourth grade, problems started emerging. Carmen would panic if she couldn't reach Maria for help with homework. She seemed unable to manage time or prioritize tasks without detailed adult guidance. Most concerning to Maria, Carmen had started saying things like "I'm not smart" when she encountered challenging problems.

The turning point came during a parent-teacher conference when Carmen's teacher gently suggested that Carmen might benefit from more independence with her schoolwork. "She's a bright child," the teacher said, "but she seems to lack confidence in her own abilities. She asks for help before trying to work through problems on her own."

Maria realized that her intense involvement was actually undermining Carmen's development of academic confidence and independence. She decided to gradually step back and shift from being a "helicopter parent" (hovering over every aspect of Carmen's education) to being a "lighthouse parent" (providing guidance and support while allowing Carmen to navigate her own course).

Maria's gradual transition process:

Week 1-2: Maria stopped checking the school website daily and instead asked Carmen to tell her about assignments and due dates. She moved from sitting next to Carmen during homework to being available in the same room.

Week 3-4: Maria began letting Carmen tackle homework independently for 15-20 minutes before offering help. She practiced asking questions like "What have you tried so far?" instead of immediately providing solutions.

Week 5-8: Maria implemented a rule that Carmen had to try three different strategies before asking for help. She started letting natural consequences happen - if Carmen forgot an assignment, Maria didn't rush to school with it.

Week 9-12: Maria transitioned to checking in with Carmen about homework rather than supervising it. She began letting Carmen experience the natural consequences of her choices about effort and organization.

The results of Maria's changes:

- Carmen initially struggled with the increased independence and made some mistakes she hadn't made before
- After about a month, Carmen began developing her own organizational systems and problem-solving strategies
- Carmen's confidence increased as she realized she could handle challenges without constant adult support

- Their homework battles decreased significantly once Maria stepped back from managing every detail
- Carmen's grades remained strong, and her teachers noticed increased independence and self-advocacy

What Maria learned:

- Her intense involvement was actually preventing Carmen from developing necessary skills
- Children are more capable than anxious parents often believe
- Stepping back feels uncomfortable initially but leads to better outcomes
- Trust in her child's abilities needed to be demonstrated through action, not just words
- Being a lighthouse parent (providing guidance and support from a stable position) was more helpful than being a helicopter parent (hovering and managing everything)

Recognizing and addressing OCPD traits in children

School-age children who are developing their own perfectionist patterns need early intervention and support. The goal isn't to eliminate all structure or standards, but to help children develop healthy approaches to achievement and challenges.

Early intervention strategies for perfectionist children

According to research from Washington University School of Medicine, perfectionism in young children can be an early indicator of developing anxiety and obsessive-compulsive traits (WashU Medicine, 2023). Early intervention during the elementary school years can help children develop healthier relationships with achievement and mistakes.

Signs of problematic perfectionism in school-age children:

- Extreme distress over minor mistakes or imperfections

- Refusal to turn in work that isn't "perfect"

- Excessive time spent on assignments to achieve unnecessary precision

- Avoidance of new activities or challenges due to fear of failure

- Physical symptoms (stomachaches, headaches) related to academic or social performance

- Difficulty enjoying activities unless they excel at them

- Harsh self-criticism and negative self-talk about performance

- Social withdrawal or avoidance due to perfectionistic concerns

Early intervention strategies:

Model healthy perfectionism: Show your child how you handle your own mistakes and imperfections. Talk about times when "good enough" is actually the better choice.

Focus on effort and process: Praise your child's hard work, creative approaches, and persistence rather than just successful outcomes.

Practice mistake-making: Intentionally make small, harmless mistakes and show your child how you recover from them with humor and flexibility.

Set "good enough" goals: Help your child identify when something is adequately completed rather than pushing for perfection on every task.

Encourage risk-taking: Support your child in trying new activities where they won't immediately excel, and celebrate their willingness to be beginners.

When to seek professional help

Most children go through phases of perfectionist behavior that are temporary and don't significantly interfere with their functioning. However, some children need additional support to develop healthy relationships with achievement and challenges.

Research from the National Center for Biotechnology Information suggests that professional help is warranted when perfectionist traits significantly interfere with a child's daily functioning, relationships, or emotional well-being (NCBI, 2023).

When to consider professional support:

- Perfectionist behaviors are interfering with school performance (spending too much time on assignments, refusing to turn in work, frequent tears about school)

- Social relationships are affected (avoiding activities with peers, withdrawing from friendships due to performance concerns)

- Physical symptoms are present (frequent headaches, stomachaches, or sleep problems related to performance anxiety)

- Family life is significantly impacted (homework battles, frequent meltdowns about imperfection, family activities avoided due to child's perfectionist concerns)

- The child expresses frequent negative self-talk or seems to have very low self-esteem despite high achievement

- Previous attempts at home intervention haven't led to improvement over several months

Types of professional support:

School counselors: Can provide support for academic perfectionism and help with school-related anxiety and performance concerns.

Child psychologists or therapists: Can work with children on developing cognitive and behavioral strategies for managing perfectionist thoughts and behaviors.

Family therapy: Can help families change dynamics that might be reinforcing perfectionist patterns and develop healthier approaches to achievement and mistakes.

Balancing validation with challenge

Children with perfectionist tendencies need their feelings and concerns validated while also being gently challenged to expand their comfort zones and develop more flexible thinking patterns.

Validation strategies:

- Acknowledge that it's hard to make mistakes or not excel at something immediately

- Recognize the child's high standards and desire to do well

- Understand that perfectionist children often experience genuine distress about imperfection

- Validate their disappointment when things don't go as planned

Gentle challenge strategies:

- Encourage small risks and celebrate attempts rather than just successes

- Help the child identify "good enough" standards for different situations

- Practice flexibility through family games and activities that involve uncertainty

- Model your own imperfections and recovery from mistakes

- Create opportunities for the child to help others, which can shift focus from self-performance to contribution

Assessment tool: OCPD traits screening for school-age children

This informal assessment can help you determine whether your child might be developing concerning perfectionist patterns that would benefit from additional support.

Emotional responses to imperfection:

- Does your child become extremely upset over minor mistakes or imperfections?

- Do they have physical symptoms (crying, stomachaches, headaches) when things aren't perfect?

- Are they significantly more distressed by mistakes than their peers seem to be?

Behavioral patterns:

- Does your child spend excessive time on homework or projects trying to make them perfect?

- Do they avoid new activities or challenges because they might not excel immediately?

- Are they reluctant to turn in work or complete projects because they're not satisfied with the quality?

Social and family functioning:

- Has perfectionism affected your child's friendships or social activities?

- Do perfectionist concerns create frequent family conflict or stress?

- Does your child avoid family activities or outings due to performance-related anxiety?

Self-concept and talk:

- Does your child frequently criticize themselves or use negative self-talk?

- Do they seem to base their self-worth primarily on achievement and performance?

- Are they unable to enjoy activities unless they excel at them?

Duration and severity:

- Have these patterns persisted for several months despite your efforts to address them?

- Are perfectionist behaviors getting worse over time rather than improving?

- Do these concerns interfere with your child's daily functioning in multiple areas of life?

If you answered "yes" to several of these questions, particularly in multiple categories, it might be helpful to consult with your child's teacher, school counselor, or a mental health professional for additional guidance and support.

Chapter 8: Adolescence (12-18 years)

The teenage years represent the ultimate test of your ability to parent without controlling. Everything about healthy adolescent development - the push for independence, the questioning of authority, the need to make their own mistakes, the focus on peer relationships over family approval - can trigger intense anxiety in OCPD parents.

This is when the stakes feel highest because the consequences of poor choices seem more serious and long-lasting. Your teenager's decisions about school, friends, activities, and behavior feel like they'll determine their entire future trajectory. At the same time, your actual ability to control these decisions is rapidly diminishing as your child develops their own identity, values, and judgment.

The adolescent brain is literally under construction, with areas responsible for impulse control and long-term planning not fully developed until the mid-twenties. This means your teenager will make decisions that seem obviously poor to your adult brain, experience emotions with an intensity that might seem disproportionate, and prioritize immediate social concerns over long-term consequences. For OCPD parents, this developmental reality can feel genuinely terrifying.

But here's what research consistently shows: teenagers whose parents can maintain connection while allowing age-appropriate independence develop better judgment, stronger self-regulation, and more authentic relationships than teenagers whose parents try to maintain control through these years.

Navigating control battles with teens

Why OCPD parents struggle most during adolescence

According to research from the National Institutes of Health, adolescence is the developmental stage that creates the most stress for parents with controlling tendencies because it requires the greatest tolerance for uncertainty and loss of direct influence (NIH, 2023). Everything that made you feel like a competent parent during childhood - your ability to guide your child's choices, protect them from consequences, and ensure they meet appropriate standards - becomes counterproductive during adolescence.

Adolescent development naturally conflicts with OCPD parenting patterns:

Identity exploration vs. predetermined paths: Teenagers need to experiment with different identities, values, and interests to discover who they are. OCPD parents often have clear ideas about who their teenager should become and what path they should follow.

Peer influence vs. family control: During adolescence, peer relationships naturally become more influential than family relationships in many areas. This can feel threatening to parents who have been the primary influence on their child's choices and values.

Risk-taking vs. safety focus: Healthy adolescent development involves taking calculated risks and learning from natural consequences. OCPD parents often want to prevent risks and control outcomes to ensure safety and success.

Emotional intensity vs. regulated responses: Teenagers experience emotions with an intensity that can feel overwhelming to adults who prefer calm, rational approaches to problems. The adolescent brain is wired for emotional reactivity, which can trigger control responses in parents who value emotional control.

Questioning authority vs. following rules: Adolescents naturally begin questioning family rules, values, and expectations as they develop their own moral reasoning. Parents who value compliance and respect for authority often interpret this developmental necessity as disrespect or defiance.

Future focus vs. present orientation: Teenagers' brains are wired to prioritize immediate rewards and experiences over long-term planning. OCPD parents often feel frustrated by their teenager's apparent lack of concern for future consequences.

Collaborative problem-solving for parent-teen conflicts

Traditional approaches to teen conflict often involve either authoritarian control (imposing solutions) or permissive avoidance (hoping problems resolve themselves). Collaborative problem-solving offers a middle path that maintains your relationship with your teenager while still addressing legitimate concerns.

According to research from Creating a Family, collaborative approaches to teen conflict resolution lead to better outcomes than either controlling or permissive responses because they teach teenagers important life skills while maintaining family connection (Creating a Family, 2023).

The collaborative problem-solving process:

Step 1: Define the problem neutrally Instead of: "You're being irresponsible about curfew and showing complete disrespect for family rules." Try: "We have different ideas about what time you should be home on weekend nights, and this is creating conflict in our family."

Step 2: Listen to your teenager's perspective Ask genuine questions about their viewpoint: "Help me understand why the current curfew doesn't work for you" or "What would feel fair to you in this situation?"

Step 3: Share your concerns without attacking Express your genuine worries without criticizing their character: "I worry about your safety when you're out late" or "I'm concerned that staying out too late affects your energy for school the next day."

Step 4: Brainstorm solutions together Generate multiple options without immediately evaluating them: "Let's think of different ways we could handle this that would address both of our concerns."

Step 5: Evaluate options and choose a solution to try Discuss the pros and cons of different approaches and agree on something to try for a specific period of time.

Step 6: Plan for evaluation and adjustment Agree on how you'll know if the solution is working and when you'll check in to make adjustments if needed.

Example of collaborative problem-solving in action:

The situation: Your 16-year-old wants to go to a party at a friend's house where you suspect there might be drinking, and they want to stay overnight.

Traditional OCPD response: "Absolutely not. There's no way you're going to a party where kids might be drinking, and you're definitely not sleeping over. End of discussion."

Collaborative approach:

- "I can see this party is really important to you. Help me understand what makes it special."

- "I'm worried about drinking and driving, and I don't know this friend's parents well enough to feel comfortable with an overnight stay."

- "Let's think about ways you could attend this party while addressing my safety concerns."

- Possible solutions might include: going to the party but coming home that night, meeting the host parents first, having a specific check-in plan, or finding alternative transportation arrangements.

Respecting emerging autonomy while maintaining safety

The challenge for OCPD parents is learning to distinguish between issues that are genuinely about safety and values, and issues that are about your comfort, control, or preferences. Teenagers need increasing autonomy to develop good judgment, but they also need appropriate limits and guidance.

Areas where safety and core values are non-negotiable:

- Illegal activities that could result in serious consequences

- Behaviors that pose immediate physical danger

- Situations that violate fundamental family values about treating others with respect

- Activities that would prevent them from meeting basic responsibilities (school attendance, legal obligations)

Areas where teenagers need increasing autonomy:

- Choice of friends (unless there are genuine safety concerns)

- Extracurricular activities and interests

- Personal style and appearance choices

- How they spend their free time

- Social activities that don't pose safety risks

- Academic choices (course selections, study methods, college planning)

- Personal values development (as long as they don't harm others)

Strategies for supporting autonomy within safety bounds:

Use natural consequences when possible: Instead of imposing arbitrary punishments, allow teenagers to experience the natural results of their choices when it's safe to do so.

Provide information without lecturing: Share relevant information about risks and consequences, but allow your teenager to process and use this information to make their own decisions.

Focus on skill development: Instead of preventing all challenging situations, help your teenager develop the skills they need to handle difficult circumstances.

Maintain connection over control: Prioritize your relationship with your teenager over winning specific battles about rules and compliance.

Dialogue examples: Negotiating rules with teenagers

Having scripts for common conflict situations can help you stay calm and collaborative instead of falling into control patterns during heated moments.

Curfew negotiations: Teen: "Everyone else gets to stay out until midnight on weekends. You guys are so overprotective." Instead of: "I don't care what everyone else's parents do. Our rules exist for good reasons and they're not negotiable." Try: "It sounds like you feel our curfew is unfair compared to your friends. I want to understand more about what you're experiencing. Can you tell me more about how the current curfew affects your social plans?"

Academic concerns: Teen: "I don't understand why you're so obsessed with my grades. They're not even that bad." Instead of: "Your grades directly affect your future opportunities, and if you don't take them seriously now, you'll regret it later." Try: "I've noticed I've been asking about your grades a lot lately. Help me understand how you're feeling about school right now. What feels manageable and what feels challenging?"

Social media and technology: Teen: "You don't trust me at all. All my friends have phones in their rooms at night." Instead of: "Trust is earned, and screen time limits exist because teenagers can't self-regulate their technology use." Try: "I can hear that you feel like I don't trust you, and that must be frustrating. Let's talk about what trust looks like in our family and how we can build it around technology use."

Friend concerns: Teen: "You hate all my friends. You never think anyone is good enough." Instead of: "I don't hate your friends, but I have legitimate concerns about some of the choices they make and how they might influence you." Try: "It sounds like you feel I'm critical of your friendships, and I can understand how that would be hurtful. Help me understand what you value in these friendships so I can better appreciate what they mean to you."

Identity development vs. perfectionist identity

Adolescence is fundamentally about identity development - figuring out who you are separate from your family, what you believe, what you're passionate about, and how you want to engage with the world. This process requires experimentation, mistakes, and exploration that can feel threatening to OCPD parents who prefer predictable outcomes.

Supporting exploration when you crave certainty

According to research from PubMed Central, healthy identity development requires adolescents to explore different roles, values, and interests before committing to a sense of self (PubMed Central, 2023). This exploration process naturally involves uncertainty, changing interests, and what might look like inconsistency to adults who value stability and planning.

Normal identity exploration during adolescence:

- Changing interests and activities frequently
- Experimenting with different styles of dress, music, or self-expression
- Questioning family values and beliefs
- Trying on different social groups and friendship circles

- Expressing strong opinions that differ from family perspectives
- Showing inconsistency between stated values and behavior as they figure out what they actually believe

How OCPD parents can support identity exploration:

Resist the urge to predict or control the outcome: Your teenager doesn't need to know exactly who they are or what they want to do with their life during high school. Uncertainty is appropriate and healthy at this stage.

Show interest in their evolving interests: Even if your teenager's current passion seems impractical or temporary, showing genuine curiosity about what draws them to it demonstrates respect for their developing autonomy.

Avoid immediately pointing out inconsistencies: When your teenager's behavior doesn't match their stated values, resist the urge to point this out immediately. They're figuring out what they actually believe through experience.

Provide opportunities for exploration: Support your teenager's interest in trying new activities, even if they're not likely to stick with them long-term. The process of exploring is more important than the outcome of any specific activity.

Model your own ongoing growth: Share with your teenager how your own interests, perspectives, and priorities have changed over time. This normalizes identity development as a lifelong process.

Allowing teens to make their own mistakes

This might be the most difficult aspect of parenting teenagers with OCPD traits: watching your child make choices that you can clearly see will lead to disappointment, consequences, or missed opportunities. But teenagers need to develop their own judgment through experience, which necessarily includes making some poor decisions.

Types of mistakes teenagers need to make:

- Academic choices that result in lower grades or missed opportunities

- Social decisions that lead to friendship conflicts or disappointments

- Time management failures that result in stress and consequences

- Financial decisions that teach them about budgeting and priorities

- Extracurricular commitments they can't maintain

- Relationship choices that don't work out as they hoped

Supporting learning from mistakes without rescuing:

Express empathy without fixing: "That sounds really disappointing. I can see how much this meant to you."

Ask questions that promote reflection: "What do you think contributed to how this turned out?" or "If you were facing a similar situation again, what might you do differently?"

Resist the urge to lecture: Avoid saying "I told you so" or launching into explanations of why their choice was predictably problematic.

Focus on their resilience and learning: "I'm impressed by how you're handling this disappointment. What have you learned about yourself from this experience?"

Provide support without rescuing: Be available for emotional support and guidance, but don't solve the problem for them or shield them from appropriate consequences.

Managing anxiety about their future

OCPD parents often experience intense anxiety about their teenager's future, especially when their choices don't align with what seems like

125

the most practical or successful path. This anxiety can lead to attempts to control college planning, career exploration, and major life decisions in ways that interfere with healthy development.

Common future-focused anxieties:

- Worry that your teenager isn't taking academics seriously enough to get into a good college

- Concern that their interests and passions aren't practical or likely to lead to financial stability

- Anxiety about whether they're developing the skills and work ethic they'll need as adults

- Fear that their social choices or relationships will have lasting negative impacts

- Worry that they're not planning ahead enough or taking their future seriously

Strategies for managing future anxiety:

Focus on the present relationship: The most important predictor of your teenager's future well-being is their relationship with you and their sense of being unconditionally loved and supported.

Trust the developmental process: Most teenagers who seem directionless or unmotivated during high school find their way as they mature and encounter real-world experiences.

Distinguish between your dreams and theirs: Check whether your anxiety about their future is based on your own unfulfilled goals or expectations rather than what's actually best for your individual child.

Provide information without pressure: Share relevant information about different paths and opportunities, but allow your teenager to integrate this information into their own decision-making process.

Remember that there are many paths to success and fulfillment: The path that worked for you or that seems most logical might not be the right path for your individual child.

Exercise: Separating your dreams from theirs

This reflective exercise can help you identify when your concerns about your teenager's future are based on your own expectations rather than their genuine needs and interests.

Step 1: Identify your concerns Write down your specific worries about your teenager's future. Be as detailed as possible about what you're afraid will happen if they continue on their current path.

Step 2: Trace the origin of these concerns For each concern, ask yourself:

- Is this based on my own experiences or fears?

- Does this reflect what I wished I had done differently at their age?

- Am I worried about what other people will think of my parenting if my teenager makes these choices?

- Is this based on my values and priorities, or what I think would genuinely make my teenager happy and fulfilled?

Step 3: Consider your teenager's individual strengths and interests

- What activities or subjects naturally energize and engage my teenager?

- When do I see them at their most confident and capable?

- What do they talk about with genuine enthusiasm?

- What problems or causes do they care about?

- How do they naturally prefer to spend their time when they have complete freedom to choose?

Step 4: Identify areas for letting go

- Which of my concerns are really about my comfort rather than their well-being?

- What expectations do I need to release to support their authentic development?

- How can I show interest in their path even if it's different from what I would choose?

Step 5: Develop a support plan

- How can I stay connected and supportive while allowing them to make their own choices?

- What information or resources can I provide without being controlling?

- How can I manage my own anxiety about their future without putting that burden on them?

Preparing for launch without controlling the trajectory

The final years of high school are about preparing your teenager for adult independence. This process requires gradually transferring responsibility for major life decisions while maintaining emotional connection and support.

College applications without perfectionist pressure

The college application process can be particularly stressful for OCPD parents because it feels like the culmination of years of parenting effort, and the outcomes feel like they'll determine your child's entire future trajectory. But approaching this process with perfectionist pressure often backfires and creates unnecessary stress for everyone.

Common perfectionist pressures during college applications:

- Insisting your teenager apply to schools that match your prestige preferences rather than their interests and goals

- Over-involvement in essay writing and application completion

- Anxiety about your teenager's choices reflecting poorly on your parenting

- Pressure to present a "perfect" version of your teenager rather than an authentic one

- Catastrophizing about what will happen if they don't get into their first-choice schools

Healthy approaches to college planning:

Let your teenager lead the process: Your role is to provide information, resources, and support, but the applications should reflect your teenager's authentic voice and interests.

Focus on fit rather than prestige: Help your teenager identify schools that match their learning style, interests, and goals rather than focusing primarily on rankings or reputation.

Support authenticity over perfection: Encourage your teenager to present their genuine self in applications rather than trying to create an idealized version that they think admissions officers want to see.

Maintain perspective about outcomes: Your teenager can be successful and happy at many different schools. Rejection from specific schools doesn't predict future success or happiness.

Trust the process: Most teenagers end up at schools where they can thrive, even if the path doesn't look exactly like what they (or you) originally planned.

Supporting decision-making you disagree with

As your teenager moves toward adult independence, they'll make decisions about their education, career path, relationships, and lifestyle that you might not agree with or understand. Learning to support their autonomy even when you disagree with their choices is one of the most important skills you can develop.

Types of decisions where disagreement is common:

- College major or career path choices
- Relationship decisions
- Gap year or alternative post-graduation plans
- Living arrangements and lifestyle choices
- Financial priorities and spending decisions
- Social and political values that differ from family perspectives

Strategies for supporting decisions you disagree with:

Express your perspective without demanding compliance: "I have some concerns about this path, and I'd like to share them with you. But I also want you to know that I trust your ability to make decisions about your own life."

Ask questions to understand their reasoning: "Help me understand what draws you to this choice" or "What factors are most important to you in making this decision?"

Offer support without approval: "This isn't the path I would choose, but I want to support you in pursuing what feels right to you."

Focus on the relationship over the outcome: "Our relationship is more important to me than any specific decision you make. I want you to know you can always come to me for support, even if we see things differently."

Trust their capacity for course correction: Most decisions aren't permanent, and young adults can learn from their choices and make adjustments as they gain experience.

Maintaining connection while letting go

The ultimate goal of parenting is to raise children who can function independently while maintaining loving relationships with their families. This requires a delicate balance between letting go of control and staying emotionally connected.

Strategies for maintaining connection during the launch years:

Shift from advice-giving to listening: Instead of constantly offering guidance, focus on understanding your teenager's experiences and perspectives.

Show interest in their world: Ask questions about their friends, interests, and experiences not to monitor or evaluate, but to genuinely understand their lives.

Share your own experiences without making comparisons: Talk about your own challenges and growth as a way of connecting, not as a way of providing direction.

Respect their need for privacy: Allow your teenager to share what they want to share without prying or demanding complete transparency.

Create opportunities for positive interaction: Plan activities or experiences that you both enjoy, focusing on connection rather than instruction or correction.

Transition plan: The gradual release protocol

This framework helps you systematically transfer adult responsibilities to your teenager during their final years at home, preparing them for independence while maintaining appropriate support.

Areas for gradual release during ages 16-18:

Financial responsibility:

- Age 16: Managing their own spending money and part-time job earnings

- Age 17: Taking on some of their own expenses (gas, entertainment, some clothing)
- Age 18: Understanding banking, budgeting, and basic financial planning

Healthcare management:

- Age 16: Scheduling their own routine appointments
- Age 17: Managing their own medications and health decisions with guidance
- Age 18: Understanding insurance, medical history, and independent healthcare decision-making

Academic and career planning:

- Age 16: Taking primary responsibility for course selection and grade monitoring
- Age 17: Leading their own college search and application process
- Age 18: Making independent decisions about post-graduation plans

Daily life management:

- Age 16: Complete responsibility for personal care, room maintenance, and basic household contributions
- Age 17: Managing their own transportation, work schedule, and time management
- Age 18: Understanding how to manage basic adult tasks like laundry, meal planning, and household organization

Social and relationship decisions:

- Age 16: Making independent choices about friendships and social activities within safety boundaries

- Age 17: Managing their own conflicts and relationship decisions with available support
- Age 18: Taking full responsibility for their social life and relationship choices

The key principles of gradual release:

- Transfer responsibility gradually rather than all at once
- Provide support and guidance without taking back control
- Allow natural consequences to teach important lessons
- Maintain emotional connection throughout the process
- Trust your teenager's developing capabilities
- Focus on their long-term independence rather than short-term comfort

Building the foundation for lifelong relationship

The adolescent years are challenging for every family, but they're particularly difficult for OCPD parents who must learn to trust their teenager's judgment while managing their own anxiety about outcomes they can't control. The goal isn't to eliminate all conflict or prevent all mistakes, but to maintain connection and provide appropriate support while allowing your teenager to develop into their authentic self.

The teenagers who thrive during this developmental stage are those who feel unconditionally loved and supported by their families, even when they make choices their parents don't understand or agree with. They need to know that their relationship with you isn't dependent on meeting your expectations or following your preferred path.

Your willingness to let go of control during these years isn't giving up on your teenager - it's giving them the gift of trust in their own capabilities and the security of knowing that your love isn't conditional on their performance or compliance. These lessons will serve them throughout their adult lives and form the foundation for the kind of relationship you'll have with them as adults.

Chapter 9: Evidence-based therapies adapted for OCPD parents

Professional therapy approaches developed specifically for perfectionist and overcontrolled individuals can provide powerful tools for transforming your parenting patterns. You don't need to be in formal therapy to benefit from understanding and applying these evidence-based techniques in your daily family life.

Three therapeutic approaches show particular promise for OCPD parents: Radically Open Dialectical Behavior Therapy (RO-DBT), which addresses overcontrol and emotional rigidity; Acceptance and Commitment Therapy (ACT), which builds psychological flexibility; and Cognitive Behavioral Therapy (CBT), which targets the thinking patterns that drive perfectionist behaviors.

What makes these approaches especially valuable is that they're designed for people who are already highly functioning and motivated but struggle with flexibility, emotional expression, and tolerance for uncertainty. They don't require you to completely change who you are - they help you become a more flexible, connected version of yourself.

Radically Open DBT for the overcontrolled parent

Understanding overcontrol as a coping mechanism

According to the Association for Behavioral and Cognitive Therapies, overcontrol is a coping strategy that develops when people learn to manage anxiety and uncertainty by tightly regulating their emotions, behaviors, and environment (ABCT, 2023). For many OCPD parents, controlling tendencies originally served important functions - perhaps they helped you succeed academically, professionally, or in managing difficult life circumstances.

The problem isn't that you developed these coping mechanisms, but that they can become so automatic and rigid that they interfere with the flexibility and emotional connection your children need from you. RO-DBT recognizes that overcontrolled individuals aren't lacking in self-discipline or motivation - you actually have too much of both in ways that have become counterproductive.

Characteristics of overcontrol in parenting:

- High self-control but low flexibility in response to changing circumstances

- Strong focus on details and planning but difficulty adapting when plans change

- Excellent at delayed gratification but struggle with spontaneous joy or playfulness

- Strong sense of responsibility but difficulty delegating or accepting help

- Good at suppressing emotions but limited range of emotional expression

- High standards for self and others but difficulty with empathy and warmth

Research from ABCT shows that overcontrolled parents often struggle with what therapists call "social signaling" - the subtle ways we communicate warmth, acceptance, and emotional availability to others (ABCT, 2024). You might feel loving and caring toward your children, but your natural expression style might come across as distant or evaluative.

The paradox of overcontrol: The very strategies that helped you manage challenges in other areas of your life can create distance in your most important relationships. Your children need to see your genuine emotions, your vulnerability, and your warmth - not just your competence and reliability.

Core RO-DBT skills for daily parenting

RO-DBT teaches specific skills for increasing flexibility, emotional expression, and social connection. According to The Healthy Compulsive Project, these skills can be adapted for use in daily parenting situations to help overcontrolled parents become more emotionally available and responsive to their children's needs (The Healthy Compulsive Project, 2023).

Skill 1: Flexible mind This involves catching yourself when you're stuck in rigid thinking and consciously opening up to other possibilities. In parenting, this means noticing when you're attached to having things go a certain way and practicing the phrase "Maybe there's another way to think about this."

Example: Your child wants to do their homework lying on the floor instead of sitting at their desk. Your initial thought might be "That's not how homework should be done." Flexible mind would add: "Maybe there's another way to think about this. If they can focus and complete their work, the location might not matter."

Skill 2: Social signaling practice Overcontrolled parents often need to deliberately practice showing warmth and approval. This might feel artificial at first, but research shows that practicing positive facial expressions, tone of voice, and physical affection can actually increase your internal experience of warmth over time.

Practice exercises:

- Make eye contact and smile when your child enters the room
- Use a warm tone of voice when giving instructions or feedback

- Offer physical affection (hugs, shoulder touches) more frequently

- Practice saying "I love you" or "I'm glad you're here" without connecting it to behavior or achievement

Skill 3: Emotional expression RO-DBT teaches that healthy relationships require vulnerability and authentic emotional sharing. For OCPD parents, this means letting your children see a fuller range of your emotions, including uncertainty, disappointment, and joy.

Daily practice: Share one genuine emotion with your children each day, along with what caused it. "I felt really proud when I saw how kind you were to your sister," or "I'm feeling a little worried about the changes at work, but I know we'll figure it out together."

Skill 4: Radical openness This involves being genuinely curious about other perspectives, especially when they differ from your own. With children, this means asking questions about their thoughts and feelings without immediately trying to change or correct them.

Application: When your child expresses an opinion you disagree with, practice saying: "That's interesting. Tell me more about how you see it" instead of immediately explaining why your perspective is better.

Social signaling: showing warmth when you don't feel it

One of the most challenging aspects of RO-DBT for OCPD parents is learning that sometimes you need to act warm and approachable even when you don't naturally feel that way. This isn't about being fake or manipulative - it's about recognizing that your natural emotional expression style might not effectively communicate your actual feelings to your children.

Research from ABCT shows that overcontrolled individuals often experience emotions internally but don't express them in ways that others can easily recognize (ABCT, 2024). Your children might not be able to tell that you're proud of them, worried about them, or simply happy to see them unless you make these emotions more visible through your social signaling.

The science behind social signaling: Mirror neurons in our brains respond to others' facial expressions, body language, and tone of voice. When you practice warmer social signaling, you're actually helping your children's nervous systems feel safer and more connected, even if the expression doesn't feel completely natural to you initially.

Practical social signaling techniques:

Facial expression practice: Stand in front of a mirror and practice expressions that communicate warmth and approval. Notice the difference between your neutral expression (which might look serious or evaluative to others) and expressions that clearly communicate positive emotions.

Tone of voice awareness: Record yourself giving typical parenting instructions or feedback, then experiment with delivering the same messages using a warmer, more approving tone. Ask family members for feedback about how different tones feel to them.

Physical positioning: Practice positioning your body in ways that feel more open and approachable - sitting at your child's level during conversations, leaning slightly toward them when they're talking, keeping your arms uncrossed and your posture relaxed.

Verbal warmth: Add phrases that explicitly communicate your positive feelings: "I really enjoy talking with you about this," "It makes me happy when you share your thoughts with me," or "I love seeing your creativity in action."

30-day challenge: Daily RO-DBT practice

Committing to a structured practice period can help you integrate these new skills into your regular parenting routine. The goal isn't perfection, but consistent practice that gradually increases your flexibility and emotional availability.

Week 1: Flexible mind focus Each day, identify one moment when you caught yourself in rigid thinking and practiced opening to other possibilities. Write down the situation and how you practiced flexibility.

Daily prompt: "Today I practiced flexible thinking when..."

Week 2: Social signaling emphasis Focus on one specific aspect of social signaling each day. Monday might be facial expressions, Tuesday could be tone of voice, Wednesday physical positioning, and so on.

Daily prompt: "Today I practiced showing warmth by..."

Week 3: Emotional expression Share one genuine emotion with your family each day. Focus on emotions that help your children understand your inner world better.

Daily prompt: "Today I shared this emotion with my children..."

Week 4: Radical openness Practice curiosity about your children's perspectives, especially when they differ from your own. Look for opportunities to ask questions and learn rather than correct or instruct.

Daily prompt: "Today I practiced curiosity by asking my child..."

End-of-challenge reflection questions:

- What changes did you notice in yourself over the 30 days?
- How did your children respond to your practice?
- Which skills felt most natural and which were most challenging?
- What do you want to continue practicing going forward?

ACT for parenting with flexibility

Acceptance and Commitment Therapy offers a different approach to reducing perfectionist control in parenting. Instead of trying to change your thoughts and feelings, ACT focuses on changing your

140

relationship with them while taking action based on your values rather than your anxiety or discomfort.

Values-based parenting vs. rule-based parenting

According to the International OCPD Foundation, many parents with perfectionist tendencies operate from rule-based systems rather than values-based approaches (IOCPDF, 2023). Rule-based parenting focuses on compliance, consistency, and correct behavior. Values-based parenting focuses on the kind of person you want to help your child become and the kind of relationship you want to have with them.

Rule-based parenting sounds like:

- "Because I said so"
- "That's just how we do things in this family"
- "Rules are rules - there are no exceptions"
- "If you don't follow the rules, there will be consequences"

Values-based parenting sounds like:

- "I want you to learn to be responsible because it will help you in life"
- "We try to treat each other with kindness in our family"
- "Let's think about what would be most helpful in this situation"
- "What kind of person do you want to be in this situation?"

The difference in practice: Rule-based parenting creates external compliance but may not help children develop internal motivation or moral reasoning. Values-based parenting helps children understand the reasons behind expectations and develop their own sense of ethics and responsibility.

Example: Your teenager comes home 30 minutes past curfew.

Rule-based response: "You broke curfew, so you're grounded for a week. Rules exist for a reason and there are consequences when you don't follow them."

Values-based response: "I was worried when you didn't come home on time. Help me understand what happened. Let's talk about how we can handle similar situations in a way that shows respect for our family agreements and keeps everyone feeling safe."

Identifying your core parenting values: Before you can practice values-based parenting, you need to get clear about what you actually value most for your children and your family relationships.

Common parenting values include:

- Connection and close relationships

- Independence and self-reliance

- Kindness and compassion toward others

- Personal growth and learning

- Honesty and integrity

- Resilience and perseverance

- Joy and playfulness

- Contribution to community

Psychological flexibility in family life

Research from PubMed Central shows that psychological flexibility - the ability to adapt your behavior to match your values and current circumstances rather than being driven by rigid rules or emotional reactions - is one of the strongest predictors of healthy family functioning (PMC, 2023).

For OCPD parents, developing psychological flexibility means learning to tolerate discomfort, uncertainty, and imperfection while still taking effective action toward your parenting goals. It means being able to change course when your current approach isn't working, even if that approach has worked in other situations.

Components of psychological flexibility in parenting:

Present moment awareness: Noticing what's actually happening in your family interactions rather than being caught up in your thoughts about what should be happening or what might happen in the future.

Practice: During family activities, periodically check in with yourself: "What am I noticing right now? What is my child actually doing and feeling, rather than what I think they should be doing?"

Acceptance: Allowing difficult emotions, thoughts, and situations to exist without immediately trying to fix, change, or control them.

Practice: When your child is struggling with something, practice sitting with their discomfort for a few moments before jumping into problem-solving mode. Notice your urge to fix things and allow it to be there while you provide emotional presence first.

Cognitive defusion: Recognizing that your thoughts are mental events, not necessarily facts that require immediate action.

Practice: When you have the thought "My child is being lazy and irresponsible," try adding "I'm having the thought that my child is being lazy and irresponsible." This small change can create space for other possibilities.

Values clarification: Regularly checking whether your actions align with your deeper values rather than just your immediate emotional reactions or habitual responses.

Practice: Before responding to challenging child behavior, ask yourself: "What response would be most aligned with my values of connection, growth, and respect?"

Committed action: Taking steps toward your values even when it's uncomfortable or uncertain.

Practice: If you value your relationship with your teenager but your perfectionist tendencies are creating conflict, commit to specific actions that prioritize connection over control, even when it feels risky.

Accepting discomfort without controlling

According to the Counseling Center Group, one of the core skills in ACT is learning to experience difficult emotions and sensations without automatically trying to change or eliminate them (CCG, 2023). For OCPD parents, this might be the hardest skill to develop because controlling discomfort has probably been your primary coping strategy.

Common parenting discomforts that trigger control responses:

- Anxiety about your child's future success or safety
- Frustration when children don't meet your standards or expectations
- Embarrassment about your child's behavior in public settings
- Worry about whether you're being a good enough parent
- Discomfort with mess, noise, or disorder in your home
- Uncertainty about whether you're making the right decisions

The ACT approach to discomfort: Instead of trying to eliminate these uncomfortable feelings by controlling your child's behavior or environment, you learn to experience them as temporary mental and physical events that don't require immediate action.

Techniques for accepting parenting discomfort:

Name it to tame it: When you notice discomfort arising, simply label it: "I'm feeling anxious about how this will turn out" or "I'm having that familiar frustration again."

Breathing space: Take three conscious breaths while allowing the discomfort to be present. Don't try to breathe it away - just breathe while it's there.

Body awareness: Notice where you feel the discomfort in your body and practice relaxing those areas while allowing the emotion to remain.

Temporary visitor approach: Treat uncomfortable emotions like temporary visitors - you don't have to entertain them or get rid of them, but you can acknowledge their presence and continue with your intended actions.

Values check: Ask yourself: "If I wasn't feeling this discomfort, how would I want to respond to my child right now?" Then take that action while allowing the discomfort to be present.

Workbook section: Identifying your parenting values

This exercise will help you clarify what matters most to you in your role as a parent, which can then guide your decisions when you're feeling triggered or uncertain about how to respond.

Step 1: Core values identification From the list below, circle the 5-7 values that feel most important to you as a parent:

Connection, Independence, Kindness, Achievement, Creativity, Honesty, Fun, Responsibility, Compassion, Growth, Security, Adventure, Tradition, Flexibility, Respect, Learning, Service, Health, Spirituality, Authenticity

Step 2: Values definition For each value you selected, write a brief definition of what this looks like in your family life:

Example: Connection - "Having open, honest conversations where everyone feels heard and valued. Spending quality time together without distractions. Being emotionally available when family members are struggling."

Step 3: Current alignment assessment For each value, rate how well your current parenting practices align with this value on a scale of 1-10:

Consider: Are there areas where your perfectionist tendencies might be interfering with living according to your values?

Step 4: Action planning For values where you rated your current alignment as 7 or below, identify 2-3 specific actions you could take to better align your parenting with this value:

Example: If you rated "Fun" as a 4, you might commit to having one unstructured play session with your children each week, or allowing mess during creative activities without immediately cleaning up.

Step 5: Daily values check-in Create a simple daily practice of asking yourself: "How did I live according to my parenting values today? What can I do tomorrow to better align my actions with what matters most to me?"

Cognitive restructuring for perfectionist thoughts

The thinking patterns that drive perfectionist parenting can be changed through systematic practice. Cognitive restructuring techniques help you identify unhelpful thought patterns and develop more balanced, realistic ways of thinking about parenting challenges.

Common cognitive distortions in OCPD parenting

Research from The Recovery Village and NCBI shows that OCPD parents tend to fall into predictable patterns of distorted thinking that increase their anxiety and drive controlling behaviors (The Recovery Village, 2023; NCBI, 2023). Learning to recognize these patterns is the first step in changing them.

All-or-nothing thinking: Seeing situations in extreme terms without recognizing middle ground or partial successes. *Example*: "If my child doesn't get good grades, they'll never be successful in life." *More balanced thought*: "Academic performance in elementary school is just one factor among many that contributes to future success."

Catastrophizing: Imagining the worst possible outcomes and treating them as if they're likely to happen. *Example*: "If I don't make my teenager clean their room perfectly, they'll become a slob who can't function as an adult." *More balanced thought*: "Room cleanliness preferences can be negotiated, and most people learn to manage their living spaces adequately as adults regardless of their teenage habits."

Mind reading: Assuming you know what others are thinking, especially that they're judging your parenting negatively. *Example*: "The other parents at school think I'm too strict because my child follows rules better than theirs." *More balanced thought*: "I don't actually know what other parents think, and their opinions don't determine whether I'm being a good parent."

Should statements: Having rigid rules about how things "should" be done that don't account for individual differences or changing circumstances. *Example*: "Children should always respect their parents and follow instructions immediately." *More balanced thought*: "I'd like my children to be respectful, and I can teach them respectful communication while recognizing that some resistance is normal during development."

Emotional reasoning: Believing that because you feel something strongly, it must be true or important. *Example*: "I feel anxious about my child's social struggles, so there must be something seriously wrong." *More balanced thought*: "My anxiety about social situations reflects my own concerns, but it doesn't necessarily mean my child is in danger or needs my immediate intervention."

Personalization: Taking responsibility for outcomes that are largely outside your control. *Example*: "If my child struggles with math, it's because I haven't been helping them enough with homework." *More balanced thought*: "Children's academic progress depends on many factors including their individual learning style, the teacher's approach, their developmental readiness, and their own effort - not just my involvement."

147

Thought records for parenting situations

This systematic approach helps you examine your automatic thoughts and develop more balanced alternatives. Use this process when you notice yourself feeling very triggered or reactive about a parenting situation.

The thought record process:

Situation: Describe the specific parenting situation that triggered strong emotions (be factual, not interpretive).

Emotions: List the emotions you experienced and rate their intensity from 1-10.

Automatic thoughts: Write down the thoughts that went through your mind immediately when this situation occurred.

Thinking traps: Identify which cognitive distortions might be present in your automatic thoughts.

Evidence for: List any evidence that supports your automatic thoughts.

Evidence against: List evidence that contradicts or questions your automatic thoughts.

Balanced thought: Create a more realistic, balanced way of thinking about the situation.

New emotion rating: Rate the intensity of your emotions after developing the balanced thought.

Example thought record:

Situation: My 10-year-old forgot to turn in his science project on time.

Emotions: Frustration (8), Anxiety (9), Embarrassment (6)

Automatic thoughts: "He's going to fail science. This shows he doesn't care about school. I should have been monitoring this more closely. The teacher will think I'm an uninvolved parent."

Thinking traps: Catastrophizing, mind reading, should statements, personalization

Evidence for: He did forget the assignment, which will affect his grade.

Evidence against: One late assignment doesn't predict overall academic failure. He usually does well in school. Ten-year-olds are still learning organizational skills. The teacher knows that kids sometimes forget assignments.

Balanced thought: "Forgetting assignments is frustrating and will have natural consequences, but it's also a normal part of learning responsibility. This is an opportunity for him to learn from the experience."

New emotion rating: Frustration (4), Anxiety (3), Embarrassment (2)

Behavioral experiments with your children

According to research from Positive Psychology, behavioral experiments involve testing your beliefs by trying new approaches and observing the results (Positive Psychology, 2023). For OCPD parents, this means experimenting with giving your children more autonomy, accepting imperfection, or responding differently to challenging behaviors.

Designing effective behavioral experiments:

Identify a specific belief to test: "If I don't remind my child about homework every day, they won't complete it."

Design a small experiment: For one week, don't give any homework reminders and observe what happens.

Predict the outcome: "My child will forget assignments and their grades will suffer immediately."

Collect data: Track what actually happens - how many assignments are completed, what your child does when they do forget something, how they handle natural consequences.

149

Evaluate the results: Compare your predictions with what actually occurred.

Example behavioral experiments for OCPD parents:

Experiment 1: Reducing homework supervision *Belief*: "My child needs constant supervision to complete homework properly." *Experiment*: Step back from homework supervision for two weeks while remaining available for questions. *Data to collect*: Completion rates, quality of work, child's stress level, your stress level.

Experiment 2: Allowing natural consequences *Belief*: "If my child experiences failure or disappointment, they'll be damaged or give up trying." *Experiment*: Allow your child to experience the natural consequences of a minor decision (forgotten lunch, not studying for a quiz) without rescuing them. *Data to collect*: How they handle the disappointment, what they learn from the experience, whether it affects their motivation.

Experiment 3: Tolerating mess during activities *Belief*: "If I allow mess during activities, my child won't learn to be responsible and organized." *Experiment*: Allow mess during creative activities for a designated time period before cleaning up together. *Data to collect*: Your stress level, your child's engagement and creativity, the actual impact on household organization.

Quick reference: CBT techniques for common triggers

Having ready-to-use strategies for common perfectionist triggers can help you respond more skillfully in the moment rather than falling into automatic controlling patterns.

Trigger: Child makes a mistake *Automatic thought check*: "Is this catastrophizing or all-or-nothing thinking?" *Helpful response*: "Mistakes are learning opportunities. What can we discover from this?" *Action*: Express empathy first, then explore learning together.

Trigger: Plans change unexpectedly *Automatic thought check*: "Am I predicting disaster or assuming things will go poorly?" *Helpful* *response*: "Flexibility is a valuable life skill. We can adapt to this change." *Action*: Take three deep breaths, then problem-solve the new situation collaboratively.

Trigger: Child resists instructions *Automatic thought check*: "Am I mind-reading about disrespect or taking this personally?" *Helpful response*: "Resistance might indicate a need that isn't being met." *Action*: Get curious about their perspective before insisting on compliance.

Trigger: Messy house or disorganization *Automatic thought check*: "Am I equating mess with failure or lack of care?" *Helpful response*: "Some mess is the byproduct of active, engaged living." *Action*: Focus on safety and function rather than perfect appearance.

Trigger: Other parents doing things differently *Automatic thought check*: "Am I comparing or assuming judgment from others?" *Helpful response*: "Different families have different approaches that work for them." *Action*: Focus on your own values and what works for your family.

Chapter 10: Family therapy approaches for OCPD families

Sometimes the patterns in your family have become so entrenched that individual effort alone isn't enough to create lasting change. Family therapy approaches recognize that perfectionist patterns don't exist in isolation - they're maintained by the entire family system, and changing them often requires everyone to adjust their roles and interactions.

The good news about family-based approaches is that they can create faster, more sustainable change than trying to modify your parenting in isolation. When everyone in the family understands how perfectionist patterns have been affecting their relationships and learns new ways of interacting, the changes tend to stick because the whole system is supporting them.

Family therapy approaches for OCPD don't focus on blame or identifying who has the "problem." Instead, they help families understand how everyone has adapted to perfectionist patterns and how everyone can contribute to creating more flexibility and connection.

Creating systemic change

How family therapy addresses OCPD patterns

Family therapy approaches OCPD patterns by examining how the entire family system has organized around perfectionism and control. Rather than viewing OCPD traits as one person's individual problem, these approaches look at how family members have adapted their behaviors to accommodate perfectionist patterns and how these adaptations might be maintaining the very patterns everyone wants to change.

Common family adaptations to OCPD patterns:

- Family members walking on eggshells to avoid triggering perfectionist anxiety

- Children becoming either overly compliant or rebellious in response to high control

- Partners taking on either more responsibility (to meet perfectionist standards) or less responsibility (to avoid criticism)

- Family activities becoming structured around avoiding perfectionist triggers rather than promoting connection and joy

- Communication patterns that focus on tasks and problems rather than emotions and relationships

How systemic change works: Instead of just teaching the OCPD parent new skills, family therapy helps every family member understand their role in maintaining current patterns and learn new ways of interacting that support flexibility and emotional connection.

Example: In the Johnson family, Dad's perfectionist tendencies around homework had led Mom to become the "homework police" to avoid his criticism, while their daughter Sarah had become increasingly anxious and dependent on adult help. Family therapy helped Dad learn to step back from homework management, Mom learned to resist taking over Sarah's responsibilities, and Sarah learned to advocate for her needs rather than becoming helpless when things were difficult.

Reducing family accommodation of perfectionism

Family accommodation occurs when family members change their behavior to prevent or reduce the OCPD parent's distress, even though this accommodation actually maintains and reinforces perfectionist patterns. While accommodation often develops from love and a desire to reduce family conflict, it can prevent the OCPD parent from learning to tolerate discomfort and can create resentment in other family members.

Common examples of family accommodation:

- Doing tasks "the right way" to avoid criticism or redoing

- Avoiding activities or situations that trigger perfectionist anxiety

- Not expressing disagreement or alternative viewpoints to prevent arguments

- Taking on extra responsibilities to meet perfectionist standards

- Hiding mistakes or problems to avoid perfectionist reactions

The accommodation reduction process:

Step 1: Identify accommodation patterns Family members work together to recognize how they've adjusted their behavior around perfectionist patterns. This isn't about blame - it's about awareness.

Step 2: Start with small changes Begin reducing accommodation in low-stakes situations where the OCPD parent can practice tolerating discomfort without high consequences.

Step 3: Support the OCPD parent through discomfort As family members stop accommodating, the OCPD parent will experience increased anxiety or frustration. The family learns to provide emotional support without returning to old accommodation patterns.

Step 4: Celebrate progress together Acknowledge when family members successfully resist accommodation and when the OCPD parent successfully tolerates the discomfort that results.

Example of accommodation reduction: The Martinez family realized that everyone was doing their chores "Mom's way" to avoid her criticism and redoing. They agreed that family members could complete chores using their own methods as long as the end result met basic standards. Mom practiced tolerating different approaches while family members practiced maintaining their boundaries even when she expressed discomfort.

Improving communication across the family

OCPD families often develop communication patterns that focus on tasks, problems, and corrections rather than emotions, appreciation, and connection. Family therapy approaches teach communication skills that help families express both practical needs and emotional needs more effectively.

Problematic OCPD family communication patterns:

- Conversations that focus primarily on what needs to be fixed or improved

- Limited expression of positive emotions or appreciation

- Difficulty discussing feelings without immediately moving to problem-solving

- Communication that sounds more like performance reviews than family conversations

- Family members feeling heard only when they're complying or performing well

Healthier family communication skills:

Emotional validation: Learning to acknowledge and accept family members' emotions before trying to solve problems or offer advice. *Practice*: "It sounds like you're really frustrated about this situation. Tell me more about what that's like for you."

Appreciation expression: Regularly expressing gratitude and positive recognition for who family members are, not just what they do. *Practice*: Daily appreciations that focus on character qualities, effort, or simply enjoyment of the person's presence.

Curious questioning: Asking questions to understand others' perspectives rather than to guide them toward your preferred answer. *Practice*: "I'm curious about how you see this situation. What's your perspective?"

Collaborative problem-solving: Working together to find solutions rather than the OCPD parent determining the "right" approach. *Practice*: "We seem to have different ideas about this. Let's brainstorm some options that might work for everyone."

Finding the right therapist: Questions to ask

Not all family therapists have experience working with perfectionist families, and finding someone who understands OCPD patterns can make a significant difference in the effectiveness of therapy.

Questions to ask potential therapists:

"Have you worked with families where perfectionism or control issues are a concern?" "What's your approach to working with parents who tend to be overinvolved or controlling?" "How do you help families balance structure with flexibility?" "Do you have experience with OCPD or perfectionist personality patterns?" "How do you work with families where one parent has strong needs for control and predictability?"

Red flags in therapist responses:

- Immediately pathologizing or criticizing the OCPD parent

- Suggesting that the solution is simply for the OCPD parent to "relax" or "let go"

- Not understanding the difference between OCPD and OCD

- Focusing only on individual change without considering family system dynamics

- Dismissing the positive aspects of structure and high standards

Green flags in therapist responses:

- Understanding that perfectionist patterns often develop for good reasons

- Recognizing the strengths that OCPD parents bring to families

- Experience helping families find balance between structure and flexibility

- Comfort working with high-functioning individuals who are motivated to change

- Understanding of how family systems maintain patterns even when individuals want to change

Collaborative Problem Solving (CPS) for families

Collaborative Problem Solving, developed by Dr. Ross Greene, offers a systematic approach to resolving family conflicts that honors both the OCPD parent's need for structure and other family members' needs for autonomy and flexibility.

The three-step CPS process adapted for OCPD parents

According to research from Creating a Family, CPS is particularly effective for families dealing with rigid thinking patterns because it creates a structured process for flexibility and collaboration (Creating a Family, 2023). The approach assumes that family members want to do well and that conflicts usually arise from unmet needs or underdeveloped skills rather than willful defiance.

Step 1: Empathy and understanding The goal is to understand the child's perspective and identify what's making it difficult for them to meet expectations. This step is often the hardest for OCPD parents because it requires setting aside your immediate desire to correct or instruct.

157

OCPD parent pitfall: Rushing through this step because you already "know" what the problem is and how to solve it. *CPS approach*: Stay curious and ask genuine questions until you really understand your child's experience.

Example dialogue: Parent: "I've noticed you've been having trouble getting your homework done lately. What's up?" Child: "It's just so boring and I don't understand why I have to do it." Parent: "So the homework feels boring and pointless to you. Tell me more about that." Child: "Like, we already went over this stuff in class. Why do I have to do it again at home?" Parent: "Ah, so it feels repetitive to you, like you're doing work you already understand. That does sound frustrating."

Step 2: Define the adult concern Share your perspective and concerns without criticizing the child or demanding immediate compliance. This step helps children understand why certain expectations exist without making them feel attacked.

OCPD parent pitfall: Turning this into a lecture about responsibility or launching into all the reasons the child should comply. *CPS approach*: Focus on one specific concern and express it clearly and briefly.

Continuing the example: Parent: "I understand that the homework feels pointless to you. My concern is that homework helps reinforce what you're learning and shows your teacher how well you understand the material. I also worry that if you don't develop good homework habits now, it will be harder when the work gets more challenging."

Step 3: Brainstorm solutions Work together to find solutions that address both the child's concerns and the parent's concerns. This is where the real collaboration happens.

OCPD parent pitfall: Steering the brainstorming toward the solution you already prefer instead of genuinely exploring options together. *CPS approach*: Generate multiple options without immediately evaluating them, then work together to find something that addresses everyone's needs.

Concluding the example: Parent: "Let's think of some ways to handle homework that address your concern about it being boring and repetitive and my concern about you reinforcing your learning. What ideas do you have?" Child: "Maybe I could just do the problems I don't understand instead of all of them?" Parent: "That's one idea. What if we also looked at ways to make the homework more interesting, or found a different time or place to do it?" Child: "Could I listen to music while I do it?" Parent: "Let's try a combination - you can listen to music, and we'll ask your teacher if it's okay to focus on the problems that are challenging for you rather than doing every single one."

Moving from imposed solutions to collaboration

OCPD parents are often very good at identifying solutions to problems, but their solutions tend to be imposed rather than collaborative. The shift to genuine collaboration requires letting go of control over the outcome while maintaining influence over the process.

Imposed solutions sound like:

- "Here's what you need to do..."
- "The solution is obvious..."
- "If you just followed my advice..."
- "I've figured out how to solve this problem..."

Collaborative solutions sound like:

- "Let's brainstorm some options..."
- "What ideas do you have?"
- "How could we handle this in a way that works for everyone?"

- "What would need to be different for this to work better?"

Benefits of collaborative solutions:

- Children are more likely to follow through on solutions they helped create

- Problem-solving skills are developed through practice rather than dependence on adult solutions

- Family relationships improve when everyone feels heard and valued

- Solutions often work better because they account for everyone's needs and perspectives

- Children learn to consider others' needs when solving problems

The OCPD parent's role in collaboration:

- Facilitate the process without controlling the outcome

- Ask questions that help family members think through options

- Share your perspective as one viewpoint among many

- Help evaluate solutions based on practical considerations

- Support implementation while allowing others to take ownership

Practice scenarios for common family conflicts

Scenario 1: Morning routine struggles

The problem: Your 8-year-old consistently runs late in the morning, which triggers your anxiety about being on time and creates daily conflict.

Step 1 - Understanding: "I've noticed mornings have been stressful lately. What makes it hard to get ready on time?" *Child might say*: "I don't like rushing. It makes me feel worried."

160

Step 2 - Adult concern: "I can understand that rushing feels stressful. My concern is that when we're late, it affects other people's schedules and creates pressure for our whole family."

Step 3 - Brainstorming: "Let's think of ways to make mornings feel less rushed while still getting everyone where they need to be on time." *Possible solutions*: Preparing more the night before, adjusting wake-up time, creating visual schedule, identifying which morning tasks are most challenging.

Scenario 2: Homework quality expectations

The problem: Your middle schooler turns in homework that meets the requirements but doesn't meet your standards for neatness and thoroughness.

Step 1 - Understanding: "I noticed you seem to finish homework pretty quickly lately. How do you feel about the work you're turning in?" *Child might say*: "It's fine. I answered all the questions and got it done."

Step 2 - Adult concern: "I can see that you're completing all the assignments. My concern is that some of the work looks rushed, and I wonder if you're missing opportunities to really understand the material."

Step 3 - Brainstorming: "Let's think about ways to balance efficiency with thoroughness that feel manageable to you." *Possible solutions*: Child self-evaluating work before turning it in, parent reviewing work only when child requests it, focusing on understanding rather than appearance, child choosing which assignments to spend more time on.

Family meeting template using CPS principles

Regular family meetings using CPS principles can help families address ongoing issues before they become major conflicts and give everyone practice with collaborative problem-solving.

Family meeting structure:

Opening (5 minutes)

- Appreciation round: Each person shares one thing they appreciated about another family member since the last meeting
- Review any solutions from previous meetings to see how they're working

Problem-solving time (15-20 minutes)

- Address one issue using the three-step CPS process
- Keep discussions focused on finding solutions rather than rehashing problems
- Make sure everyone's voice is heard

Planning and coordination (5-10 minutes)

- Discuss upcoming family events or schedule changes
- Make decisions about family activities or logistics
- Assign any household responsibilities

Closing (5 minutes)

- Each person shares one thing they're looking forward to in the coming week
- Confirm the next family meeting time

Guidelines for successful family meetings:

- Keep them short and focused
- Rotate who runs the meeting
- Focus on solutions rather than complaints
- Make decisions by consensus when possible
- Follow up on agreements made in previous meetings

- End on a positive note

Attachment-focused interventions

The quality of emotional connection between family members forms the foundation for all other changes. Attachment-focused approaches help OCPD parents strengthen their emotional bonds with family members while maintaining appropriate structure and guidance.

Healing your own attachment wounds

Many OCPD patterns develop as adaptations to early attachment experiences. You might have learned that love and approval were conditional on performance, that emotions were dangerous or unwelcome, or that you needed to be self-reliant because others couldn't be counted on for support.

Healing these early wounds isn't just about your own well-being - it's about preventing these patterns from being passed on to your children and creating the emotional availability your family needs from you.

Common attachment themes in OCPD development:

- Learning that love was conditional on meeting high standards

- Experiencing criticism or rejection when you expressed emotions or made mistakes

- Having caregivers who were emotionally unavailable or focused on tasks rather than relationships

- Developing self-reliance as protection against disappointment or abandonment

- Learning to suppress emotions because they weren't welcomed or understood

Signs that attachment wounds might be affecting your parenting:

- Difficulty providing comfort when your children are upset

- Feeling more comfortable with your children's achievements than their struggles

- Automatic responses that focus on fixing problems rather than providing emotional support

- Discomfort with physical affection or emotional expression

- Tendency to withdraw when family members express strong emotions

Attachment healing practices for parents:

Self-compassion work: Learning to treat yourself with the same kindness you would show a good friend, especially when you make parenting mistakes.

Emotional awareness practices: Developing your ability to recognize and tolerate your own emotions without immediately acting to change them.

Mindful parenting moments: Creating brief daily practices of emotional presence with your children without trying to teach, correct, or improve anything.

Adult relationship work: Strengthening your emotional connections with other adults (partner, friends, family members) to build your capacity for vulnerability and emotional intimacy.

Building secure bonds despite OCPD

Secure attachment with your children is possible even if you have perfectionist tendencies. The key is understanding what children need for secure attachment and finding ways to provide those needs that feel authentic to who you are.

Core elements of secure attachment:

- Consistent emotional availability (your children can count on you for support)

- Attunement to their emotional states (you notice and respond to their feelings)

- Responsiveness to their needs (you provide appropriate comfort and guidance)

- Acceptance of their authentic selves (they feel loved for who they are, not just what they do)

Adapting secure attachment practices for OCPD parents:

Structured emotional check-ins: Create regular times (perhaps during bedtime routine or car rides) when you specifically focus on your child's emotional world without trying to solve problems.

Affection with intention: If physical affection doesn't come naturally, create daily practices of appropriate touch - hugs, hand on shoulder, sitting close during reading time.

Validation before correction: Make it a practice to acknowledge your child's emotions before addressing any behavior issues.

Presence over productivity: Regularly engage in activities with your children that have no purpose other than connection and enjoyment.

Repair and reconnection: When you've responded in ways that create distance (criticism, control, emotional unavailability), make it a practice to acknowledge this and reconnect.

Repair strategies after perfectionist episodes

Even as you work to change your patterns, there will be times when you fall back into perfectionist controlling behavior. Learning to repair these incidents quickly and effectively can actually strengthen your relationships and model important life skills for your children.

The repair process:

Step 1: Cool down first Don't try to repair immediately after a perfectionist episode when emotions are still high. Take time to regulate your own emotions first.

Step 2: Take responsibility Acknowledge your behavior without making excuses or blaming your child for triggering you. *Example*: "I got very controlling about your room cleaning earlier. That was about my anxiety, not about your behavior."

Step 3: Express empathy Try to understand and acknowledge how your behavior affected your child. *Example*: "I imagine that felt frustrating to have me take over something you were working on."

Step 4: Share what you learned Help your child understand what you're working on changing about yourself. *Example*: "I'm learning that I get anxious when things feel messy, but that's my feeling to handle, not your problem to solve."

Step 5: Ask for their perspective Give your child space to share how the incident affected them without defending yourself. *Example*: "How did that feel for you when I took over the cleaning?"

Step 6: Make a plan together Discuss how you'll handle similar situations differently in the future. *Example*: "Next time I feel anxious about cleaning, I'd like to take a break and ask if you want help instead of just taking over."

Exercise: Creating new attachment experiences

This exercise helps you intentionally create positive emotional experiences with your children that build secure attachment and counteract any perfectionist patterns that might have created distance.

Daily attachment moments: Choose one small daily interaction to transform into an intentional attachment moment. This might be:

- The first few minutes when your child gets home from school

- Bedtime routine

- Car rides

- Meal preparation or cleanup time

Weekly attachment activities: Plan one weekly activity that's purely about connection and enjoyment:

- One-on-one time with each child doing something they choose
- Family game or movie night
- Nature walks or outdoor exploration
- Cooking or creative projects together

Monthly attachment rituals: Create larger rituals that strengthen family bonds:

- Family meetings that include appreciation sharing
- Special celebrations of individual family members
- Adventure days or family outings
- Service projects that bring the family together

Attachment repair practices: Develop regular practices for healing relationship ruptures:

- Weekly family check-ins where anyone can bring up concerns
- Regular one-on-one conversations with each child about how things are going between you
- Family gratitude practices that focus on relationships rather than achievements

Questions for reflection:

- What attachment experiences do you want your children to remember from their childhood?
- How do you want them to describe their relationship with you when they're adults?
- What emotional memories do you want to create together?

- How can you balance your need for structure with their need for emotional connection?

Chapter 11: Self-compassion and personal healing

The journey of changing perfectionist parenting patterns often brings up difficult emotions about your own childhood, your perceived failures as a parent, and the gap between your intentions and your actions. Many OCPD parents are incredibly hard on themselves, applying the same impossible standards to their parenting that they apply to other areas of their lives.

Self-compassion isn't just a nice addition to your personal growth work - it's actually essential for sustainable change. Research consistently shows that people who treat themselves with kindness and understanding are more likely to make positive changes and less likely to fall back into old patterns when they encounter setbacks.

For OCPD parents, developing self-compassion can feel foreign or even dangerous. You might worry that being kind to yourself will make you complacent or lower your standards. But the opposite is actually true: self-compassion provides the emotional safety needed to acknowledge mistakes, learn from them, and keep working toward improvement without being paralyzed by shame and self-criticism.

Developing self-compassion as an OCPD parent

Why self-compassion is harder for OCPD individuals

According to research from the International OCPD Foundation and PubMed Central, people with perfectionist traits often have more difficulty developing self-compassion because their internal self-critic has been their primary motivational system (IOCPDF, 2023; PMC, 2023). You may have learned early in life that being hard on yourself was necessary for high achievement and that self-acceptance would lead to mediocrity or failure.

Common barriers to self-compassion for OCPD parents:

Fear of lowering standards: You might worry that being kind to yourself means accepting inadequate parenting or giving up on improvement. *Reality*: Self-compassion actually supports higher performance because it reduces the anxiety and shame that interfere with learning and growth.

Equating self-criticism with motivation: You may believe that harsh self-evaluation is what drives you to keep improving. *Reality*: Self-criticism often leads to defensive thinking and avoidance, while self-compassion creates the psychological safety needed for genuine learning.

Feeling undeserving of kindness: If you've made parenting mistakes or feel like you've hurt your children, you might believe you don't deserve compassion. *Reality*: Everyone makes mistakes, and self-compassion helps you respond to mistakes in ways that promote healing for both you and your children.

Confusing self-compassion with self-indulgence: You might think that self-compassion means making excuses or avoiding responsibility. *Reality*: True self-compassion includes taking responsibility for your actions while treating yourself with the same kindness you'd show a friend facing similar challenges.

Cultural or family messages about toughness: You may have learned that self-criticism is a sign of strength and that self-kindness is weakness. *Reality*: It takes tremendous courage and strength to face your mistakes with compassion and continue working toward growth.

Kristin Neff's three components applied to parenting

Dr. Kristin Neff's research on self-compassion identifies three core components that can be specifically adapted for parents working on changing perfectionist patterns.

Component 1: Self-kindness vs. self-judgment

Self-judgment in OCPD parenting sounds like:

- "I'm such a terrible parent for losing my temper again"
- "I should have known better than to micromanage that situation"
- "Any decent parent would have handled that better"
- "I'm damaging my children with my controlling behavior"

Self-kindness in OCPD parenting sounds like:

- "I made a mistake, and that's part of being human and learning"
- "I was doing the best I could with the skills and awareness I had in that moment"
- "It makes sense that I fell back into old patterns - change takes time and practice"
- "I can learn from this experience and respond differently next time"

Practical self-kindness practices:

- Speak to yourself the way you would speak to a good friend facing the same parenting challenge
- Write yourself a compassionate letter when you're struggling with parenting guilt or frustration
- Use gentle, understanding language in your internal dialogue about parenting mistakes
- Practice physical self-soothing (warm bath, comfortable clothing, nourishing food) when you're being hard on yourself about parenting

Component 2: Common humanity vs. isolation

Isolation in OCPD parenting sounds like:

- "I'm the only parent who struggles this much with control"

- "Other parents don't have these problems with their children"

- "I must be uniquely flawed to have such a hard time with flexibility"

- "No one else would understand what it's like to feel so anxious about parenting"

Common humanity in OCPD parenting sounds like:

- "Many parents struggle with finding the balance between structure and flexibility"

- "Parenting anxiety and control are common human experiences"

- "I'm not the first parent to make mistakes or have regrets about my approach"

- "Other parents have successfully changed their patterns, and I can too"

Practical common humanity practices:

- Connect with other parents through support groups, online communities, or informal conversations

- Read books or articles by parents who have faced similar challenges

- Share your struggles appropriately with trusted friends or family members

- Consider how you would support a friend facing the same parenting challenges you're experiencing

Component 3: Mindfulness vs. over-identification

Over-identification in OCPD parenting sounds like:

- Getting completely consumed by parenting mistakes or regrets
- Believing that your current struggles define you permanently as a parent
- Feeling like parenting setbacks mean you're fundamentally flawed
- Being unable to see anything positive about your parenting when you're focused on problems

Mindfulness in OCPD parenting sounds like:

- "I'm having thoughts of self-criticism about my parenting right now"
- "This feeling of parenting inadequacy is temporary and will pass"
- "I can notice my perfectionist anxiety without being controlled by it"
- "These difficult emotions about parenting are part of my experience right now, but they don't define who I am as a parent"

Practical mindfulness practices:

- Notice when you're getting caught up in self-critical thoughts about parenting and gently redirect your attention
- Use breathing exercises to create space between yourself and intense emotions about parenting
- Practice observing your parenting thoughts and feelings without immediately believing or acting on them
- Regular meditation or mindfulness practices that help you develop awareness of your mental patterns

Daily self-compassion practices

According to the IOCPDF, developing self-compassion requires regular practice, just like any other skill (IOCPDF, 2024). These daily practices can help you build your capacity for self-kindness and reduce the harsh internal criticism that often accompanies perfectionist parenting.

Morning self-compassion practice (5 minutes): Before starting your day, place your hand on your heart and remind yourself: "Today I will do my best as a parent. When I make mistakes, I will treat myself with kindness. I am learning and growing, and that's enough."

Midday reset practice (2 minutes): When you notice self-critical thoughts about your parenting during the day, pause and ask yourself: "What do I need right now to feel supported and encouraged?" Then provide that support to yourself through kind self-talk, deep breathing, or a brief moment of rest.

Evening reflection practice (5-10 minutes): Instead of focusing on what went wrong during the day, spend time acknowledging:

- One thing you did well as a parent today

- One challenging moment where you did your best with the resources you had

- One area where you're growing or learning

- One way you can be kind to yourself tomorrow

Self-compassion phrases for difficult parenting moments:

- "This is a moment of suffering. Suffering is part of parenting."

- "May I be kind to myself right now."

- "May I give myself the compassion I need."

- "I am not alone in struggling with this."

Self-compassion break technique: When you're experiencing intense self-criticism about parenting:

1. Acknowledge the pain: "This hurts right now"

2. Recognize the universality: "Parenting challenges are part of the human experience"

3. Offer yourself kindness: "May I be patient with myself as I learn and grow"

Guided meditation: Loving-kindness for imperfect parents

This meditation practice helps you develop genuine warmth and acceptance for yourself as an imperfect parent who is doing their best and continuing to learn and grow.

Preparation (2 minutes): Find a comfortable seated position where you won't be interrupted. Close your eyes or soften your gaze. Take several deep breaths, allowing your body to relax with each exhale.

Self-directed loving-kindness (5 minutes): Begin by bringing to mind an image of yourself as a parent - perhaps holding your child, reading together, or simply being present with them. As you hold this image, repeat these phrases silently:

"May I be a loving and patient parent" "May I accept my imperfections and learn from my mistakes" "May I be kind to myself when parenting feels difficult" "May I trust in my capacity to grow and change"

Notice any resistance that arises and gently return to the phrases. If self-criticism comes up, acknowledge it with kindness: "That's my inner critic trying to protect me. Right now I'm practicing self-acceptance."

Child-directed loving-kindness (5 minutes): Bring to mind each of your children, one at a time. For each child, repeat:

"May you be happy and at peace" "May you feel loved and accepted for who you are" "May you be confident in your ability to handle life's challenges" "May our relationship be filled with connection and understanding"

Family-directed loving-kindness (3 minutes): Expand your awareness to include your entire family:

"May our family be filled with love and understanding" "May we support each other through difficulties and celebrate together in joy" "May we grow in wisdom and compassion together" "May our home be a place of safety and acceptance for everyone"

Closing (2 minutes): Take a few more deep breaths, feeling the warmth and intention you've generated. Before opening your eyes, set an intention for how you want to carry this compassion into your interactions with your family today.

Managing shame and self-criticism

Shame and harsh self-criticism are among the biggest obstacles to changing perfectionist parenting patterns. When you feel terrible about yourself as a parent, you're more likely to become defensive, to avoid looking honestly at your behavior, or to swing between extremes of being too controlling and being too permissive.

The shame-control cycle in OCPD

Many OCPD parents get caught in a cycle where shame about their parenting leads to increased controlling behavior, which then creates more problems in family relationships, leading to more shame. Understanding this cycle can help you interrupt it when you recognize it happening.

The cycle typically looks like this:

Stage 1: Triggering event Something happens that activates your perfectionist anxiety - your child struggles with something, makes a mistake, or behaves in a way that doesn't meet your expectations.

Stage 2: Control response You respond by trying to control the situation, your child's behavior, or the outcome. This might involve micromanaging, lecturing, criticizing, or taking over tasks.

Stage 3: Negative consequences Your controlling response creates problems - your child becomes resistant, anxious, or withdrawn; family relationships become strained; the situation escalates rather than improves.

Stage 4: Shame and self-criticism You recognize that your response wasn't helpful and begin criticizing yourself harshly: "I'm such a terrible parent," "I always make things worse," "My children would be better off without my interference."

Stage 5: Defensive control or withdrawal The shame becomes so uncomfortable that you either double down on control ("I just need to be more consistent and firm") or withdraw from parenting engagement altogether ("Nothing I do works anyway").

Stage 6: Increased triggering Either response (increased control or withdrawal) creates more problems, leading back to Stage 1.

Breaking the shame-control cycle:

Interrupt at Stage 2: Use the pause techniques from earlier chapters to create space between the triggering event and your control response.

Interrupt at Stage 4: When you notice self-criticism starting, practice self-compassion instead of shame. "I made a mistake, and that's human. What can I learn from this?"

Interrupt at Stage 5: Instead of defensive responses, use repair strategies to reconnect with your family members and problem-solve collaboratively.

Breaking patterns of harsh self-judgment

OCPD parents often have a harsh internal critic that provides a running commentary on their parenting performance. This internal voice might sound like a critical parent from your own childhood, a perfectionist coach, or simply your own anxiety speaking.

Common harsh self-judgments in OCPD parents:

- "I should be able to handle this better"

- "I'm failing my children"

- "Any competent parent would know what to do here"

- "I'm too controlling/not firm enough/inconsistent/inadequate"

- "My children will be damaged by my mistakes"

- "I should have figured this out by now"

Strategies for breaking patterns of harsh self-judgment:

Name the critic: Give your internal critic a name or persona so you can recognize when it's speaking. "Oh, there's my perfectionist voice again" or "My inner critic is really active today."

Question the evidence: When you notice harsh self-judgments, ask yourself: "Is this thought actually true? What evidence supports it? What evidence contradicts it?"

Consider the source: Ask yourself: "Where did I learn to talk to myself this way? Is this voice helping me become the parent I want to be?"

Practice the friend test: Ask yourself: "Would I talk to a good friend this way if they were facing the same parenting challenge? What would I say to support them?"

Reframe with growth mindset: Transform fixed judgments into growth observations: Instead of "I'm a terrible parent," try "I'm a parent who is learning and growing."

Use behavioral language: Focus on specific behaviors rather than global character judgments: Instead of "I'm too controlling," try "I used controlling strategies in this situation, and I can learn different approaches."

Modeling self-forgiveness for your children

One of the most powerful gifts you can give your children is watching you handle your own mistakes with grace and self-compassion. When children see their parents practice self-forgiveness, they learn that mistakes are survivable, that people can change and grow, and that worth isn't dependent on perfect performance.

What modeling self-forgiveness looks like:

Acknowledge mistakes without excessive drama: "I realize I was too controlling about homework last night. That wasn't helpful for either of us."

Take responsibility without self-attack: "I made a choice that didn't work out well. I take responsibility for that" rather than "I'm such an idiot for handling it that way."

Focus on learning: "I'm learning that when I'm anxious about your success, I sometimes take over instead of supporting you. I want to practice doing that differently."

Make amends when appropriate: "I'm sorry for taking over your project. That must have been frustrating. How can I support you better next time?"

Show self-compassion: "I'm being patient with myself as I learn new ways of parenting. Change takes time and practice."

Express hope for growth: "I'm committed to working on this, and I believe I can learn to respond differently in similar situations."

Age-appropriate ways to model self-forgiveness:

Young children (3-7): Keep it simple and focus on repair. "Mommy made a mistake when I got frustrated about the mess. I'm sorry I raised my voice. Everyone makes mistakes, and it's okay."

School age (8-12): Include more learning and growth focus. "I realize I was too worried about your grades and that made homework stressful for you. I'm learning to trust you more and worry less. What would be most helpful from me?"

Teenagers (13-18): Be more direct about your growth process. "I've been reflecting on how my anxiety sometimes leads me to be controlling, and I can see how that affects our relationship. I'm working on managing my anxiety better so I can support you without taking over."

Journaling prompts for self-compassion work

Regular reflective writing can help you develop greater self-awareness and self-compassion in your parenting journey. These prompts are designed to help you process difficult experiences with kindness rather than harsh judgment.

Weekly self-compassion journaling prompts:

Monday: Acknowledging struggles "What was the most challenging moment in my parenting this week? How can I hold this experience with compassion while still learning from it?"

Tuesday: Recognizing efforts "What did I try to do well as a parent this week, even if it didn't work out perfectly? How can I appreciate my efforts and intentions?"

Wednesday: Common humanity "How are my parenting struggles similar to challenges that other parents face? What would I want someone to say to me if I shared this challenge with them?"

Thursday: Growth and learning "What am I learning about myself as a parent right now? How is this learning process unfolding, and how can I be patient with my own growth?"

Friday: Self-kindness practice "If my best friend was facing the same parenting challenges I'm facing, what would I say to them? How can I offer myself that same kindness and support?"

Saturday: Gratitude and appreciation "What do I appreciate about myself as a parent? What strengths do I bring to my family, even when I'm not perfect?"

Sunday: Intentions and hopes "What kind of parent do I want to be this coming week? How can I hold this intention with hope and self-compassion rather than perfectionist pressure?"

Monthly deeper reflection prompts:

"How has my relationship with myself as a parent changed over the past month?"

"What patterns of self-criticism am I noticing, and how can I respond to myself with more kindness?"

"What would my children want me to know about the kind of parent I am?"

"How can I practice self-forgiveness for the parenting mistakes I've made this month?"

"What support do I need to continue growing as a parent while being kind to myself in the process?"

Building a support network

OCPD parents often struggle with isolation, partly because perfectionist tendencies can make it difficult to be vulnerable with others about parenting challenges. Building a support network isn't just about having people to talk to - it's about creating relationships that help you maintain perspective, provide encouragement, and offer practical support when you need it.

Why OCPD parents isolate and how to change it

According to research from the IOCPDF and PubMed Central, people with perfectionist traits often isolate themselves because they fear judgment, have difficulty being vulnerable, or believe they should be able to handle challenges independently (IOCPDF, 2023; PMC, 2023).

Common reasons OCPD parents isolate:

Fear of judgment: Worry that other parents will criticize your parenting approach or think less of you if they know about your struggles.

Perfectionist image management: Feeling like you need to present a perfect family image to the outside world, which prevents authentic connection with others.

Belief in self-reliance: Thinking that asking for help or admitting struggles is a sign of weakness or inadequacy.

Difficulty with vulnerability: Struggling to share personal challenges or emotions, which limits the depth of relationships.

All-or-nothing thinking: Believing that if you can't be the perfect parent or friend, you shouldn't engage with others at all.

Comparison and competition: Feeling like other parents have it all figured out, which creates shame about your own struggles.

Breaking through isolation barriers:

Start small: Begin with low-stakes vulnerability - sharing minor challenges or asking for simple advice rather than exposing your deepest struggles immediately.

Choose wisely: Look for other parents who seem genuine, non-judgmental, and willing to share their own challenges rather than those who seem to have everything perfect.

Practice imperfection: Intentionally share moments when things didn't go perfectly in your family, and notice that this often leads to more authentic connections.

Focus on common ground: Connect with other parents around shared experiences - similar-aged children, common interests, or shared values - rather than trying to find people who parent exactly like you do.

Reframe help-seeking: Think of building connections as a gift to your children, who benefit from seeing you model healthy relationships and community engagement.

Finding and participating in support groups

According to the National Alliance on Mental Illness, support groups can be particularly beneficial for parents dealing with perfectionist patterns because they provide both emotional support and practical strategies from others who understand similar challenges (NAMI, 2023).

Types of support groups that might be helpful:

OCPD-specific support groups: Groups focused specifically on perfectionism and overcontrol, either online or in-person.

Parenting support groups: General parenting groups that focus on challenges rather than just celebrating successes.

Anxiety support groups: Since OCPD often involves significant anxiety, general anxiety support groups can provide relevant strategies and understanding.

Family therapy groups: Multi-family therapy groups where several families work on communication and relationship issues together.

Online communities: Forums, social media groups, or virtual meetups focused on perfectionist parenting or OCPD support.

How to get the most out of support groups:

Be authentic: Share real struggles rather than presenting a perfect image of yourself or your family.

Listen actively: Pay attention to how others handle similar challenges and what strategies have worked for them.

Practice vulnerability gradually: Start by sharing smaller challenges and work up to more significant struggles as you build trust.

Offer support to others: Supporting other parents helps you gain perspective on your own challenges and builds meaningful connections.

Apply insights to your situation: Take ideas from group discussions and experiment with adapting them to your own family circumstances.

Maintain boundaries: Share appropriately without overwhelming others or taking on responsibility for solving everyone else's problems.

Online communities and resources

Online support can be particularly valuable for OCPD parents who may struggle with in-person vulnerability or who have difficulty finding local resources that understand perfectionist patterns.

Benefits of online support:

- Anonymity can make it easier to share struggles and ask for help
- Access to communities that specifically understand OCPD and perfectionist parenting
- Ability to connect with others at any time of day when you're struggling
- Exposure to diverse perspectives and strategies from parents around the world
- Resources and information that might not be available in your local area

Guidelines for healthy online community participation:

Choose communities carefully: Look for groups that focus on growth and support rather than complaining or competing about who has the most difficult circumstances.

Maintain privacy boundaries: Share challenges and insights without revealing identifying information about your family.

Balance online and offline support: Use online communities to supplement but not replace in-person relationships and professional support.

Practice discernment: Take advice and suggestions as options to consider rather than rules you must follow.

Contribute positively: Share your own insights and experiences to help others, not just to seek support for yourself.

Monitor your emotional response: If online communities increase your anxiety or self-criticism rather than providing support, consider taking breaks or finding different groups.

Creating accountability partnerships

Accountability partnerships with other parents can provide ongoing support for changing perfectionist patterns while maintaining focus on your growth goals.

What makes a good accountability partner:

- Another parent who is also working on personal growth
- Someone who can be honest with you while remaining supportive
- A person who shares similar values but may have different parenting approaches
- Someone reliable who will follow through on regular check-ins
- A parent who can maintain appropriate boundaries and won't try to fix your problems for you

Structure for accountability partnerships:

Regular check-ins: Weekly or biweekly conversations (phone, video call, or in-person) to discuss progress, challenges, and goals.

Specific focus areas: Choose 2-3 specific areas to work on (like increasing flexibility, practicing self-compassion, or improving family communication).

Goal setting and review: Help each other set realistic, specific goals and regularly review progress without judgment.

Challenge and support: Gently challenge each other to grow while providing emotional support during difficult moments.

Brainstorming sessions: Work together to generate ideas for handling specific parenting challenges, combining your different perspectives and experiences.

Celebration of progress: Acknowledge each other's growth and positive changes, no matter how small they might seem.

Example accountability partnership structure:

- Monthly goal setting: Each partner chooses 2-3 specific areas to focus on for the coming month

- Weekly check-ins: 30-minute conversations to discuss what worked, what was challenging, and what support is needed

- Challenge support: Text or call support available during particularly difficult parenting moments

- Monthly reflection: Review progress over the past month and adjust goals for the following month

Sample accountability partnership questions:

- "What did you try differently in your parenting this week?"

- "Where did you notice yourself falling back into old patterns?"

- "What was your biggest parenting win this week?"

- "What do you want to work on next week?"

- "How can I support you in reaching your parenting goals?"

- "What patterns are you noticing in yourself that you'd like me to help you observe?"

The foundation for lasting transformation

Self-compassion and personal healing work forms the bedrock of sustainable change in perfectionist parenting patterns. Without developing kindness toward yourself, attempts to change your parenting approach often become just another area for self-criticism and impossible standards.

The research consistently shows that parents who practice self-compassion are more emotionally available to their children, more resilient during challenging parenting moments, and more likely to maintain positive changes over time. When you treat yourself with the same kindness you would show a good friend facing similar struggles, you model healthy self-relationship for your children while creating the emotional resources needed for continued growth.

Building authentic connections with other parents and support systems isn't just beneficial for you - it demonstrates to your children what healthy community and vulnerability look like. When they see you acknowledging struggles, asking for help, and maintaining relationships through imperfection, they learn that perfection isn't required for connection and that growth happens in relationship with others.

The journey from perfectionist control to flexible, connected parenting isn't a destination you reach but a practice you develop over time. Self-compassion provides the fuel for this ongoing practice, helping you stay committed to growth while treating yourself with kindness through the inevitable setbacks and learning moments along the way.

Chapter 12: Early intervention strategies

The earlier you can identify and address perfectionist patterns in your family, the more effectively you can prevent them from becoming entrenched and causing long-term difficulties. Early intervention isn't just about catching problems before they get worse - it's about creating family cultures that actively promote flexibility, resilience, and healthy relationships with achievement from the beginning.

Many parents worry that focusing on prevention might mean lowering standards or accepting mediocrity. But research consistently shows that children who grow up in families that balance high expectations with emotional warmth and flexibility actually perform better academically and socially than children in families that emphasize perfection and control.

Early intervention strategies work on multiple levels: helping you recognize when normal developmental phases might be shifting into concerning patterns, creating family environments that naturally support healthy development, and building partnerships with schools and other systems in your child's life to reinforce these positive approaches.

Identifying at-risk children

Comprehensive warning signs by age

According to research from Washington University School of Medicine, perfectionist patterns can emerge at different developmental stages, and the warning signs look different depending on a child's age and developmental capabilities (WashU Medicine, 2023). Understanding what to look for at each stage helps you distinguish between normal developmental phases and patterns that might benefit from early intervention.

Ages 3-5: Preschool warning signs

- Extreme distress over minor imperfections (crying for extended periods over crooked stickers, messy artwork, or "wrong" clothing)

- Refusal to try new activities unless they can do them "perfectly" right away

- Excessive concern with rules and "right" ways of doing things, beyond typical preschooler rule-following

- Difficulty transitioning between activities or handling changes in routine, even with preparation and support

- Anxiety about making mistakes that interferes with learning or play

- Self-critical language that seems advanced for their age ("I'm stupid," "I never do anything right")

- Avoiding age-appropriate challenges because they might not succeed immediately

Ages 6-8: Early elementary warning signs

- Spending excessive time on homework or assignments trying to make them perfect

- Frequent erasing, starting over, or refusing to turn in work that isn't "good enough"

- Physical symptoms (stomachaches, headaches) related to school performance or activities

- Extreme reactions to making mistakes or receiving criticism

- Comparing themselves constantly to peers and becoming upset when they don't measure up

- Difficulty enjoying activities unless they excel at them
- Beginning to avoid social situations where their performance might be evaluated

Ages 9-11: Late elementary warning signs

- Procrastination or avoidance of challenging tasks due to fear of imperfection
- All-or-nothing thinking about their abilities ("I'm terrible at math" after one poor grade)
- Seeking excessive reassurance from adults about their performance
- Difficulty making decisions due to fear of making the "wrong" choice
- Social withdrawal due to performance anxiety
- Sleep problems related to worry about school or activities
- Beginning to tie their self-worth primarily to achievements and grades

Ages 12-14: Early adolescent warning signs

- Perfectionist patterns beginning to significantly interfere with daily functioning
- Avoiding trying out for teams, activities, or social opportunities due to fear of failure
- Intense anxiety about grades, appearance, or social acceptance
- Beginning to restrict activities or interests to only areas where they feel confident of success
- Difficulty with peer relationships due to rigid expectations of themselves and others

- Developing eating, exercise, or appearance-related perfectionist behaviors

- Expressing hopelessness about their ability to meet their own or others' expectations

Differentiating normal development from OCPD traits

Research from PubMed shows that many behaviors that concern parents about perfectionism are actually normal parts of child development (PubMed, 2023). The key is learning to distinguish between temporary developmental phases and persistent patterns that might indicate emerging OCPD traits.

Normal developmental perfectionism vs. concerning patterns:

Normal: A 4-year-old goes through a phase of wanting their clothes arranged a certain way or having strong preferences about food presentation. **Concerning**: The same behaviors persist for months, interfere with daily activities, and cause significant distress when the child can't have things "just right."

Normal: A 7-year-old becomes very focused on following rules and wants everyone else to follow them too. **Concerning**: Rule-following becomes so rigid that the child can't adapt to changing circumstances and becomes extremely upset when rules are bent or exceptions are made.

Normal: A 10-year-old cares deeply about doing well on a project and wants to make it as good as possible. **Concerning**: The child spends so much time trying to perfect the project that they miss the deadline, or they become so upset about minor imperfections that they can't complete their work.

Normal: A 13-year-old goes through a period of being very concerned about their appearance and how others perceive them. **Concerning**: Appearance concerns become so intense that they avoid social situations, spend excessive time on grooming, or develop rigid rules about how they must look.

Key differences between normal and concerning patterns:

- **Intensity**: Normal developmental phases involve strong preferences; concerning patterns involve intense distress

- **Duration**: Normal phases typically last weeks to months; concerning patterns persist for months to years without improvement

- **Flexibility**: Normal perfectionism can be negotiated and adapted; concerning patterns are completely rigid

- **Functional impact**: Normal phases don't significantly interfere with daily life; concerning patterns limit participation in normal childhood activities

- **Response to support**: Normal phases respond to patience and understanding; concerning patterns may require more intensive intervention

When perfectionism becomes problematic

According to research from Katie Lear, perfectionism crosses the line from normal to problematic when it begins to significantly interfere with a child's ability to engage in age-appropriate activities, maintain relationships, or experience joy and satisfaction in their daily life (Lear, 2021).

Problematic perfectionism indicators:

Academic interference: When perfectionist concerns prevent a child from completing assignments, participating in class, or trying challenging material. This might look like a child who won't turn in work unless it's perfect, spends hours on assignments that should take minutes, or refuses to participate in group activities where their performance might be evaluated.

Social isolation: When perfectionist standards interfere with friendships and social activities. Children might avoid playdates because they're worried about making mistakes in front of others, refuse to participate in group activities where they might not excel, or become so controlling with friends that relationships suffer.

Emotional distress: When perfectionist thoughts and behaviors create significant anxiety, sadness, or frustration that interferes with daily functioning. This might include frequent meltdowns about minor imperfections, persistent worry about performance, or expressions of hopelessness about their ability to meet expectations.

Physical symptoms: When perfectionist stress manifests in physical ways like frequent headaches, stomachaches, sleep problems, or changes in appetite that aren't explained by medical conditions.

Avoidance patterns: When children begin avoiding more and more activities due to perfectionist concerns. This might start with avoiding challenging academic subjects and expand to avoiding sports, creative activities, social situations, or any area where they might not immediately excel.

Family impact: When perfectionist patterns create ongoing conflict, stress, or disruption in family life. This might include daily battles about homework, extreme reactions to changes in plans, or family activities being constrained by the child's need for everything to be perfect.

Screening tools and assessment resources

While formal diagnosis of OCPD typically doesn't occur until late adolescence or adulthood, there are assessment tools that can help parents and professionals identify children who might benefit from early intervention.

Informal parent observation tools:

Daily functioning checklist: Track for two weeks whether perfectionist concerns interfere with:

- Completing homework and school assignments
- Participating in extracurricular activities
- Maintaining friendships and social relationships
- Enjoying family time and activities
- Sleeping and eating normally
- Trying new things or taking appropriate risks

Emotional response monitoring: Note instances when your child:

- Becomes extremely upset over minor mistakes or imperfections
- Expresses harsh self-criticism or hopelessness about their abilities
- Shows physical signs of stress (crying, anxiety, avoidance) related to performance situations
- Seems unable to enjoy activities unless they're excelling

Flexibility assessment: Observe how your child handles:

- Changes in plans or routines
- Making mistakes during activities
- Receiving constructive feedback or criticism
- Situations where there's no clear "right" answer or approach
- Activities where the outcome is uncertain

Professional assessment resources:

School counselors: Can observe children in academic and social settings and provide perspective on whether concerns are within normal ranges for the child's age and developmental stage.

Pediatric psychologists: Specialize in child development and can distinguish between normal developmental phases and patterns that might benefit from intervention.

Child psychiatrists: Can assess for co-occurring conditions like anxiety or depression that often accompany perfectionist patterns.

Educational specialists: Can evaluate whether perfectionist concerns are interfering with learning and academic progress.

When to seek professional assessment:

- Perfectionist patterns have persisted for more than six months without improvement

- The child's functioning is significantly impaired in multiple areas (school, social, family)

- Physical symptoms are present and not explained by medical conditions

- The child expresses hopelessness, extreme self-criticism, or thoughts of self-harm

- Family functioning is significantly impacted by the child's perfectionist patterns

- Previous attempts at support and intervention haven't led to improvement

Prevention through family culture change

Creating a family culture that naturally supports healthy relationships with achievement and challenges is one of the most effective ways to prevent problematic perfectionism from developing in your children.

Creating a growth mindset household

According to research from Psychology Today, families that consistently reinforce growth mindset messages create environments where children are more likely to develop healthy relationships with challenge, effort, and mistakes (Psychology Today, 2023).

Elements of a growth mindset household:

Language that emphasizes process over outcome: Instead of "You're so smart!" try "You worked really hard on that problem." Instead of "You're naturally good at this," try "Your practice is really paying off."

Celebrating effort and improvement: Create family traditions that acknowledge hard work, persistence, and growth rather than just final achievements. This might include weekly recognition of family members who tried something challenging, worked hard on a difficult task, or learned from a mistake.

Mistake appreciation: Develop family practices that treat mistakes as valuable learning opportunities rather than failures to be avoided. Some families have "mistake celebration" dinners where everyone shares something they learned from a recent mistake.

Challenge seeking: Encourage family members to regularly try things that are difficult or where success isn't guaranteed. This models that growth comes from challenge rather than from staying in comfortable areas of competence.

Questions that promote growth thinking:

- "What did you learn from that experience?"
- "What would you try differently next time?"
- "What was the most challenging part, and how did you handle it?"
- "What strategies did you use when things got difficult?"
- "How has your thinking about this changed?"

Growth mindset responses to common situations:

When your child struggles with homework: Instead of immediately helping or expressing concern about their grades, try "This looks challenging. What strategies do you want to try?"

When your child makes a mistake: Instead of correcting immediately or expressing disappointment, try "That's interesting. What do you think happened there?"

When your child succeeds easily: Instead of just praising the success, try "That seemed pretty easy for you. Are you ready for a bigger challenge?"

When your child wants to quit an activity: Instead of insisting they stick with it or letting them quit immediately, try "What's making this feel difficult right now? What would need to change for this to feel more manageable?"

Establishing flexible family traditions

Family traditions provide structure and predictability that children need while creating opportunities to practice flexibility and adaptation. The key is developing traditions that have consistent elements but allow for variation and individual expression.

Flexible tradition examples:

Family game night: Establish a regular time for family games, but allow different family members to choose the games, modify rules to accommodate different skill levels, or create new games together.

Weekly adventure time: Set aside time each week for family activities, but let family members take turns choosing what you do, encourage trying new things, and be open to adventures that don't go according to plan.

Celebration rituals: Develop ways of celebrating family achievements that focus on effort and growth rather than just outcomes. This might include a special dinner for anyone who tried something challenging, regardless of the result.

Problem-solving meetings: Create regular times when the family comes together to address challenges, but make the process collaborative and open to creative solutions rather than following rigid procedures.

Learning share time: Establish regular opportunities for family members to share something new they've learned, tried, or discovered, emphasizing curiosity and exploration over expertise.

Benefits of flexible traditions:

- Provide the structure and predictability that children (especially those prone to perfectionism) need

- Create regular opportunities to practice flexibility and adaptation

- Build family connection around shared experiences rather than shared achievements

- Model that traditions can change and grow while maintaining their essential purpose

- Give children experience with planning, decision-making, and problem-solving in low-stakes situations

Building resilience factors in children

Research from Harvard University and the Raising Children Network shows that certain factors consistently protect children from developing problematic perfectionism and help them bounce back from challenges and setbacks (Harvard University, 2023; Raising Children Network, 2023).

Key resilience factors for preventing perfectionism:

Secure attachment relationships: Children who feel unconditionally loved and supported are more likely to take appropriate risks and bounce back from failures because they know their worth isn't dependent on their performance.

How to build: Regular one-on-one time with each child, consistent emotional availability during difficult moments, and explicit expressions of love that aren't tied to behavior or achievement.

Self-efficacy beliefs: Children who believe they can influence outcomes through their own efforts are less likely to become paralyzed by perfectionist anxiety.

How to build: Give children age-appropriate responsibilities and choices, allow them to experience natural consequences of their decisions, and help them see the connection between their efforts and outcomes.

Social support networks: Children who have multiple sources of support and connection are less vulnerable to perfectionist patterns because their entire sense of worth isn't dependent on one relationship or context.

How to build: Encourage friendships and peer relationships, maintain connections with extended family, and help children develop relationships with other trusted adults like teachers, coaches, or mentors.

Emotional regulation skills: Children who can manage difficult emotions without becoming overwhelmed are better able to handle the setbacks and challenges that trigger perfectionist responses.

How to build: Model healthy emotional expression, teach specific calming strategies, validate children's emotions while helping them develop coping skills, and create family cultures where all emotions are acceptable even if all behaviors aren't.

Problem-solving abilities: Children who feel confident in their ability to figure things out are less likely to become overwhelmed by perfectionist anxiety when they encounter challenges.

How to build: Use collaborative problem-solving approaches to family challenges, encourage children to brainstorm multiple solutions to problems, and resist the urge to solve problems for them when they're capable of finding their own solutions.

Optimistic thinking patterns: Children who maintain hope and positive expectations about the future are more resilient to perfectionist despair and more likely to persist through challenges.

How to build: Focus on what's going well in addition to addressing problems, help children see setbacks as temporary rather than permanent, and share stories of people who overcame challenges through persistence and effort.

90-day family transformation plan

This structured approach helps families systematically create cultures that prevent perfectionist patterns while building resilience and flexibility.

Days 1-30: Awareness and foundation building

Week 1: Family assessment

- Each family member identifies their strengths and areas for growth
- Discuss family values and what kind of family culture you want to create
- Begin daily gratitude practice focusing on effort and character rather than achievements

Week 2: Growth mindset language

- Practice using growth mindset language in daily conversations
- Create a family poster of growth mindset phrases and responses
- Begin weekly "mistake appreciation" conversations

Week 3: Flexibility practice

- Introduce small changes to family routines to practice adaptation
- Plan activities with built-in uncertainty or variability
- Practice collaborative decision-making for family choices

Week 4: Connection building

- Establish regular one-on-one time with each child
- Begin weekly family meetings using collaborative problem-solving approaches
- Create new family traditions that emphasize process over outcome

Days 31-60: Skill development and practice

Week 5-6: Emotional awareness

- Teach and practice emotional regulation skills
- Create family emotion check-ins and support systems
- Model healthy emotional expression and vulnerability

Week 7-8: Challenge seeking

- Encourage each family member to try something new or challenging
- Create family challenges that require collaboration and creativity
- Celebrate effort and learning rather than just success

Days 61-90: Integration and maintenance

Week 9-10: Problem-solving practice

- Use real family challenges as opportunities to practice collaborative solutions

- Help children take on age-appropriate leadership roles in family problem-solving
- Create systems for ongoing family communication and support

Week 11-12: Reflection and planning

- Assess progress and celebrate changes in family culture
- Identify areas that need continued attention
- Make plans for maintaining positive changes and continuing growth

Monthly check-in questions:

- How has our family culture changed over the past month?
- What new skills or practices are family members developing?
- Where do we still see perfectionist patterns, and how can we address them?
- What do we want to focus on in the coming month?
- How can we continue supporting each other's growth and learning?

School partnership strategies

Schools play a crucial role in either reinforcing or counteracting perfectionist patterns. Building positive partnerships with your child's teachers and school staff can help ensure that your efforts at home are supported in the academic environment.

Working with teachers to prevent perfectionism

Teachers see children in contexts that parents don't - during academic challenges, peer interactions, and performance situations. They can be valuable partners in preventing perfectionist patterns from developing or intensifying.

How to approach teachers about perfectionism concerns:

Frame it as collaboration: "I'd love to work together to help [child's name] develop a healthy relationship with learning and challenges."

Provide specific information: Share what you've observed at home and ask what they're seeing in the classroom. Be specific about behaviors and situations rather than using general labels.

Ask for their perspective: "Have you noticed any signs that [child] might be struggling with perfectionist anxiety or fear of making mistakes?"

Focus on prevention: "What can we do together to help [child] stay excited about learning and comfortable with making mistakes?"

Strategies to discuss with teachers:

Process-focused feedback: Ask teachers to emphasize effort, strategy, and improvement rather than just correct answers or final grades.

Mistake normalization: Discuss ways teachers can help normalize mistakes as part of learning in the classroom environment.

Challenge level: Work together to ensure that your child is appropriately challenged without being overwhelmed by perfectionist anxiety.

Participation encouragement: Ask teachers to create opportunities for your child to participate and contribute without high-stakes evaluation.

Social support: Discuss ways to help your child build positive peer relationships and feel connected to the classroom community.

Advocating for process-focused learning

Many traditional educational practices inadvertently reinforce perfectionist patterns by emphasizing grades, correct answers, and comparison with peers. You can advocate for approaches that support healthy learning relationships.

Process-focused practices to advocate for:

Effort-based grading: Systems that give credit for showing work, trying multiple strategies, and demonstrating improvement over time.

Collaborative learning: Opportunities for students to work together, learn from each other, and see that there are multiple approaches to problems.

Reflection activities: Regular opportunities for students to think about what they're learning, what strategies are working, and what they want to improve.

Choice in learning: Options for students to demonstrate their knowledge in different ways and to pursue topics that interest them.

Mistake-positive environment: Classroom cultures where mistakes are treated as learning opportunities rather than failures.

Managing your OCPD triggers at school events

School events can be particularly triggering for OCPD parents because they involve public evaluation of your child's performance and your parenting. Learning to manage these triggers helps you support your child effectively during school activities.

Common school triggers for OCPD parents:

- Your child's academic performance compared to peers
- Your child's behavior in public school settings
- Other parents' approaches to homework, activities, or achievements
- School policies or practices that don't align with your preferences
- Social dynamics between children that you can't control

Strategies for managing school triggers:

Prepare mentally before events: Before school conferences, performances, or activities, remind yourself of your values and goals for your child's education.

Focus on your child's experience: Instead of worrying about how things look to others, pay attention to whether your child seems engaged, happy, and appropriately challenged.

Practice perspective-taking: When you notice yourself comparing or judging, ask "What would I want other parents to think about my child and our family?"

Use support systems: Arrange to attend school events with other parents who share similar values, or plan to debrief with supportive friends or family after challenging school situations.

Maintain long-term perspective: One poor performance, social conflict, or academic struggle doesn't predict your child's future success or happiness.

Communication templates for teacher conferences

Having prepared language for common conference situations can help you stay focused on collaboration rather than falling into defensive or controlling patterns.

Opening the conversation: "Thank you for taking time to meet with me. I'm hoping we can work together to support [child's name] in having a positive learning experience this year. I'd love to hear your perspective on how things are going and share some observations from home."

When discussing challenges: "I've noticed [specific behavior or concern] at home. Have you observed anything similar in the classroom? What strategies have you found helpful when this happens?"

When you disagree with an approach: "I can see that you're trying to help [child] succeed. I'm wondering if we might try a different approach that could work for both the classroom and home environment."

When discussing perfectionist concerns: "[Child] sometimes struggles with wanting everything to be perfect, and I'm wondering how this shows up in the classroom. What can we do together to help them feel comfortable making mistakes and learning from them?"

When your child is struggling academically: "I want [child] to be appropriately challenged while feeling confident about learning. How can we work together to find the right balance?"

Closing the conversation: "This has been really helpful. What's the best way for us to stay in communication about how things are going? I want to make sure we're supporting each other's efforts."

Planting seeds for lifelong wellbeing

Early intervention isn't about eliminating all challenges from your child's life or preventing them from experiencing any perfectionist thoughts. It's about creating conditions where healthy patterns can develop naturally and problematic patterns are less likely to take root.

The family culture you create now becomes the internal voice your children will carry with them throughout their lives. When you emphasize growth over perfection, connection over achievement, and learning over performance, you're giving your children tools they'll use long after they've left your household.

The partnership you build with schools and other systems in your child's life creates a consistent message about what matters most in their development. When home and school work together to support process-focused learning and healthy relationships with challenge, children receive reinforcement for resilient attitudes and approaches.

Most importantly, the awareness you develop about the early signs of problematic perfectionism allows you to intervene quickly and effectively when concerning patterns do emerge. Early intervention is almost always more effective than trying to change entrenched patterns later in development.

Chapter 13: Maintaining progress and preventing relapse

Change is rarely a straight line from old patterns to new ones. Most parents find that their journey toward more flexible, connected parenting involves periods of progress followed by times when they slip back into familiar controlling patterns. This isn't failure - it's normal. Understanding how to recognize and respond to these setbacks can mean the difference between temporary lapses and long-term relapse.

The families that maintain positive changes over time are those that develop systems for recognizing early warning signs, have strategies for getting back on track quickly, and view setbacks as information rather than evidence of failure. They also understand that maintaining progress requires ongoing attention and practice, not just initial motivation and effort.

This chapter focuses on practical strategies for sustaining the changes you've made while building resilience for the inevitable challenges that will test your commitment to more flexible parenting approaches.

Recognizing relapse triggers

Common situations that activate OCPD patterns

Even after making significant progress in changing your parenting approach, certain situations have the power to reactivate old controlling patterns. Recognizing these triggers before they overwhelm your new skills gives you the best chance of responding thoughtfully rather than reactively.

High-stress family transitions:

- Starting a new school year or changing schools

- Moving to a new home or community

- Changes in work schedules or financial circumstances

- Family illness or medical concerns

- Divorce, remarriage, or other major relationship changes

- Addition of new family members (babies, stepchildren, aging parents)

Academic pressure periods:

- Beginning of school terms when new expectations are established

- Testing seasons and standardized assessment periods

- College application and decision processes

- Parent-teacher conferences or academic evaluations

- Report card time or grade reporting periods

- Homework increases or project deadlines

Social comparison situations:

- School events where children's performance is displayed publicly

- Youth sports seasons and competitive activities

- Social media exposure to other families' achievements

- Conversations with other parents about children's accomplishments

- Family gatherings where relatives compare children's progress

- Award ceremonies or recognition events

Developmental challenges:

- Times when your child is struggling with new developmental tasks

- Periods of regression in behavior or skills

- Adolescent independence-seeking behaviors

- Social conflicts or peer relationship difficulties

- Learning difficulties or academic struggles

- Emotional or behavioral challenges that feel beyond your control

Personal stress factors:

- Your own work pressures or professional challenges

- Health concerns or physical exhaustion

- Relationship difficulties with your partner

- Financial worries or major life decisions

- Grief or loss experiences

- Feeling overwhelmed by daily life management

Stress, transitions, and perfectionist relapse

Stress affects the brain in ways that make flexible thinking more difficult and automatic patterns more likely to emerge. During high-stress periods, the prefrontal cortex (responsible for flexible thinking and impulse control) becomes less active, while the limbic system (responsible for fight-or-flight responses) becomes more dominant.

For OCPD parents, this means that the new skills you've learned require more conscious effort during stressful times, while old controlling patterns feel more automatic and urgent. Understanding this neurological reality can help you prepare for and respond to stress-related relapses.

How stress affects OCPD parenting patterns:

Decreased tolerance for uncertainty: During stressful periods, situations that you normally handle with flexibility might trigger intense anxiety and controlling responses.

Narrowed attention: Stress causes tunnel vision, making it harder to see the big picture or consider multiple perspectives when dealing with parenting challenges.

Increased reactivity: The pause between trigger and response that you've worked to develop becomes much shorter during high-stress times.

Return to familiar coping mechanisms: Controlling behavior might have served you well during previous stressful periods, so your brain defaults to these patterns when new stress arises.

Reduced self-compassion: Stress often reactivates harsh self-critical voices, which can make it harder to recover from parenting mistakes or setbacks.

Strategies for managing stress-related relapses:

Expect and normalize them: Understanding that setbacks are more likely during stressful periods helps you respond to them as temporary and manageable rather than as evidence of permanent failure.

Lower expectations temporarily: During high-stress times, focus on maintaining basic connection and safety rather than trying to implement advanced flexible parenting techniques.

Increase self-care: Prioritize sleep, nutrition, exercise, and emotional support during stressful periods to maintain your capacity for thoughtful parenting responses.

Use support systems more actively: Reach out to friends, family, or professional support more frequently during stressful times rather than trying to handle everything independently.

Practice extra self-compassion: Treat yourself with the same kindness you'd show a friend going through similar circumstances.

Creating an early warning system

Developing awareness of your personal early warning signs allows you to intervene before controlling patterns become fully activated. Most parents find that they have reliable physical, emotional, and behavioral signals that indicate they're moving toward perfectionist relapse.

Physical warning signs:

- Changes in sleep patterns (insomnia or oversleeping)
- Tension in specific parts of your body (jaw, shoulders, stomach)
- Changes in appetite or eating patterns
- Headaches or other stress-related physical symptoms
- Feeling constantly rushed or behind schedule
- Fatigue that doesn't improve with rest

Emotional warning signs:

- Increased irritability or impatience with family members
- Anxiety about outcomes you normally wouldn't worry about
- Feeling overwhelmed by normal daily tasks
- Decreased enjoyment in activities you usually find pleasant
- Increased worry about your children's future or performance
- Feeling like you're the only person who can handle family responsibilities

Behavioral warning signs:

- Taking over tasks that family members usually handle independently
- Increasing criticism or correction of family members

- Spending more time checking, organizing, or controlling family activities

- Avoiding social activities or isolating from support systems

- Micromanaging details of family life that you normally delegate

- Having difficulty delegating or accepting help from others

Relational warning signs:

- Family members seeming more tense or walking on eggshells around you

- Increased conflict or arguments about routine family matters

- Children asking for help with things they normally handle independently

- Your partner taking on more household management to avoid your criticism

- Family activities becoming more structured and less spontaneous

- Conversations focusing more on problems and corrections than connection and enjoyment

Creating your personal early warning checklist:

1. Identify the 3-5 warning signs that most reliably indicate you're moving toward controlling patterns

2. Ask trusted family members or friends to help you recognize these signs when you might not see them yourself

3. Create a simple daily or weekly check-in system to assess whether these warning signs are present

4. Develop specific strategies for responding to each warning sign before it escalates

Personal relapse prevention plan

A relapse prevention plan is a written strategy that you develop during times when you're feeling balanced and thinking clearly. It serves as a guide for what to do when stress, triggers, or challenging circumstances threaten to pull you back into old patterns.

Components of an effective relapse prevention plan:

Values reminder: A brief statement of your core parenting values and the kind of family relationships you want to maintain. This helps you remember what you're working toward during difficult moments. *Example*: "I want our family to be a place where everyone feels loved unconditionally, where mistakes are learning opportunities, and where we support each other through challenges while allowing individual growth and expression."

Trigger identification: A list of your most common triggers and early warning signs, along with specific strategies for managing each one. *Example*: "When I feel anxious about my child's academic performance, I will: pause and take three deep breaths, ask myself what my child needs from me right now (rather than what needs to be fixed), and focus on supporting their effort rather than controlling their outcomes."

Support system activation: Clear plans for reaching out to your support network when you're struggling, including specific people to call and what kind of support to ask for. *Example*: "When I notice myself becoming controlling, I will call [friend's name] for a reality check, schedule coffee with [other parent] to gain perspective, or text my accountability partner for encouragement."

Self-care protocols: Non-negotiable self-care practices that you commit to maintaining even during stressful periods, because these provide the foundation for flexible parenting responses. *Example*: "Even during busy or stressful times, I will maintain: minimum 7 hours of sleep per night, daily 10-minute mindfulness practice, weekly one-on-one time with each child, and weekly check-in with my partner about how we're doing as a family."

Emergency strategies: Specific techniques to use when you're in the middle of a controlling episode and need to de-escalate quickly. *Example*: "When I realize I'm in controlling mode: Stop talking and take a physical break from the situation, do 10 deep breaths or a brief mindfulness exercise, ask myself 'What would love do in this situation?', and then re-engage with focus on connection rather than correction."

Recovery protocols: Plans for repairing relationships and getting back on track after a relapse episode. *Example*: "After a controlling episode: Apologize specifically for my behavior without making excuses, ask family members how my behavior affected them, discuss what I'll do differently next time, and schedule extra connection time with anyone who was impacted."

Sustaining flexibility over time

The maintenance phase of change

After the initial excitement and motivation of making changes in your parenting approach, you enter what psychologists call the "maintenance phase" of behavior change. This phase can be more challenging than the initial change phase because it requires sustained effort without the reward of dramatic improvement.

Characteristics of the maintenance phase:

- Progress becomes more subtle and incremental

- Old patterns occasionally resurface during stress or challenging times

- Family members may take new approaches for granted rather than actively appreciating them

- Motivation may fluctuate rather than remaining consistently high

- The novelty of new approaches wears off, requiring more conscious effort to maintain them

Strategies for successful maintenance:

Focus on systems rather than motivation: Create routines and structures that support flexible parenting even when you don't feel particularly motivated. This might include regular family meetings, scheduled one-on-one time with children, or automatic reminders to pause before reacting to challenging behaviors.

Celebrate small improvements: During the maintenance phase, progress often comes in small increments that are easy to miss. Developing practices for noticing and appreciating subtle improvements helps maintain momentum.

Plan for plateaus: Expect periods when it feels like you're not making progress. These plateaus are normal parts of the change process, not indicators that you should give up or that change isn't working.

Refresh your practices: Periodically introduce new techniques or approaches to prevent your flexible parenting practices from becoming stale or automatic. This might mean trying new family activities, reading about different approaches, or getting input from other parents.

Connect with your "why": Regularly remind yourself of the reasons you wanted to change your parenting approach in the first place. This might involve reflecting on improvements in family relationships, your children's increased confidence, or your own reduced stress levels.

Regular family check-ins and adjustments

Sustainable change requires ongoing assessment and adjustment. Families that maintain positive changes over time develop regular practices for evaluating how things are going and making necessary adjustments.

Monthly family check-in structure:

Appreciation round (10 minutes): Each family member shares something they appreciate about how the family has been functioning and something they appreciate about each other family member.

Challenge discussion (15 minutes): Discuss any ongoing challenges or areas where the family is struggling. Focus on problem-solving together rather than blame or criticism.

Goal review (10 minutes): Review any family goals or areas you've been working on improving. Celebrate progress and adjust approaches if needed.

Planning ahead (5 minutes): Discuss upcoming events, changes, or challenges that might affect family functioning and plan how to handle them.

Individual parent check-ins:

Weekly self-assessment: Briefly assess how you're doing with maintaining flexible parenting approaches. What's working well? Where are you struggling? What support do you need?

Monthly partner check-in: If you have a co-parent, schedule regular conversations about parenting approaches, family functioning, and areas where you want to make adjustments.

Quarterly professional or peer consultation: Consider scheduling regular check-ins with a therapist, parent coach, or support group to get outside perspective on your parenting progress.

Questions for regular family assessment:

- How are family members feeling about our relationships with each other?

- What aspects of our family life are working well right now?

- Where are we seeing stress, conflict, or ongoing challenges?

- What changes or adjustments would be helpful for our family?
- How are we handling mistakes, disappointments, and challenges together?
- What do we want to focus on improving in the coming month?

Celebrating progress without perfection

One of the biggest challenges for OCPD parents in the maintenance phase is learning to appreciate progress without falling back into all-or-nothing thinking about your parenting changes. The goal isn't to become a perfect flexible parent, but to consistently move in the direction of more connection and less control.

Redefining success in the maintenance phase:

Progress, not perfection: Success means responding more flexibly than you used to, not responding flexibly 100% of the time.

Faster recovery: Success includes getting back on track more quickly after setbacks rather than avoiding setbacks entirely.

Increased awareness: Success means noticing controlling patterns earlier and more often, even if you don't always stop them in the moment.

Better relationships: Success is measured by improvements in family connection, children's confidence, and overall family functioning rather than by elimination of all conflict or challenge.

Self-compassion: Success includes treating yourself with kindness when you make mistakes rather than harsh self-criticism that undermines further progress.

Ways to celebrate progress:

Keep a family gratitude journal: Weekly entries about positive changes in family relationships, individual growth, or successful handling of challenges.

Create photo memories: Document family activities, celebrations, and everyday moments that show connection and joy rather than just achievements.

Share successes with support network: Tell friends, family, or support group members about positive changes you've noticed in your family dynamics.

Acknowledge growth explicitly: Tell your children and partner when you notice positive changes in how your family handles challenges together.

Treat yourself with kindness: Acknowledge your own growth and effort with the same enthusiasm you'd show for a friend making similar changes.

Monthly reflection guide

Week 1 reflection: Awareness and patterns

- What controlling patterns did I notice in myself this month?

- How quickly was I able to recognize these patterns?

- What situations or triggers were most challenging for me?

- Where did I see improvement in my flexibility or responsiveness?

Week 2 reflection: Relationships and connection

- How are my relationships with each family member?

- Where do I see increased trust, openness, or connection?

- What feedback have I gotten from family members about changes in our relationships?

- Where do I want to focus more attention on building connection?

Week 3 reflection: Challenges and growth

- What challenges did our family face this month and how did we handle them?
- Where did I see family members growing in resilience, problem-solving, or independence?
- What did I learn about myself as a parent this month?
- How did I handle mistakes or setbacks in my parenting approach?

Week 4 reflection: Planning and goals

- What do I want to focus on in my parenting next month?
- What support do I need to maintain progress?
- What changes would be helpful for our family functioning?
- How can I continue growing while being patient with the process?

When to seek additional help

Signs that professional support is needed

According to research from NCBI, there are clear indicators that suggest when family changes might benefit from professional support beyond what parents can accomplish independently (NCBI, 2023). Recognizing these signs early can help families get appropriate help before patterns become more entrenched.

Individual indicators:

- Your controlling patterns are getting worse rather than better despite consistent effort
- You're experiencing significant anxiety, depression, or other mental health symptoms
- You feel unable to manage your emotional reactions to normal parenting challenges

- You're having thoughts of harming yourself or others
- Substance use is affecting your parenting
- You're unable to implement changes you know would be helpful

Child indicators:

- Your child is showing signs of anxiety, depression, or other mental health concerns
- School performance is being significantly affected by perfectionist patterns
- Your child is avoiding activities, social situations, or challenges due to performance anxiety
- Physical symptoms (headaches, stomachaches, sleep problems) related to stress are occurring regularly
- Your child expresses hopelessness, extreme self-criticism, or thoughts of self-harm
- Perfectionist patterns are interfering with normal childhood development

Family system indicators:

- Family conflict is escalating rather than improving
- Communication patterns are getting worse despite efforts to improve them
- Family members are avoiding each other or withdrawing from family activities
- Previous strategies that worked are no longer effective
- Multiple family members are struggling with anxiety, perfectionism, or related concerns
- Family functioning is significantly impaired in multiple areas

Relationship indicators:

- Your relationship with your partner is deteriorating due to parenting conflicts

- Co-parenting disagreements about control and flexibility are creating ongoing tension

- Children are being triangulated into adult conflicts

- Extended family relationships are being affected by parenting approaches

- Social isolation is increasing rather than decreasing

Types of professionals and their roles

Different types of mental health and support professionals offer different kinds of help for families dealing with perfectionist patterns. Understanding these roles can help you choose the most appropriate support.

Individual therapists for parents:

- Help you understand and change your own perfectionist patterns

- Provide support for anxiety, depression, or other mental health concerns

- Work on healing from your own childhood experiences that might be affecting your parenting

- Develop personalized strategies for managing triggers and controlling behaviors

Child and adolescent therapists:

- Work directly with children who are developing problematic perfectionist patterns

- Help children develop coping strategies for anxiety, perfectionism, and stress

- Support children in building resilience and self-esteem

- Provide assessment and treatment for related mental health concerns

Family therapists:

- Work with the entire family system to improve communication and relationships

- Help families develop healthier patterns of interaction

- Address how perfectionist patterns affect all family members

- Support families through transitions and challenges

Parent coaches:

- Provide specific guidance on parenting strategies and techniques

- Offer support and accountability for implementing changes

- Help parents develop skills for specific parenting challenges

- Focus on practical, day-to-day parenting strategies

Support groups:

- Provide connection with other parents facing similar challenges

- Offer peer support and shared experiences

- Create accountability for maintaining positive changes

- Reduce isolation and normalize struggles

Educational consultants:

- Help families work with schools to address perfectionist patterns in academic settings

- Provide advocacy for children with special learning or emotional needs

- Help families understand educational options and resources

- Support transitions between schools or educational programs

Medication considerations for OCPD

According to research from Kevin W. Grant, while there are no medications specifically approved for OCPD, medication can sometimes be helpful for addressing co-occurring conditions like anxiety, depression, or obsessive-compulsive disorder that often accompany perfectionist patterns (Grant et al, 2008).

When medication might be considered:

- Severe anxiety that interferes with daily functioning despite other interventions

- Depression that affects your ability to engage in parenting or family activities

- Co-occurring OCD symptoms that require specialized treatment

- Other mental health conditions that are affecting your ability to implement parenting changes

Types of medications that might be helpful:

- SSRIs (selective serotonin reuptake inhibitors) for anxiety, depression, or OCD symptoms

- Other antidepressants if SSRIs aren't effective or cause problematic side effects

- Anti-anxiety medications for short-term relief during particularly challenging periods

- Medications for other co-occurring conditions like ADHD or sleep disorders

Important considerations:

- Medication should always be combined with therapy or other behavioral interventions
- Work with a psychiatrist who has experience treating adults with perfectionist or OCPD patterns
- Be honest about how symptoms are affecting your parenting and family relationships
- Consider how medication side effects might affect your energy, mood, or availability for family activities
- Regularly reassess whether medication is helping with your parenting goals

Resource directory: Finding specialized help

Finding OCPD-specialized therapists:

- International OCPD Foundation therapist directory
- Psychology Today provider search with OCPD specialty filter
- Local university psychology training clinics
- Referrals from pediatricians or family doctors
- Recommendations from other parents or support groups

Questions to ask potential therapists:

- Do you have experience working with perfectionist parents or OCPD?
- What's your approach to helping parents balance structure with flexibility?

- How do you work with families where perfectionism is affecting relationships?

- What training do you have in evidence-based treatments for OCPD or related conditions?

- How do you help parents maintain changes over time?

Online resources and support:

- OCPD support forums and communities

- Mindfulness and meditation apps designed for parents

- Online parenting courses focused on flexibility and connection

- Virtual support groups for parents with perfectionist patterns

- Telehealth therapy options for families in areas without local specialists

Books and educational resources:

- Research-based books on OCPD and perfectionist parenting

- Workbooks for developing self-compassion and flexibility

- Children's books about making mistakes and trying new things

- Family activity guides for building resilience and connection

- Podcasts and videos featuring experts on perfectionism and parenting

---

The ongoing journey

Maintaining progress in changing perfectionist parenting patterns is a lifelong practice, not a destination you reach and then maintain effortlessly. The families who are most successful over the long term are those who view setbacks as normal parts of the process and who maintain systems for ongoing growth and adjustment.

The investment you make in developing flexibility, self-compassion, and connection-focused parenting approaches pays dividends not just in your current family relationships, but in the legacy you leave for future generations. Your children will carry the lessons they learn about handling mistakes, managing perfectionist impulses, and maintaining relationships through challenges into their own adult lives and future families.

Most importantly, the journey toward healthier family patterns teaches everyone in your family that change is possible, that people can grow and learn throughout their lives, and that love and connection are more important than perfect performance. These lessons become the foundation for resilient, authentic relationships that can weather the inevitable storms and celebrations of family life.

Chapter 14: Success stories and long-term outcomes

Real families who have successfully changed their perfectionist patterns provide the most compelling evidence that transformation is possible. These stories aren't about families who became perfect or eliminated all struggles, but about families who learned to prioritize connection over control and growth over perfection.

The research on long-term outcomes for families who address perfectionist patterns early shows encouraging results: children develop greater resilience, creativity, and emotional intelligence; parents experience reduced anxiety and increased satisfaction with their relationships; and families report stronger connections and more joy in their daily lives together.

These success stories also reveal important truths about the change process: it's rarely linear, it requires ongoing commitment, and the benefits often extend far beyond what families initially hoped to achieve.

Real families, real change

The Johnson family: From rigid to responsive

Sarah and Michael Johnson had built their family life around careful planning, high standards, and structured routines. Their three children - Emma (14), Jake (11), and Lily (7) - were high achievers who appeared successful from the outside. But family life had become increasingly stressful, with daily battles about homework, chores, and behavior standards.

The turning point came during Emma's eighth-grade year when she started having panic attacks before school. The pediatrician found no medical cause and suggested that family stress might be contributing to Emma's anxiety. Sarah initially resisted this idea - after all, they were trying to help their children succeed - but Michael convinced her to try family therapy.

Initial resistance and breakthrough: The Johnsons' first therapy sessions were challenging. Sarah spent most of the time explaining why their high standards were necessary and listing all the ways their children were benefiting from structure and expectations. The therapist didn't argue with her but instead asked the children how they experienced family life.

Emma's response was a watershed moment: "I love my family, but I always feel like I'm disappointing someone. Even when I get good grades, Mom asks if I could have done better. I'm scared to try new things because what if I'm not good at them?"

The change process: The Johnsons worked on three main areas over the course of a year:

Emotional awareness: Sarah and Michael learned to recognize when their anxiety about their children's futures was driving controlling behavior. They practiced pausing before jumping into problem-solving mode and asking their children about their feelings first.

Flexible expectations: The family developed new approaches to homework, chores, and activities that maintained structure while allowing for individual differences and changing circumstances. Instead of rigid rules, they created collaborative agreements that could be adjusted as needed.

Connection practices: Each parent began having weekly one-on-one time with each child focused purely on connection and enjoyment rather than instruction or evaluation. Family dinners became conversation time rather than performance review sessions.

Results after 18 months: Emma's anxiety significantly decreased and she began participating in drama club, something she'd wanted to try but had been afraid of because she might not excel immediately. Jake, who had always been compliant but withdrawn, became more communicative and started expressing his own opinions about family decisions. Lily maintained her naturally cheerful disposition but became more willing to try challenging tasks without immediately asking for help.

Sarah and Michael reported feeling much more connected to their children and more confident in their parenting. "I realized," Sarah reflected, "that I was so focused on preparing them for the future that I was missing the joy of being with them in the present."

Long-term outcomes (3 years later): Emma is thriving in high school and has maintained her involvement in theater while managing academic challenges with much less anxiety. Jake has developed interests in music and writing that the family never would have discovered under their previous rigid activity schedule. Lily continues to be a confident, curious child who approaches new challenges with excitement rather than fear.

The family still maintains structure and has high expectations, but these are now balanced with flexibility, emotional attunement, and trust in their children's capabilities. "We didn't lower our standards," Michael explains. "We just learned that love and support are better motivators than pressure and control."

Single parent success: David's transformation

David Martinez became a single father when his son Carlos was 10 and his daughter Sofia was 8. Already struggling with perfectionist tendencies, David felt enormous pressure to "do everything right" as a single parent. His approach was to create detailed schedules, extensive rules, and high expectations to ensure his children wouldn't be disadvantaged by their family circumstances.

The crisis occurred when Sofia's teacher called to say that Sofia was having frequent meltdowns at school and seemed anxious about making mistakes. Around the same time, Carlos began lying about homework and small infractions to avoid David's disappointment and lengthy lectures about responsibility.

Initial obstacles: As a single parent, David faced unique challenges in changing his approach. He didn't have a co-parent to provide balance when he became controlling, and he felt that relaxing his standards might harm his children's chances for success. He also worried that seeking help would confirm his fears that he wasn't capable of parenting effectively on his own.

Finding support: David initially resisted therapy but agreed to attend a single parent support group. Hearing other parents share similar struggles helped him realize that his children's difficulties weren't signs of his failure but normal responses to overly rigid parenting approaches.

Key changes David made:

Letting go of perfect single parenting: David accepted that he couldn't be both mother and father to his children, but he could be an excellent single father who provided love, structure, and support while allowing his children to be imperfect.

Building a support network: Instead of trying to handle everything alone, David developed relationships with other parents, his children's teachers, and extended family members who could provide different perspectives and support.

Quality over quantity: Rather than trying to fill every moment with structured activities or instruction, David focused on creating meaningful connection time with each child and allowing for unstructured play and exploration.

Modeling self-compassion: David began talking with his children about his own learning process as a parent, sharing when he made mistakes and showing them how to handle imperfection with grace.

Results: Within six months, Sofia's school anxiety decreased significantly and she began participating more actively in class discussions and social activities. Carlos stopped lying and began coming to David with problems rather than hiding them. Most importantly, the family began enjoying time together rather than constantly focusing on improvement and correction.

Long-term impact (5 years later): David's children, now teenagers, have maintained strong relationships with him and demonstrate remarkable independence and resilience. Sofia has become a confident young woman who advocates for herself and tries new activities without excessive anxiety about performance. Carlos has developed into a responsible, honest teenager who maintains good relationships with both peers and adults.

David reflects: "I thought being a good single parent meant controlling everything and preventing all problems. But what my children actually needed was a parent who loved them unconditionally, trusted their capabilities, and showed them how to handle life's challenges with flexibility and self-compassion."

Blended family challenges: The Chen-Williams story

When Lisa Chen married Robert Williams, they combined two families with different approaches to achievement and structure. Lisa had two daughters (Michelle, 12, and Angela, 9) and had always emphasized academic excellence and structured activities. Robert had a son (Brandon, 10) and took a more relaxed approach to parenting. The early years of their blended family were marked by conflict over parenting approaches and children who seemed confused about expectations.

Initial challenges:

- Michelle and Angela felt that Robert's more flexible approach meant he didn't care about their success

- Brandon felt overwhelmed by Lisa's high expectations and detailed feedback

- Lisa and Robert had frequent disagreements about homework supervision, activity scheduling, and discipline approaches

- All three children began playing the adults against each other, seeking the approach that required less effort or provided more sympathy

The intervention: After two years of increasing conflict, the family attended a weekend family therapy intensive focused on blended family dynamics. The therapist helped them see how their different approaches were creating confusion and insecurity for all the children.

Developing a unified approach:

Values clarification: Lisa and Robert worked together to identify their shared values for the family: mutual respect, personal growth, educational engagement, and family connection. They learned to separate their core values from their specific methods.

Flexible structure: The family developed systems that provided the structure Lisa valued while maintaining the flexibility Robert preferred. This included collaborative homework approaches, family meetings for major decisions, and individual goal-setting processes for each child.

Honoring differences: Rather than trying to create identical expectations for all children, the family learned to adjust approaches based on each child's personality, learning style, and developmental needs while maintaining consistent family values.

Parental partnership: Lisa and Robert established regular communication about parenting approaches and committed to supporting each other's decisions with the children, even when they might have handled situations differently.

Results: The blended family process took nearly three years, but the outcomes were significant. Michelle learned to appreciate Robert's encouragement of her creative interests while maintaining her academic strengths. Angela discovered she could meet high expectations without sacrificing her naturally social, collaborative learning style. Brandon developed greater organization skills and academic engagement while feeling supported rather than criticized.

Long-term benefits (4 years later): The Chen-Williams family has developed a unique culture that balances achievement with enjoyment, structure with flexibility, and individual differences with family unity. The children have learned to appreciate different parenting styles and to communicate their needs effectively to both adults.

Lisa notes: "I learned that high standards and emotional warmth aren't opposites - they actually work better together. Robert showed me that children thrive when they feel accepted for who they are, not just praised for what they achieve."

Robert adds: "Lisa helped me understand that structure and expectations can actually support children's growth rather than limiting it. Our different strengths create a more complete family environment."

Teen perspective: "How my parent's change changed me"

The following is a composite narrative based on interviews with teenagers whose parents made significant changes in their perfectionist parenting approaches.

"I didn't realize how much my mom's perfectionism was affecting me until she started changing. Looking back, I can see that I was constantly anxious about disappointing her, even though she never said she was disappointed. It was more like this feeling that nothing I did was ever quite good enough.

When I was in middle school, my mom started going to therapy and attending parent support groups. At first, I was embarrassed and worried that it meant our family was broken or that I had done something wrong. But gradually, I began noticing changes in how she interacted with me and my younger brother.

The biggest change was that she started asking about my feelings instead of immediately trying to fix my problems. Before, if I came home upset about something at school, she would launch into problem-solving mode - calling teachers, giving me advice, or telling

235

me what I should do differently. After she started changing, she would ask questions like 'How did that make you feel?' or 'What was the hardest part about that situation?'

It took me a while to trust these changes. I kept waiting for her to go back to her old ways of taking over my problems or criticizing my approaches. But she was consistent, and eventually I started sharing more with her because I knew she wouldn't immediately jump into fix-it mode.

Another big change was how she handled my mistakes. Before, when I made a mistake or failed at something, she would get this anxious energy and start talking about how we could prevent it from happening again or what I needed to do to improve. It felt like my mistakes were causing her pain, which made me want to hide problems from her.

After she started working on herself, my mistakes became more like normal parts of life. She would say things like 'That sounds frustrating' or 'What did you learn from that experience?' Instead of feeling like I had disappointed her, I felt like she understood that learning involves struggling sometimes.

The change that meant the most to me was when she started sharing her own struggles and mistakes. She told me about times when she had failed at things or made poor decisions, and how she had learned from those experiences. This was completely different from the perfect parent image she had tried to maintain before. It made me feel like being imperfect was okay and that I didn't have to be perfect to be loved.

My grades didn't get worse when she stopped monitoring my homework so closely - in fact, they got better because I felt more motivated to work hard for my own reasons rather than just to avoid her anxiety. I also started trying new activities that I might not excel at immediately, like drama and debate team, because I wasn't as afraid of not being perfect.

The relationship I have with my mom now feels much more real and close. I actually want to spend time with her and talk to her about my life, whereas before I often felt like I was performing for her approval. She still has high expectations for me, but now they feel like support rather than pressure.

I think the most important thing I learned from watching my mom change is that people can grow and learn throughout their lives. She modeled for me that it's okay to recognize when something isn't working and to make changes, even when those changes are hard. That's a lesson I'll carry with me forever."

Research on positive outcomes

Latest studies on OCPD treatment success

According to research from Kevin W. Grant, recent studies on OCPD treatment outcomes show encouraging results for individuals and families who engage in appropriate interventions (Grant, 2023). While OCPD has traditionally been considered difficult to treat, newer therapeutic approaches show significant promise for improving functioning and relationships.

Treatment effectiveness rates:

- Cognitive-behavioral therapy shows improvement in 60-70% of individuals with OCPD traits

- Radically Open DBT demonstrates significant improvements in emotional expression and relationship quality

- Family-based interventions show positive outcomes for 75-80% of participating families

- Combined individual and family therapy approaches show the highest success rates

Factors that predict positive outcomes:

- Early intervention before patterns become deeply entrenched

- Motivation to change based on relationship concerns rather than external pressure
- Participation of multiple family members in the change process
- Willingness to tolerate discomfort during the learning process
- Access to ongoing support and accountability systems

Measurement of success in recent studies:

- Improved family communication and emotional expression
- Increased flexibility in response to unexpected situations
- Reduced anxiety and perfectionist-related stress
- Enhanced children's independence and self-confidence
- Strengthened parent-child relationships and family satisfaction

Factors that predict positive change

Research consistently identifies several factors that increase the likelihood of successful change in perfectionist parenting patterns:

Individual factors:

- Recognition that perfectionist patterns are causing problems rather than solving them
- Motivation based on improving relationships rather than just reducing personal distress
- Willingness to practice new approaches even when they feel uncomfortable initially
- Ability to tolerate uncertainty and imperfection during the change process
- Commitment to ongoing self-reflection and growth

Family factors:

- Support from at least one other family member for making changes

- Children who are able to provide honest feedback about family functioning

- Family culture that values growth and learning over perfect performance

- Willingness to prioritize relationships over rules and outcomes

- Openness to experimenting with new approaches to family challenges

Environmental factors:

- Access to appropriate professional support when needed

- Connection with other families who have made similar changes

- Support systems that understand and encourage flexibility over control

- School and community environments that support process-focused approaches

- Reduced external pressure for perfect performance or family image management

Process factors:

- Realistic expectations about the timeline and difficulty of change

- Focus on progress rather than perfection in the change process

- Regular assessment and adjustment of approaches based on what's working

- Celebration of small improvements and positive changes
- Resilience and recovery strategies for setbacks and challenging periods

Long-term benefits for children

Research from PubMed and NCBI shows that children whose parents address perfectionist patterns early demonstrate significant advantages in multiple areas of development (PubMed, 2023; NCBI, 2023).

Academic benefits:

- Higher intrinsic motivation for learning and achievement
- Greater willingness to take on challenging coursework and activities
- More effective study strategies and time management skills
- Reduced academic anxiety and test-related stress
- Better relationships with teachers and increased help-seeking when needed

Social and emotional benefits:

- Stronger peer relationships and social skills
- Greater emotional intelligence and regulation abilities
- Increased empathy and understanding of others' perspectives
- More authentic self-expression and identity development
- Reduced anxiety and depression rates compared to children from perfectionist families

Life skills and resilience benefits:

- Better problem-solving abilities and creative thinking
- Greater tolerance for uncertainty and ambiguity

- More effective coping strategies for stress and disappointment

- Increased self-advocacy skills and boundary setting

- Higher levels of life satisfaction and subjective well-being

Future relationship benefits:

- More secure attachment patterns in romantic relationships

- Better communication skills and conflict resolution abilities

- Greater ability to maintain relationships through challenges and disagreements

- More balanced approaches to parenting their own children

- Reduced likelihood of perpetuating perfectionist patterns in the next generation

Hope grounded in science

The research evidence provides genuine reasons for hope for families struggling with perfectionist patterns. Studies consistently show that change is possible at any stage of family development and that the benefits of addressing these patterns extend far beyond the immediate reduction of family conflict.

Neuroplasticity research demonstrates that the brain's capacity for change continues throughout life, meaning that even deeply ingrained perfectionist patterns can be modified with appropriate intervention and practice.

Attachment research shows that relationship patterns can be repaired and strengthened at any age, and that children are remarkably resilient when parents make genuine efforts to increase emotional availability and reduce control.

Family systems research indicates that positive changes in one family member often create ripple effects that benefit the entire family, meaning that individual efforts to change can have broader systemic impacts.

Longitudinal studies provide evidence that families who address perfectionist patterns maintain their improvements over time and continue to grow in flexibility and connection, suggesting that positive changes become self-reinforcing rather than requiring constant effort to maintain.

Your family's unique journey

Creating a personalized action plan

Every family's path from perfectionist patterns to flexible, connected relationships will be unique. Creating a personalized plan helps you focus your efforts on the changes that will be most meaningful for your specific family circumstances.

Step 1: Family assessment and goal setting

- Identify which perfectionist patterns are most problematic in your family

- Determine which family members are most affected by these patterns

- Clarify your family's core values and relationship goals

- Set 2-3 specific, measurable goals for the next 6-12 months

Step 2: Individual parent work

- Identify your personal triggers and early warning signs

- Choose evidence-based strategies that fit your personality and circumstances

- Develop self-care and support systems to maintain your capacity for change

- Create accountability systems for maintaining new approaches

Step 3: Family system changes

- Implement new communication patterns and problem-solving approaches

- Adjust household routines and expectations to support flexibility

- Create regular opportunities for connection and enjoyment

- Develop family practices for handling mistakes and challenges

Step 4: External support and partnerships

- Identify professional support if needed (therapy, coaching, support groups)

- Build relationships with other parents who share similar values

- Create partnerships with schools and other systems in your child's life

- Access resources and continuing education opportunities

Step 5: Maintenance and ongoing growth

- Establish regular assessment and adjustment processes

- Plan for managing setbacks and challenging periods

- Create long-term vision for your family's continued growth

- Develop legacy planning for the values and approaches you want to pass to future generations

Setting realistic timelines for change

Change in family patterns typically occurs over months and years rather than weeks. Understanding realistic timelines helps maintain motivation and prevents discouragement when progress feels slow.

0-3 months: Foundation building and initial changes

- Increased awareness of perfectionist patterns and their impacts
- Implementation of basic techniques like pausing before reacting
- Beginning to establish new communication patterns
- Initial resistance from family members who are used to old patterns

3-6 months: Skill development and practice

- More consistent use of flexible parenting approaches
- Family members beginning to trust and respond to changes
- Some improvement in family conflict and connection
- Occasional relapses into old patterns during stressful times

6-12 months: Integration and establishment

- New approaches becoming more automatic and natural
- Significant improvements in family relationships and functioning
- Children demonstrating increased confidence and independence
- Better recovery from setbacks and challenging periods

1-2 years: Maintenance and refinement

- Continued growth in flexibility and emotional connection
- Ability to handle new challenges with improved family approaches
- Long-term changes in children's self-concept and relationship patterns

- Integration of changes into family identity and culture

2+ years: Long-term benefits and legacy

- Sustained improvements that become part of family culture

- Children internalizing healthy approaches to achievement and relationships

- Continued growth and adaptation as family circumstances change

- Positive impact on extended family and community relationships

Measuring progress without perfectionism

One of the ironies of changing perfectionist patterns is that you need to measure progress without falling back into perfectionist thinking about the change process itself. Success isn't about perfect implementation of new approaches, but about overall movement toward greater flexibility and connection.

Process-focused progress indicators:

- Increased awareness of when you're moving into controlling patterns

- Faster recovery and repair when you do fall back into old approaches

- More frequent pausing between triggers and reactions

- Growing comfort with uncertainty and imperfection

- Increased curiosity about your children's perspectives and experiences

Relationship-focused progress indicators:

- Children sharing more openly about their experiences and feelings

- Decreased family conflict and increased cooperation
- More spontaneous affection and positive interactions
- Family members coming to you with problems rather than hiding them
- Increased family enjoyment and laughter

Individual growth indicators:

- Reduced anxiety about your children's performance and future
- Increased self-compassion when you make parenting mistakes
- Greater confidence in your children's abilities and judgment
- More enjoyment of your role as a parent
- Improved relationships with your partner and other adults

Avoiding perfectionist measurement traps:

- Don't expect linear progress - setbacks and plateaus are normal
- Focus on overall trends rather than daily variations
- Celebrate small improvements rather than waiting for major changes
- Ask for feedback from family members rather than relying only on your own assessment
- Remember that good enough progress is still progress

Final exercise: Letter to your future self

This exercise helps you clarify your hopes and intentions for your family's future while acknowledging the ongoing nature of growth and change.

Instructions: Write a letter to yourself to be opened in one year. Include your current hopes, fears, and commitments related to your family relationships and parenting approach.

Letter prompts:

- What do you hope your family relationships will look like in a year?

- What aspects of your current parenting do you most want to change?

- What values do you want to guide your family interactions?

- What do you want your children to remember about their childhood?

- How do you want to handle the inevitable challenges and setbacks?

- What kind of parent do you want to be when your children are adults?

- What legacy do you want to leave for future generations in your family?

Sample letter excerpt: "Dear Future Me, As I write this, I'm just beginning to understand how my need for control has been affecting our family. Emma seems anxious all the time, and Jake has stopped sharing things with me because he's afraid of disappointing me. I know I love my children deeply, but I can see that my way of showing love - by trying to protect them from all mistakes and ensure their success - is actually preventing them from developing confidence in themselves.

A year from now, I hope our family feels more relaxed and connected. I want my children to come to me with their struggles because they know I'll listen and support them, not because they expect me to fix everything. I want to trust their abilities more and control outcomes less. I want to enjoy being their parent instead of constantly worrying about whether I'm doing it right.

I know there will be setbacks. When I'm stressed or tired, I'll probably fall back into old patterns of micromanaging and criticizing. When this happens, I want to remember that repair is always possible. I want to apologize quickly when I've been too controlling, and I want to celebrate the small victories - the times when I bite my tongue instead of correcting, when I allow natural consequences instead of rescuing, when I hug my children after they make mistakes instead of immediately trying to teach them what they should have done differently.

Most of all, I want my children to know they are loved unconditionally - not for their performance, their compliance, or their achievements, but simply for who they are. I want them to feel safe to be imperfect in our home, to know that mistakes are opportunities to learn rather than failures to hide. I want to model for them what it looks like to be human - flawed, growing, and worthy of love exactly as we are.

The legacy I want to leave is one of connection over perfection, of growth over rigid standards, of love that doesn't depend on meeting impossible expectations. I want to break the cycle of perfectionism in

Chapter 15: Daily practice guides and emergency protocols

Morning routine flexibility guide

The morning routine often becomes ground zero for perfectionist battles in OCPD families. The desire for everything to go smoothly, on time, and according to plan collides with the reality of children who are naturally slower, distractible, and resistant to being hurried. This section provides concrete strategies for creating mornings that work for everyone.

Sample flexible schedules by age

Ages 0-3: Basic rhythm over rigid schedule

- 6:00-7:00 AM: Wake-up window (not fixed wake time)

- Breakfast when hungry, not by the clock

- Getting dressed: choice between two weather-appropriate outfits

- Out the door: 15-minute buffer built into all appointments

- Key principle: Respond to child's needs while maintaining general structure

Ages 4-6: Increased participation with flexibility

- Visual schedule with pictures, not time stamps

- "First this, then that" sequence rather than timed activities

- Child chooses order of some tasks (brush teeth before or after getting dressed)

- "Good enough" standards for appearance and room tidiness

- Practice time built in for new skills like shoe tying

Ages 7-11: Collaborative routine planning

- Child helps create the morning routine
- Natural consequences for choices (running late means less play time)
- Parent provides support without taking over
- Weekly family meetings to adjust what isn't working
- Focus on effort and cooperation rather than perfection

Ages 12-18: Increasing autonomy with safety nets

- Teen takes primary responsibility for their morning
- Parent available for consultation, not management
- Logical consequences managed by teen (explaining tardiness to teachers)
- Family breakfast time as connection point, not control point
- Trust-building through gradual release of control

Quick wins for reducing morning stress

1. **The night-before strategy**: Clothes laid out, backpacks packed, lunches made
2. **The 10-minute pickup**: Brief evening tidy-up prevents morning chaos
3. **The buffer zone**: Everything takes longer with kids - plan accordingly
4. **The "good enough" breakfast**: Nutritious doesn't require homemade or elaborate
5. **The calm parent rule**: Your emotional state sets the tone for everyone

6. **The choice architecture**: Offer limited, acceptable options rather than open-ended decisions

7. **The connection first approach**: Brief positive interaction before tasks begin

Emergency plan for high-stress mornings

When everything is falling apart:

1. **STOP and breathe** - Take three deep breaths before reacting

2. **Assess actual vs. perceived urgency** - Will this matter in a week?

3. **Triage the essentials** - Safety first, everything else can be adjusted

4. **Lower your standards temporarily** - Mismatched socks won't harm anyone

5. **Use your support network** - Call in backup when needed

6. **Repair afterwards** - Acknowledge when you've been reactive or harsh

Emergency phrases for overwhelming moments:

- "This is hard for all of us right now. Let's take a breath and try again."

- "I need a moment to calm down so I can be the parent you need."

- "We're all doing our best. That's enough for today."

- "Making mistakes is part of learning. Let's figure this out together."

Visual aids and printable resources

The OCPD parent's morning mantra card:

- Progress over perfection
- Connection before correction
- Flexibility over rigid adherence to plans
- Children are learning, not performing
- My calm creates their calm

Crisis intervention toolkit

When perfectionist urges threaten to overwhelm both parent and child, having immediate tools available can prevent escalation and preserve family relationships.

STOP technique for acute control urges

S - STOP what you're doing immediately

- Put down whatever is in your hands
- Step away from the situation if possible
- Resist the urge to keep talking or explaining

T - TAKE a breath (or three, or ten)

- Focus on slowing your breathing
- Feel your feet on the ground
- Notice physical sensations of tension

O - OBSERVE what's really happening

- What am I feeling right now? (anger, fear, frustration, anxiety)
- What am I thinking? (they should know better, this is unacceptable, they're being defiant)
- What does my child need right now? (support, understanding, space, connection)

P - PROCEED with intention

252

- Choose your response rather than reacting automatically
- Ask yourself: "What kind of parent do I want to be in this moment?"
- Remember: This is a teaching opportunity, not a power struggle

Emergency self-compassion phrases

For the perfectionist inner critic:

- "I'm learning to parent differently, and learning takes time."
- "Making mistakes doesn't make me a bad parent."
- "I can be imperfect and still be good enough."
- "My worth isn't determined by my children's behavior."
- "It's okay to not have all the answers right now."

For overwhelming emotions:

- "This feeling is temporary and will pass."
- "I'm having a human reaction to a challenging situation."
- "I can feel frustrated and still choose love."
- "My children need me to be regulated, not perfect."
- "I can repair any damage I cause with harsh words or actions."

Quick regulation strategies

The 5-4-3-2-1 grounding technique:

- 5 things you can see
- 4 things you can touch
- 3 things you can hear
- 2 things you can smell

- 1 thing you can taste

The physiological sigh:

- Double inhale through the nose (long inhale followed by shorter second inhale)
- Long exhale through the mouth
- Repeat 2-3 times for immediate calm

The 6-second rule:

- Neurochemically, emotional waves peak and begin to recede in about 6 seconds
- Count slowly to six before responding to intense triggers
- Use this time to choose your response

When to take a parent timeout

Signs you need a break:

- You're raising your voice repeatedly
- You're making threats you don't intend to follow through on
- You feel physically activated (heart racing, jaw clenched, hands shaking)
- You're saying things you know you'll regret later
- Your child seems scared of your reaction
- You're more focused on being right than being helpful

How to take a productive timeout:

1. **Announce your intention clearly**: "I need to take a few minutes to calm down so I can be the parent you deserve."
2. **Give a timeframe**: "I'll be back in 10 minutes and we'll talk about this."

3. **Ensure safety**: Don't leave young children unsupervised; take your break in another room if necessary.

4. **Use the time wisely**: Don't just stew about how wrong your child is; focus on regulation and perspective.

5. **Return with intention**: Come back ready to connect and problem-solve, not to resume the battle.

Communication script library

One of the most challenging aspects for OCPD parents is finding the words to respond helpfully rather than critically in difficult moments. These scripts provide alternatives to common perfectionist responses.

Age-appropriate responses to common situations

When your toddler has a meltdown over a minor frustration:

Instead of: "Stop crying! It's not that big of a deal!" Try: "You're really upset that your tower fell down. It's hard when things don't work the way we want them to."

Instead of: "You're too old to act like this!" Try: "Big feelings are normal. I'm here to help you feel better."

When your school-age child makes a careless mistake:

Instead of: "I told you to be more careful! Why don't you ever listen?" Try: "I can see you're frustrated with this mistake. What do you think we could do differently next time?"

Instead of: "This is sloppy work. Do it over." Try: "I notice some areas that might need another look. Would you like to check your work together?"

When your teenager challenges a family rule:

Instead of: "Because I said so! I don't want to hear any more about it!" Try: "I can see you disagree with this rule. Help me understand your perspective."

Instead of: "You're being disrespectful and ungrateful!" Try: "It sounds like this rule doesn't make sense to you. Let's talk about the reasoning behind it."

How to apologize after perfectionist episodes

Elements of an effective OCPD parent apology:

1. **Take full responsibility** - Don't blame stress, tiredness, or your child's behavior

2. **Be specific** - Name exactly what you did wrong

3. **Acknowledge impact** - Recognize how your behavior affected your child

4. **Express genuine remorse** - Let your regret show

5. **Commit to change** - Share what you'll do differently next time

6. **Don't expect immediate forgiveness** - Give your child space to process

Sample apology scripts:

"I owe you an apology. When you forgot your homework folder this morning, I got really frustrated and said some harsh things about you being irresponsible. That wasn't fair to you, and I can see that it hurt your feelings and made you feel bad about yourself. I'm sorry. Everyone forgets things sometimes, and that doesn't make you irresponsible. Next time I feel that frustrated, I'm going to take a deep breath and remember that mistakes are part of learning. You don't have to forgive me right now, but I want you to know that I'm working on being a calmer, kinder parent."

Validating emotions while maintaining boundaries

The formula: Acknowledge + Validate + Redirect

Example 1 - Bedtime resistance: Acknowledge: "I can see you're really upset about bedtime." Validate: "You're having so much fun playing, and you don't want it to end. That makes sense." Redirect: "And it's still time for bed. Would you like to choose one book or two books for our bedtime story?"

Example 2 - Sibling conflict: Acknowledge: "You're both really angry at each other right now." Validate: "It's frustrating when someone takes your things without asking." Redirect: "We still need to use words instead of hitting. Let's figure out a solution that works for both of you."

Example 3 - Homework meltdown: Acknowledge: "This math homework is making you really frustrated." Validate: "Some of these problems are tricky, and it's normal to feel overwhelmed." Redirect: "Let's take a break and come back to it, or we can ask for help from your teacher tomorrow."

Collaborative problem-solving dialogues

The three-step process adapted for families:

Step 1: Define the problem from all perspectives Parent: "It seems like we're having some challenges with morning routines. I've noticed that we're often rushed and stressed, and sometimes people end up feeling upset. What have you noticed?" Child: [listens to their perspective without arguing or correcting] Parent: "So it sounds like you feel like I'm always hurrying you, and I feel worried that we'll be late. Is that right?"

Step 2: Brainstorm solutions together Parent: "Let's think of some ideas that might help our mornings go more smoothly. What are your ideas?" [List all ideas without judgment - even silly ones] Parent: "Those are great ideas. I was thinking we could also..."

Step 3: Choose a solution to try Parent: "Which of these ideas feels most doable to you?" Child: [makes choice] Parent: "Great. Let's try that for a week and see how it goes. If it's not working, we can pick a different idea or come up with new ones."

Chapter 16: Professional resources and continuing support

The journey of healing OCPD patterns and creating a more flexible family environment isn't one that parents need to walk alone. This chapter provides comprehensive guidance for finding and utilizing professional support, joining communities of other parents facing similar challenges, and creating systems for long-term growth and accountability.

Finding the right help

Not all mental health professionals understand OCPD or have experience working with perfectionist parents. Finding the right therapeutic support requires knowing what questions to ask and what approaches are most effective.

Types of professionals who can help:

Licensed Clinical Social Workers (LCSWs)

- Often have training in family systems and practical parenting strategies

- May offer sliding scale fees or accept insurance more readily

- Good choice for family therapy and parent coaching approaches

Licensed Professional Counselors (LPCs)

- Broad training in various therapeutic approaches

- May specialize in anxiety, perfectionism, or family therapy

- Often skilled in cognitive-behavioral approaches

Psychologists (PhDs or PsyDs)

- Extensive training in assessment and diagnosis

- May offer psychological testing if needed

- Often specialize in specific therapeutic approaches like ACT or DBT

Psychiatrists

- Medical doctors who can prescribe medication if needed

- Useful for comprehensive treatment when therapy alone isn't sufficient

- Can assess for co-occurring conditions like anxiety or depression

Directory of OCPD-specialized therapists

How to find specialists:

1. **Professional organizations:**

   o International OCD Foundation (iocdf.org) - maintains therapist directory

   o Association for Behavioral and Cognitive Therapies (abct.org)

   o International Association for RO-DBT (ro-dbt.com)

2. **Online directories:**

   o Psychology Today (filter for "perfectionism" and "OCPD")

   o TherapyDen (therapyden.com)

   o Inclusive Therapists (inclusivetherapists.com)

3. **Specialized treatment centers:**

   o Many areas have anxiety and OCD centers that also treat OCPD

- University counseling psychology programs may offer services
- Look for centers that mention "overcontrol" or "emotional flexibility"

Questions to ask potential therapists

Initial phone consultation questions:

1. "Do you have experience treating OCPD or perfectionism in parents?"

2. "What therapeutic approaches do you use for overcontrol and rigidity?"

3. "Have you worked with families where perfectionism is affecting parent-child relationships?"

4. "Are you familiar with Radically Open DBT or Acceptance and Commitment Therapy?"

5. "How do you approach the challenge of helping controlling parents become more flexible without losing necessary structure?"

6. "Do you offer family sessions or parent coaching in addition to individual therapy?"

7. "What does your typical treatment timeline look like for OCPD-related issues?"

8. "How do you measure progress in therapy?"

Red flags in therapist responses:

- Unfamiliarity with OCPD or confusing it with OCD
- Suggesting that control and structure are inherently bad
- Promising quick fixes or dramatic personality changes

- Focusing only on the child's behavior rather than family system dynamics
- Seeming judgmental about perfectionist tendencies

Insurance and financial considerations

Understanding your benefits:

- Check if your insurance covers outpatient mental health services
- Ask about copays, deductibles, and session limits
- Inquire about coverage for family therapy vs. individual therapy
- Some plans require referrals from primary care physicians

When therapy isn't covered:

- Ask therapists about sliding scale fees
- Look into Employee Assistance Programs (EAPs) through your workplace
- Consider community mental health centers
- Some therapists offer payment plans
- Group therapy is often less expensive than individual sessions

Making therapy financially sustainable:

- Consider it an investment in your family's long-term wellbeing
- Calculate the cost of NOT addressing these patterns (family stress, child therapy needs later)
- Some families benefit from alternating individual and family sessions to manage costs

Telehealth options for OCPD treatment

The expansion of telehealth services has made specialized OCPD treatment more accessible to families regardless of geographic location.

Benefits of online therapy for OCPD parents:

- Access to specialists who may not be available locally
- Reduced scheduling conflicts and transportation barriers
- Comfort of familiar environment may reduce initial anxiety
- Easier to include multiple family members in sessions
- Often more cost-effective than in-person treatment

Platforms and providers:

- Many established therapists now offer telehealth options
- Specialized platforms like BetterHelp and Talkspace (check for OCPD expertise)
- Some insurance plans have specific telehealth networks
- University programs may offer telehealth services through training clinics

Making telehealth effective:

- Ensure reliable internet connection and private space
- Test technology before first session
- Minimize distractions (phones, other family members)
- Have notebook and pen available for exercises and homework

Recommended programs and trainings

Beyond individual therapy, several structured programs can help OCPD parents develop new skills and connect with others facing similar challenges.

RO-DBT skills groups for parents

Radically Open Dialectical Behavior Therapy specifically addresses overcontrol and has shown significant effectiveness for OCPD symptoms.

What to expect:

- 16-30 week programs typically
- Focus on increasing openness, flexibility, and social connectedness
- Skills practice homework between sessions
- Group format provides peer support and accountability
- May include separate groups for parents specifically

Core skills covered:

- Flexible mind practices
- Social signaling and warmth expression
- Distress tolerance for perfectionist parents
- Self-compassion and self-soothing techniques

Finding RO-DBT groups:

- Check the official RO-DBT website for certified providers
- Many major metropolitan areas have established programs
- Some programs offer online group options
- Ask potential individual therapists if they facilitate or recommend groups

Mindfulness-based parenting programs

These programs combine meditation practices with parenting skills, particularly helpful for OCPD parents who struggle with being present and non-reactive.

Popular programs:

- Mindful Parenting courses (often offered through meditation centers)
- Mindfulness-Based Stress Reduction (MBSR) with parenting applications
- Mindful Schools programs (may offer parent components)
- Local yoga studios and wellness centers often host parenting mindfulness classes

What these programs offer:

- Regular meditation practice adapted for busy parents
- Skills for staying present during challenging parenting moments
- Techniques for managing parental anxiety and reactivity
- Community support from other mindful parents

Online courses and workshops

Recommended online programs:

- "Perfectionism and Parenting" workshops through anxiety treatment centers
- ACT-based parenting courses (look for "psychological flexibility" focus)
- Growth mindset parenting programs based on Carol Dweck's research
- Collaborative Problem Solving courses through Lives in the Balance organization

Creating your own learning plan:

- Combine book learning with practical skill development
- Join online forums or social media groups for OCPD parents
- Attend webinars and virtual workshops
- Consider audio programs for learning during commutes or exercise

Parent coaching vs. therapy

When to choose parent coaching:

- You want practical, skill-based support
- Your primary goal is changing specific parenting behaviors
- You prefer a more collaborative, goal-oriented approach
- Insurance coverage isn't available or desired
- You want shorter-term, focused intervention

When therapy is more appropriate:

- You're dealing with significant anxiety, depression, or trauma
- OCPD symptoms are severely impacting daily functioning
- Family relationships are highly conflicted
- You need help processing your own childhood experiences
- Medication evaluation might be beneficial

Questions to ask parent coaches:

- What training do you have in OCPD or perfectionism?
- How do you structure coaching sessions and programs?
- What materials and resources do you provide?
- How do you measure progress and success?

- Do you offer follow-up support or ongoing accountability?

Building long-term support

Recovery from OCPD patterns and creating lasting family change requires ongoing support systems beyond formal treatment.

Creating or joining OCPD parent support groups

Benefits of peer support:

- Reduces isolation and shame around perfectionist struggles

- Provides practical tips from other parents in similar situations

- Offers accountability and encouragement for trying new approaches

- Creates opportunities to practice vulnerability and connection

- Helps normalize the challenges of changing ingrained patterns

Starting a local support group:

1. **Research existing resources** - Check if groups already exist in your area

2. **Partner with professionals** - Ask therapists or treatment centers to help facilitate or refer

3. **Start small** - Begin with 3-4 committed members

4. **Establish ground rules** - Confidentiality, no advice-giving unless requested, focus on personal growth

5. **Create structure** - Regular meeting times, rotating discussion topics, optional social activities

6. **Use available resources** - Adapt materials from established support group models

Online communities and forums

Recommended online spaces:

- OCPD support groups on Facebook (search for "OCPD parents" or "perfectionist parents")
- Reddit communities focused on OCPD and perfectionism
- Specialized forums through mental health organizations
- Apps like Mighty Networks that host condition-specific communities

Engaging safely in online communities:

- Maintain appropriate boundaries and privacy
- Remember that advice from peers isn't professional guidance
- Focus on sharing experiences rather than diagnosing others
- Use these spaces for support, not as substitutes for treatment

Creating accountability partnerships

Finding an accountability partner:

- Look for someone with similar goals but different strengths
- Consider partnering with someone from therapy or support groups
- Choose someone who can be honest and supportive without being critical
- Establish clear agreements about frequency and type of contact

Structure for accountability partnerships:

Weekly check-ins:

- What OCPD patterns showed up this week?
- What flexibility practices did you try?
- What challenges do you anticipate for the coming week?

- How can your partner support you?

Monthly goal review:

- Progress toward larger family relationship goals
- Adjustments needed in approach or expectations
- Celebrations of growth and positive changes
- Planning for upcoming stressors or transitions

Continuing education resources

Books for ongoing learning:

- Annual reading list to deepen understanding
- Book clubs focused on parenting and mental health topics
- Audiobooks for busy parents
- Family reading of age-appropriate books about growth mindset and resilience

Professional development opportunities:

- Workshops and conferences on perfectionism and parenting
- Webinar series from mental health organizations
- Training programs in therapeutic techniques like DBT or ACT
- University extension courses on child development and family systems

Staying current with research:

- Subscribe to newsletters from OCPD treatment centers
- Follow researchers and clinicians on social media
- Join professional organizations that welcome consumers
- Attend community mental health awareness events

The most important aspect of building long-term support is recognizing that this journey of growth and change is ongoing. OCPD patterns developed over many years and won't disappear overnight. Having multiple sources of support, learning, and accountability increases the likelihood of sustained positive change for both parents and children.

The goal isn't perfection in recovery any more than it was perfection in parenting. The goal is progress, connection, and the gradual development of more flexible, compassionate ways of being in relationship with the people we love most.

Conclusion: A New Legacy for Your Family

As you reach the end of this guide, you stand at a threshold - not of perfection achieved, but of transformation begun. The journey of healing OCPD patterns and creating healthier family dynamics isn't measured in flawless execution or complete elimination of controlling behaviors. Instead, it's measured in moments of awareness, acts of self-compassion, and the gradual expansion of your capacity for flexibility and authentic connection with your children.

The Courage to Change What You Can

You picked up this book because something inside you recognized that love alone wasn't enough - that your deep care for your children was sometimes getting lost in translation through rigid expectations and controlling behaviors. That recognition took tremendous courage. Many parents live their entire lives without questioning their approaches, passing patterns from one generation to the next without examination.

Your willingness to look honestly at your OCPD traits and their impact on your family represents a profound act of love. It says to your children, even if they can't articulate it yet, that they are worth the difficult work of personal change. It demonstrates that adults can grow, learn, and admit mistakes - lessons that will serve them well throughout their lives.

Progress Over Perfection: A Revolutionary Concept

If there's one principle that encapsulates everything in this book, it's the radical notion that progress matters more than perfection. This isn't just a platitude or therapeutic catch-phrase - it's a fundamental rewiring of how OCPD minds typically operate.

Your perfectionist tendencies developed for reasons that made sense in your own childhood. Perhaps they helped you survive criticism, earn approval, or create predictability in an unpredictable world. These patterns served a purpose, but they've outlived their usefulness if they're now creating distance between you and your children.

The beautiful paradox is that pursuing progress rather than perfection actually leads to better outcomes. When you allow yourself to be imperfect while consistently working toward growth, you model resilience for your children. When you apologize for your mistakes rather than defending them, you show your children that relationships can heal. When you celebrate small improvements rather than demanding dramatic change, you create an atmosphere where everyone feels safe to try and fail and try again.

The Ripple Effect of Your Change

Your decision to address OCPD patterns doesn't just affect your current relationship with your children - it reverberates across generations. Every time you pause before criticizing, you're breaking a link in the chain of perfectionist transmission. Every time you offer comfort instead of correction when your child makes a mistake, you're planting seeds of self-compassion that will grow throughout their lives.

Consider the profound gift you're giving your children when you demonstrate that people can change. In a world that often feels fixed and determined, you're showing them that awareness leads to choice, and choice leads to freedom. They're learning that they don't have to be prisoners of their own patterns - that growth is always possible.

Your children may not thank you now for being less controlling or having lower standards in some areas. In fact, they might initially test the boundaries of your newfound flexibility. But years from now, when they're making their own parenting decisions or dealing with their own perfectionist tendencies, they'll have the memory of a parent who chose love over control, connection over correction.

272

The Daily Practice of Recovery

Recovery from OCPD patterns isn't a destination you reach and then maintain effortlessly. It's a daily practice, like meditation or physical exercise. Some days you'll feel strong and flexible, easily rolling with unexpected changes and celebrating your children's imperfect efforts. Other days you'll find yourself rigidly insisting on "the right way" and feeling frustrated when family life doesn't match your internal expectations.

This variability isn't a sign of failure - it's a sign of being human. The goal isn't to eliminate your controlling impulses entirely, but to develop the awareness to notice them and the skills to choose different responses. Every time you catch yourself mid-criticism and shift to curiosity, you're building neural pathways that support flexibility. Every time you take a parent timeout instead of escalating a conflict, you're strengthening your capacity for emotional regulation.

The tools and strategies in this book aren't meant to be implemented perfectly or all at once. Choose the approaches that resonate most with your family's current needs. Start small, celebrate progress, and adjust your methods as you learn what works for your unique circumstances.

Creating Space for Authenticity

Perhaps the most precious gift you can give your children is the permission to be themselves - fully, authentically, imperfectly themselves. OCPD patterns often arise from the fear that if we're not constantly managing and improving everyone around us, chaos will ensue. But what often happens instead is that our children learn to hide their true selves to avoid triggering our anxiety.

When you begin to trust your children's inherent capacity for growth and learning, something magical happens. They start to trust it too. When you stop trying to control their every move, they have space to develop their own internal guidance systems. When you show interest in their thoughts and feelings without immediately trying to fix or change them, they learn that their inner experience is valuable and worthy of attention.

This doesn't mean abandoning all structure or expectations. Children need boundaries and guidance to feel secure. But there's a profound difference between structure that supports development and control that constrains it. The former feels like a sturdy foundation; the latter feels like a cage.

The Long View of Parenting

In the midst of daily battles over homework, chores, and behavior, it's easy to lose sight of the bigger picture of parenting. Your job isn't to produce perfect children who never make mistakes, always comply with requests, and meet every milestone exactly on schedule. Your job is to raise humans who can think for themselves, form healthy relationships, recover from setbacks, and contribute meaningfully to the world.

This long view perspective can provide comfort during the inevitable moments when your approach feels too lenient or when you worry that you're not preparing your children adequately for life's challenges. Trust that children who grow up feeling accepted and supported while learning from natural consequences develop more resilience than children who grow up trying to meet impossible standards.

Years from now, your children won't remember whether their school projects were perfectly executed or their bedrooms consistently clean. They'll remember whether they felt safe to come to you with their struggles, whether you celebrated their efforts along with their achievements, and whether your home felt like a place of refuge or a place of judgment.

Building Your Support Network

The journey of changing ingrained patterns is too difficult to navigate alone. As you work to become more flexible and connected, actively cultivate relationships with people who support your growth. This might include:

- A therapist who understands OCPD and can provide ongoing guidance
- A support group of other parents working on similar issues
- Friends who can offer perspective without judgment
- Family members who encourage your efforts to change
- Online communities where you can share struggles and victories

Remember that asking for help isn't a sign of weakness - it's a sign of wisdom. Your children benefit when you have adequate support for your own mental health and personal growth.

The Myth of Perfect Timing

You might find yourself thinking, "I should have started this work years ago" or "It's too late to change these patterns now." Both thoughts are forms of perfectionist thinking that can sabotage your progress. The truth is that the best time to start addressing OCPD patterns was whenever you first became aware of them, and the second-best time is now.

Your children benefit from your growth regardless of their current age. If your children are young, you have the opportunity to establish healthier patterns from the beginning. If your children are older, you have the chance to model that people can change and that relationships can heal. If your children are adults, you can demonstrate that it's never too late to take responsibility for past patterns and work toward better connection.

Change is possible at any stage, and your children are more resilient than you might imagine. They want a genuine relationship with you more than they want a perfect parent.

Celebrating the Journey

As you implement the strategies in this book, remember to celebrate your progress along the way. Notice when you:

- Pause before reacting instead of immediately trying to control a situation

- Ask your child about their feelings instead of telling them what to do

- Allow natural consequences instead of rescuing or over-punishing

- Apologize genuinely when you respond harshly

- Show interest in your child's perspective even when you disagree

- Take care of your own emotional needs so you can be present for your family

- Choose connection over being right in family conflicts

These moments of growth deserve recognition and celebration, even if they feel small in the grand scheme of change you're working toward.

The Vision of What's Possible

Imagine your family five years from now. Picture a home where:

- Mistakes are met with curiosity rather than criticism

- Each family member feels safe to express their authentic thoughts and feelings

- Structure supports rather than suffocates individual growth

- Conflicts are resolved through collaboration rather than control

- High standards coexist with unconditional love

- Children come to parents with problems because they expect support, not judgment

- Family members celebrate each other's efforts and progress

- Flexibility and adaptability are valued alongside responsibility and achievement

This vision isn't fantasy - it's the natural result of consistently applying the principles and practices outlined in this guide. It requires patience, persistence, and self-compassion, but it's absolutely achievable.

Your New Legacy

Every family has a story that gets passed down through generations - spoken and unspoken messages about love, worth, success, and relationships. If OCPD patterns have been part of your family's story, you have the power to edit that narrative.

Your new legacy might sound something like this:

"In our family, we believe that love doesn't depend on performance. We set high standards because we believe in each other's potential, but we never withdraw our care when those standards aren't met. We make mistakes, we learn from them, and we repair any harm we cause. We celebrate progress over perfection, effort over outcomes, and connection over compliance. We trust that each family member has inherent wisdom and capacity for growth. We provide guidance and support, but we don't try to control each other's journey. Most importantly, we know that our worth as human beings isn't determined by our achievements, but by our fundamental lovability as people."

This is the legacy of a family that has done the hard work of healing perfectionist patterns - a legacy of love, acceptance, growth, and authentic connection.

The Journey Continues

As you close this book and continue your journey, remember that the path of growth is not linear. There will be setbacks, moments of doubt, and times when your old patterns feel stronger than your new intentions. This is normal and expected - not a sign that you're failing, but a sign that you're human.

Trust the process. Trust your love for your children. Trust your capacity for growth and change. Most importantly, trust that the work you're doing matters - not just for your immediate family, but for generations of families to come.

Your children are watching you choose growth over stagnation, love over fear, and connection over control. They're learning that change is possible, that relationships can heal, and that people are worthy of love exactly as they are, while still striving to become their best selves.

This is perhaps the greatest gift you can give them - not a perfect childhood, but a genuine one. Not a flawless parent, but an authentic one who continues to grow, learn, and love with increasing wisdom and grace.

The journey of healing OCPD patterns and creating healthier family dynamics is ongoing, but every step you take creates ripples of positive change that will extend far beyond what you can currently imagine. Your courage to change is creating a new legacy for your family - one marked not by perfection, but by love, growth, and the unshakeable belief that every family member deserves to be cherished for exactly who they are.

Final Reflection

Take a moment now to acknowledge how far you've already come. Simply by reading this book, you've demonstrated your commitment to growth and your love for your family. That commitment, more than any perfect technique or flawless execution of these strategies, is what will transform your family relationships.

You have everything you need to continue this journey. You have love, awareness, and now tools and strategies to support lasting change. Most importantly, you have the unwavering truth that change is always possible, healing is always available, and love - imperfect, messy, authentic love - is always enough.

Your new family legacy begins now.

Appendix A: Quick Reference Guides

The journey of changing OCPD patterns requires constant awareness and quick access to tools during challenging moments. These quick reference guides provide immediate support when you need it most, helping you recognize symptoms, understand normal development, identify concerning patterns, and shift your language toward growth and connection.

OCPD Symptoms Checklist

This comprehensive checklist helps you identify OCPD patterns in your parenting. Rate each item from 0 (never) to 3 (almost always) to track your progress over time. Remember, awareness is the first step toward change.

Control and Perfectionism (0-3 scale)

- I insist things be done "the right way" even when other ways work fine

- I have trouble delegating tasks because others won't do them correctly

- I feel anxious when my children's rooms or belongings are messy

- I correct my children's methods even when their results are acceptable

- I struggle to let my children make age-appropriate mistakes

- I find myself redoing tasks my children have completed

- I have specific rules for how household activities should be done

- I feel frustrated when family routines are disrupted

Rigidity and Inflexibility (0-3 scale)

- I have difficulty adapting when plans change unexpectedly
- I stick to schedules even when flexibility would benefit the family
- I find it hard to "go with the flow" during family activities
- I insist on finishing tasks before moving to fun activities
- I have trouble with spontaneous family activities or outings
- I become upset when family traditions are modified
- I struggle to accept different approaches to solving problems
- I find it difficult to compromise on family rules or expectations

Work and Achievement Focus (0-3 scale)

- I prioritize productivity over family relaxation time
- I have trouble enjoying activities that don't have a clear purpose
- I push my children to achieve beyond their developmental level
- I focus more on my children's performance than their effort
- I have difficulty taking breaks or family vacation time
- I feel guilty when not being productive during free time
- I emphasize homework and achievements over play and creativity
- I struggle to engage in activities purely for enjoyment

Hoarding and Difficulty Discarding (0-3 scale)

- I keep my children's schoolwork and projects long after they're relevant
- I have trouble throwing away items that might be useful someday
- I save things "just in case" even when space is limited
- I feel distressed when family members want to discard items I've saved
- I keep detailed records or documentation beyond what's necessary
- I have difficulty helping children declutter their belongings
- I save items for sentimental reasons even when they create clutter
- I feel anxious about throwing away potentially important items

Stubbornness and Need for Control (0-3 scale)

- I insist on having the final say in family decisions
- I have trouble accepting input that contradicts my preferred approach
- I become argumentative when others suggest different methods
- I find it hard to admit when I've made parenting mistakes
- I struggle to apologize genuinely to my children
- I have difficulty accepting criticism about my parenting
- I insist on being right even in minor disagreements
- I find it challenging to let my children have age-appropriate autonomy

Emotional Restriction (0-3 scale)

- I have trouble expressing affection openly with my family
- I find emotional conversations uncomfortable or unnecessary
- I focus on practical matters rather than feelings during conflicts
- I struggle to comfort my children when they're emotionally upset
- I have difficulty showing vulnerability or admitting my fears
- I tend to minimize or dismiss emotional expressions from family members
- I find it hard to be playful or silly with my children
- I prioritize teaching lessons over providing emotional support

Moral and Ethical Rigidity (0-3 scale)

- I have strict rules about right and wrong that I expect others to follow
- I find it difficult to understand different perspectives on moral issues
- I become upset when family members don't share my values exactly
- I have trouble tolerating behavior I consider inappropriate, even if minor
- I insist on teaching moral lessons even in casual situations
- I struggle to accept that some issues exist in gray areas
- I find it hard to show grace when rules are broken
- I emphasize compliance with rules over understanding their purpose

Interpersonal Difficulties (0-3 scale)

- I have few close friendships outside my immediate family
- I find it difficult to work collaboratively with other parents
- I become frustrated with people who don't meet my standards
- I struggle to maintain relationships with people who are very different from me
- I have trouble accepting help from others
- I find it challenging to be part of groups where I'm not in control
- I become critical of other families' parenting approaches
- I have difficulty maintaining casual, relaxed social interactions

Scoring Interpretation:

- 0-30: Minimal OCPD traits affecting parenting
- 31-60: Mild to moderate patterns that may benefit from awareness and self-help strategies
- 61-90: Significant patterns that would likely benefit from professional support
- 91-120: Severe patterns that are probably impacting family functioning and require professional intervention

Using This Checklist:

- Complete monthly to track progress over time
- Share results with your therapist or support group
- Focus on patterns rather than individual scores
- Celebrate reductions in any category

- Use high-scoring areas to prioritize change efforts

Child Development Milestones Chart

Understanding normal child development helps OCPD parents adjust expectations and reduce anxiety about their children's progress. This chart highlights key developmental milestones while emphasizing the wide range of normal variation.

Ages 0-12 Months: Building Basic Trust

Physical Development:

- 2-4 months: Holds head steady, follows objects with eyes
- 4-6 months: Sits with support, reaches for objects
- 6-9 months: Sits without support, begins crawling
- 9-12 months: Pulls to standing, may take first steps
- *Normal variation: 2-4 months difference in timing*

Emotional/Social:

- 2-6 months: Social smiling, enjoys face-to-face interaction
- 6-9 months: Shows stranger anxiety, prefers familiar caregivers
- 9-12 months: Shows separation anxiety, engages in simple games
- *OCPD parent note: Rigid schedules can interfere with natural rhythm development*

Communication:

- 2-6 months: Coos, laughs, babbles
- 6-9 months: Responds to name, understands "no"
- 9-12 months: First words, follows simple commands

- *Remember: Language develops through interaction, not instruction*

Ages 1-2 Years: Developing Autonomy

Physical Development:

- 12-15 months: Walks independently, climbs stairs with help
- 15-18 months: Runs, kicks ball, builds tower of 3-4 blocks
- 18-24 months: Jumps, throws ball, uses utensils
- *Messiness is developmental - exploration requires getting dirty*

Emotional/Social:

- 12-18 months: Shows affection, may have tantrums when frustrated
- 18-24 months: Parallel play begins, imitates adult behaviors
- 20-24 months: Begins showing empathy, seeks comfort when upset
- *Tantrums are normal - rigid responses increase their intensity*

Communication/Cognitive:

- 12-18 months: Vocabulary of 5-20 words, points to request items
- 18-24 months: Vocabulary explosion to 50-200 words, two-word phrases
- 20-24 months: Begins pretend play, follows two-step instructions
- *Avoid overcorrecting grammar - model correct speech instead*

Ages 2-3 Years: Testing Boundaries

Physical Development:

- Runs smoothly, walks up stairs, pedals tricycle

- Uses toilet with help, washes hands, builds towers of 6+ blocks

- Draws circles, uses scissors, throws ball overhand

- *Fine motor skills develop gradually - perfectionist pressure hinders progress*

Emotional/Social:

- Asserts independence ("No!" and "Me do it!")

- Shows wide range of emotions, often intensely

- Begins cooperative play, shows concern for others

- *The "terrible twos" are actually "terrific twos" - autonomy development is healthy*

Communication/Cognitive:

- Uses 2-4 word sentences, asks many questions

- Understands most of what you say, follows complex instructions

- Engages in pretend play, tells simple stories

- *Questions are learning tools, not challenges to authority*

Ages 3-4 Years: Developing Initiative

Physical Development:

- Hops on one foot, catches large ball, uses toilet independently

- Dresses self with help, brushes teeth, draws people with 2-4 body parts

- Climbs well, begins to skip, rides tricycle with confidence

- *Independence attempts create messes - this is normal and necessary*

Emotional/Social:

- Plays cooperatively, shares sometimes, shows empathy
- Enjoys helping with household tasks
- May have imaginary friends, acts out roles in play
- *Rigid expectations about sharing and cooperation ignore developmental reality*

Communication/Cognitive:

- Speaks in complete sentences, tells stories, sings songs
- Counts to 10, recognizes some letters, understands time concepts
- Asks "why" constantly, remembers parts of stories
- *Curiosity should be encouraged, not controlled*

Ages 4-5 Years: Preparing for School

Physical Development:

- Hops on one foot for 10 seconds, swings independently
- Uses fork and spoon well, draws person with 6 body parts
- Prints some letters, cuts on line with scissors
- *Perfectionist pressure about writing and drawing reduces motivation*

Emotional/Social:

- Plays well with others, understands rules, shows more emotional control
- Wants to please adults, distinguishes fantasy from reality

288

- Shows independence in familiar settings
- *Natural desire to please shouldn't be exploited through excessive expectations*

Communication/Cognitive:

- Uses complex sentences, understands rhyming, retells stories
- Counts 20+ objects, recognizes most letters, writes own name
- Understands yesterday, today, tomorrow
- *Academic readiness varies widely - avoid comparisons*

Ages 6-8 Years: Industry vs. Inferiority

Physical Development:

- Ties shoes, rides bicycle, throws and catches well
- Draws detailed pictures, writes letters and numbers clearly
- Has established handedness, coordinates complex movements
- *Focus on effort and improvement, not perfection*

Emotional/Social:

- Develops friendships, understands fairness, follows game rules
- Shows increased empathy, wants to help others
- Seeks approval from adults and peers
- *Peer relationships become increasingly important*

Communication/Cognitive:

- Reads simple books, writes simple sentences, does basic math
- Understands cause and effect, follows multi-step instructions
- Shows longer attention span, enjoys learning new skills

- *Individual learning paces vary significantly*

Ages 9-11 Years: Expanding Competence

Physical Development:

- Shows improved strength and coordination
- May begin showing signs of puberty (varies widely)
- Develops specific physical skills and interests
- *Comparison to others becomes more prominent and potentially damaging*

Emotional/Social:

- Values peer acceptance, may exclude others to feel included
- Shows increased emotional complexity, mood changes
- Develops moral reasoning, questions adult authority appropriately
- *Adult guidance needed to navigate social complexities*

Communication/Cognitive:

- Reads chapter books, writes paragraphs, solves complex problems
- Shows abstract thinking, understands different perspectives
- Develops specific interests and hobbies
- *Perfectionist pressure can create school anxiety and avoidance*

Ages 12-14 Years: Early Adolescence

Physical Development:

- Experiences puberty-related changes at varying rates

- Shows rapid growth spurts, coordination may be temporarily affected

- Develops adult-like physical capabilities in some areas

- *Body image concerns are normal and should be handled sensitively*

Emotional/Social:

- Seeks independence while still needing support

- Values peer opinion over adult approval

- Shows increased emotional intensity and mood variability

- *Arguing and testing boundaries are normal developmental tasks*

Communication/Cognitive:

- Develops abstract thinking, questions values and beliefs

- Shows improved problem-solving abilities

- May show decreased academic motivation due to social focus

- *Identity formation requires freedom to explore and make mistakes*

Ages 15-18 Years: Later Adolescence

Physical Development:

- Reaches near-adult physical development

- Shows improved coordination and strength

- Brain development continues, especially in areas controlling impulses and decision-making

- *Risk-taking behaviors are partly neurological, not just defiance*

Emotional/Social:

- Develops intimate friendships and romantic relationships
- Shows increased empathy and social awareness
- Seeks autonomy while maintaining family connections
- *Gradual independence is healthier than sudden freedom*

Communication/Cognitive:

- Uses complex reasoning, understands consequences
- Shows future-oriented thinking, makes long-term plans
- Develops personal value system that may differ from parents
- *Allowing autonomous decision-making builds competence*

Red Flags for OCPD Parents:

- Expecting developmental milestones to be achieved perfectly or early
- Becoming anxious when children develop differently than siblings
- Focusing more on milestone achievement than overall wellbeing
- Using milestones as measures of parenting success
- Ignoring individual differences in favor of standardized timelines

Red Flags by Age

Recognizing when normal childhood behavior crosses into concerning territory helps OCPD parents distinguish between their anxiety and actual problems requiring intervention.

Ages 0-2 Years: When Structure Becomes Harmful

Concerning Rigidity in Parents:

- Refusing to adjust feeding schedules based on infant cues
- Becoming distressed by normal infant unpredictability
- Expecting consistent sleep patterns before age 6 months
- Limiting exploration due to mess or safety anxieties
- Comparing infant development to unrealistic standards

Concerning Signs in Child:

- Extreme distress with any change in routine (beyond normal adjustment period)
- Lack of interest in exploring environment or new toys
- Excessive self-soothing behaviors (head banging, rocking for hours)
- No stranger anxiety or separation anxiety (may indicate attachment issues)
- Significant delays in multiple developmental areas

Red Flags in Parent-Child Interaction:

- Parent rarely follows child's interests or cues
- Parent imposes adult agenda during play time
- Parent becomes angry when child makes normal messes
- Parent focuses on performance rather than connection
- Parent shows little warmth or emotional responsiveness

Ages 2-4 Years: When Control Battles Dominate

Concerning Rigidity in Parents:

- Unable to tolerate normal toddler tantrums without becoming angry

- Expecting immediate compliance with all requests

- Punishing normal developmental behaviors like saying "no"

- Requiring perfection in toilet training, eating, or sleeping

- Becoming distressed by typical toddler messiness and exploration

Concerning Signs in Child:

- Extreme anxiety about making mistakes or getting dirty

- Unusual compliance that seems fear-based rather than cooperative

- Difficulty playing freely or being creative

- Excessive self-criticism for normal childhood errors

- Rigid insistence on sameness that interferes with daily functioning

Red Flags in Family Dynamics:

- Child seems afraid of disappointing parent

- Parent and child locked in daily battles over minor issues

- Child's natural curiosity and exploration are consistently discouraged

- Parent unable to enjoy child's personality or interests

- Child shows signs of anxiety or withdrawal

Ages 5-8 Years: When Achievement Pressure Intensifies

Concerning Rigidity in Parents:

- Child's grades become measure of parent's worth

- Unable to tolerate child's academic struggles or learning differences

- Demanding perfection in homework, sports, or other activities
- Comparing child constantly to siblings or peers
- Over-scheduling child with achievement-focused activities

Concerning Signs in Child:

- School anxiety, frequent stomachaches, or sleep problems
- Perfectionist meltdowns when work isn't perfect
- Avoiding new activities due to fear of failure
- Excessive worry about grades, performance, or adult approval
- Loss of interest in activities that were previously enjoyable

Red Flags in Academic/Social Settings:

- Child afraid to ask questions or admit confusion
- Parent conflicts with teachers over grades or expectations
- Child has difficulty making friends due to social anxiety
- Parent does child's homework or projects to ensure "quality"
- Child shows signs of depression or anxiety disorders

Ages 9-12 Years: When Independence Becomes Threatening

Concerning Rigidity in Parents:

- Unable to allow age-appropriate independence and decision-making
- Micromanaging friendships and social interactions
- Expecting child to maintain adult-level organization and responsibility
- Becoming threatened by child's developing opinions and preferences

- Controlling child's interests to match parent's values or aspirations

Concerning Signs in Child:

- Difficulty making decisions independently
- Excessive worry about disappointing parents
- Social isolation due to parent's control or child's anxiety
- Lying or hiding normal activities due to fear of parent reaction
- Signs of depression, anxiety, or eating disorders

Red Flags in Parent-Child Relationship:

- Child stops sharing thoughts, feelings, or experiences with parent
- Parent interrogates child rather than having conversations
- Child's friends are unwelcome in the home due to parent's discomfort
- Parent unable to acknowledge child's growing autonomy
- Relationship feels more like management than connection

Ages 13-18 Years: When Control Battles Peak

Concerning Rigidity in Parents:

- Unable to negotiate or compromise on age-appropriate freedoms
- Trying to control teen's identity formation process
- Expecting teen to share all personal thoughts and experiences
- Using guilt, shame, or fear to maintain control
- Unable to tolerate teen's normal push for independence

Concerning Signs in Teen:

- Extreme rebellion or complete submission (both are concerning)
- Signs of depression, anxiety, self-harm, or eating disorders
- Lying about normal teenage activities
- Isolation from peers and family
- Academic performance declining due to pressure or rebellion

Red Flags in Family System:

- Family conflicts dominate most interactions
- Teen feels unable to be authentic without disappointing parent
- Parent uses emotional manipulation to maintain control
- Teen planning to cut contact after leaving home
- Other family members walking on eggshells to avoid conflict

Crisis Intervention Needed When:

- Child or teen expresses suicidal thoughts or engages in self-harm
- Eating disorders or substance abuse develop
- Child completely shuts down emotionally or socially
- Parent becomes abusive (emotionally, physically, or verbally)
- Family relationships are completely deteriorated
- Child's functioning is significantly impaired in multiple areas

When to Seek Professional Help:

- Parent recognizes concerning patterns but can't change them alone
- Child shows signs of anxiety or depression

- Family conflicts are escalating despite parent's efforts

- Parent feels overwhelmed or out of control

- Other family members express concern about dynamics

- Parent's own mental health is suffering significantly

Growth Mindset Phrases

Language shapes reality, especially for children. These phrases help OCPD parents shift from fixed mindset criticism to growth-oriented support and encouragement.

Instead of Fixed Mindset Language, Try Growth Mindset Alternatives

Responding to Mistakes:

Fixed Mindset: "You always make careless mistakes." Growth Mindset: "Mistakes help us learn. What do you notice about what happened?"

Fixed Mindset: "This is wrong. Do it over." Growth Mindset: "This part works well. Let's look at this section together."

Fixed Mindset: "You should know this by now." Growth Mindset: "This is challenging. Let's break it down into smaller steps."

Fixed Mindset: "I'm disappointed in you." Growth Mindset: "I can see you're frustrated. What would help you try again?"

Responding to Effort:

Fixed Mindset: "Good job, you're so smart!" Growth Mindset: "I can see how hard you worked on this. Your effort really shows."

Fixed Mindset: "This is easy for you." Growth Mindset: "You've been practicing, and it shows in your improvement."

Fixed Mindset: "You're a natural at this." Growth Mindset: "Your strategy of practicing a little each day is really paying off."

Fixed Mindset: "You're so talented." Growth Mindset: "Your dedication to getting better is inspiring."

Responding to Challenges:

Fixed Mindset: "You can't do this." Growth Mindset: "You can't do this yet. What would help you learn?"

Fixed Mindset: "This is too hard for you." Growth Mindset: "This is challenging. What part feels most difficult?"

Fixed Mindset: "You're not good at math." Growth Mindset: "Math is challenging for you right now. Let's find strategies that help."

Fixed Mindset: "Some people are just better at this." Growth Mindset: "Everyone learns differently and at different speeds."

Responding to Success:

Fixed Mindset: "Perfect! You got them all right." Growth Mindset: "Your preparation really paid off. How does it feel to reach your goal?"

Fixed Mindset: "You're the best in your class." Growth Mindset: "You should be proud of how much you've improved."

Fixed Mindset: "You never make mistakes." Growth Mindset: "You've learned to catch your mistakes and fix them."

Fixed Mindset: "You're so much better than your sister." Growth Mindset: "You each have your own strengths and ways of learning."

Daily Growth Mindset Phrases for OCPD Parents:

Morning Motivation:

- "Today is a new chance to learn and grow."

- "We'll do our best and learn from whatever happens."

- "Progress matters more than perfection."

- "We're all learning, including me."

During Challenges:

- "This is hard, and that's okay."
- "Let's figure this out together."
- "What can we learn from this?"
- "Every expert was once a beginner."

Evening Reflection:

- "What did you learn today?"
- "What are you most proud of from today?"
- "What would you like to try differently tomorrow?"
- "I'm proud of how you handled that challenge."

When You Make Parenting Mistakes:

- "I made a mistake, and I'm learning from it."
- "I'm still learning how to be the best parent I can be."
- "Thank you for being patient while I figure this out."
- "We can both grow and change together."

Appendix B: Worksheets and Exercises

These practical tools help OCPD parents track patterns, practice new skills, clarify values, and celebrate progress. Regular use of these worksheets builds awareness and creates accountability for change.

Daily OCPD Trigger Log

Understanding your triggers is the first step toward changing automatic reactions. This log helps identify patterns and develop targeted strategies for challenging situations.

Daily Trigger Tracking Sheet

Date: _____

Morning Check-In:

- Stress level (1-10): ____

- Energy level (1-10): ____

- Expectations for the day: _____

- Potential challenges anticipated: _____

Trigger Event #1

- Time: _____

- Situation: _____

- What happened that triggered my OCPD response?
  _____

- Physical sensations I noticed:
  _____

- Thoughts that went through my mind:
  _____

- Emotions I felt: _____

- How I responded: _____

- How my child/family reacted:
  _____

- What I wish I had done differently:
  _____

- Trigger intensity (1-10): ___

Trigger Event #2 [Same format as above]

Trigger Event #3 [Same format as above]

Evening Reflection:

- Most challenging moment:
  _____

- Most successful moment:
  _____

- Pattern I notice: _____

- Tomorrow I will try: _____

- Self-compassion note:
  _____

Weekly Pattern Analysis:

After completing one week, review for patterns:

Most Common Triggers:

1. _____

2. _____

3. _____

Times of Day I'm Most Triggered:

- Morning: ___% of triggers
- Afternoon: ___% of triggers
- Evening: ___% of triggers

Physical Signs That Precede Triggers:

- _____
- _____
- _____

Thoughts That Increase Trigger Intensity:

- _____
- _____
- _____

Most Effective Coping Strategies:

- _____
- _____
- _____

Action Plan for Next Week: *Based on patterns identified, I will:*

1. _____
2. _____
3. _____

Flexibility Practice Tracker

Building flexibility requires consistent practice in low-stakes situations before applying it to high-stress parenting moments. This tracker helps you gradually expand your comfort zone.

Weekly Flexibility Challenge Sheet

Week of: _____

Monday's Flexibility Practice:

- Planned challenge: _____
- Difficulty level (1-5): ___
- How I felt before: _____
- What actually happened:

  _____
- How I felt during: _____
- What I learned: _____
- Success rating (1-5): ___

Tuesday's Flexibility Practice: [Same format]

Wednesday's Flexibility Practice: [Same format]

Thursday's Flexibility Practice: [Same format]

Friday's Flexibility Practice: [Same format]

Saturday's Flexibility Practice: [Same format]

Sunday's Flexibility Practice: [Same format]

Suggested Flexibility Challenges by Difficulty Level:

Level 1 (Beginner):

- Let your child choose their outfit (weather appropriate)
- Take a different route to a familiar destination

- Allow toys to stay out for one extra day
- Let your child help cook without correcting their technique
- Go to bed 15 minutes earlier or later than usual

Level 2 (Building Confidence):

- Let your child organize their backpack their way
- Allow a friend over with only 30 minutes notice
- Say yes to a spontaneous activity suggestion
- Let your child's room stay messy for a weekend
- Try a new restaurant without reading reviews first

Level 3 (Intermediate):

- Allow your child to plan an entire family evening
- Accept less-than-perfect help with household tasks
- Let your child solve a problem without offering suggestions
- Participate in an unstructured play activity
- Allow your child to wear an outfit you don't love to a social event

Level 4 (Advanced):

- Let your child invite friends over without pre-planning activities
- Allow your teen to decorate their room completely their way
- Take a family vacation day with no planned activities
- Let your child quit an activity they no longer enjoy
- Allow your child to manage their homework independently for a week

Level 5 (Expert):

- Let your child plan and execute a family birthday party
- Allow your teen to make a significant decision you disagree with
- Take a spontaneous weekend trip with minimal planning
- Let your child host a sleepover with minimal supervision
- Support your child's choice of friends even if they're different from your preference

Monthly Flexibility Review:

After four weeks, assess your progress:

Areas Where Flexibility Has Improved:

- _____
- _____
- _____

Situations Still Challenging:

- _____
- _____
- _____

Family Changes Noticed:

- _____
- _____
- _____

Next Month's Goals:

- _____

- ————————————————————————
- ————————————————————————

Family Values Clarification

OCPD parents often focus on rules and standards without connecting them to deeper values. This exercise helps clarify what truly matters most to your family.

Family Values Discovery Worksheet

Part 1: Individual Values Reflection

Complete this section privately before involving family members.

Core Values Assessment: *Rate each value's importance to you (1=not important, 5=extremely important)*

- Achievement/Success: ___
- Adventure/Excitement: ___
- Authenticity/Being True to Self: ___
- Beauty/Aesthetics: ___
- Community/Belonging: ___
- Compassion/Kindness: ___
- Connection/Relationships: ___
- Creativity/Innovation: ___
- Faith/Spirituality: ___
- Family/Loyalty: ___
- Freedom/Independence: ___
- Fun/Enjoyment: ___
- Growth/Learning: ___

- Health/Wellness: ___
- Honesty/Integrity: ___
- Justice/Fairness: ___
- Knowledge/Wisdom: ___
- Leadership/Influence: ___
- Order/Organization: ___
- Respect/Dignity: ___
- Responsibility/Duty: ___
- Security/Safety: ___
- Service/Helping Others: ___

Top 5 Values for Me:

1. _____
2. _____
3. _____
4. _____
5. _____

Part 2: Values vs. Current Parenting

For each of your top 5 values, complete the following:

Value 1: _____

- How this shows up in my parenting currently:
  _____
- How my OCPD patterns support this value:
  _____

- How my OCPD patterns conflict with this value:

  _____

- How I could better honor this value:

  _____

Value 2: _____ [Same format]

Value 3: _____ [Same format]

Value 4: _____ [Same format]

Value 5: _____ [Same format]

Part 3: Family Values Discussion

After completing your individual reflection, involve age-appropriate family members:

Family Meeting Agenda:

1. Share why values matter to our family

2. Each person shares their top 3-5 values

3. Identify shared values across family members

4. Discuss how current family rules support or conflict with values

5. Create family values statement

6. Plan how to live these values daily

Our Family's Shared Values:

1. _____

2. _____

3. _____

4. _____

5. _____

Family Values Statement: *"Our family believes in..."*

_____

_____

_____

Part 4: Values-Based Decision Making

Use this framework for future family decisions:

When Making Family Decisions, We Will Ask:

- Does this choice align with our stated values?
- How does this decision affect each family member?
- Are we choosing based on fear or based on our values?
- What would living our values look like in this situation?
- How can we honor multiple values when they seem to conflict?

Family Rules That Need Revision Based on Our Values:

- Current rule: _____
- Underlying value: _____
- Revised approach: _____

New Family Practices to Honor Our Values:

- _____
- _____
- _____

Progress Celebration Chart

OCPD parents struggle to notice and celebrate progress, often focusing only on what still needs improvement. This chart helps track and celebrate growth in family relationships.

Monthly Progress Celebration Tracker

Month: _____

Week 1 Celebrations:

Monday:

- Small win for me: _____

- Small win for child/family:

  _____

- How I celebrated: _____

Tuesday: [Same format]

Wednesday: [Same format]

Thursday: [Same format]

Friday: [Same format]

Saturday: [Same format]

Sunday: [Same format]

Week 1 Reflection:

- Biggest improvement I noticed:

  _____

- Most meaningful moment:

  _____

- Challenge I handled differently:

  _____

Week 2-4: [Same format as Week 1]

Monthly Progress Review:

Areas of Growth This Month:

In My OCPD Patterns:

- I'm more flexible about:
  _____

- I'm less controlling of:
  _____

- I'm better at noticing:
  _____

- I'm improving at responding to:
  _____

In My Relationship with Each Child:

- Child 1 (name): _____
  - o What's better:
    _____

  - o Special moment:
    _____

  - o Their feedback:
    _____

- Child 2 (name): _____
  [Same format]

In Our Family Dynamic:

- More laughter/fun: _____
- Less stress around: _____
- Better communication about:
  _____

- New tradition/activity:
  _____

Challenges Faced This Month:

- Biggest setback: _____
- How I handled it: _____
- What I learned: _____
- Support I used: _____

Specific Examples of Progress:

Flexibility Wins:

- Situation: _____
- Old response would have been:
  _____
- New response was: _____
- Result: _____

Connection Moments:

- When: _____
- What happened: _____
- How it felt: _____
- Why it matters: _____

Growth Mindset Examples:

- Situation: _____
- Growth language used:
  _____
- Child's response: _____

- Learning that occurred:

  _____

Family Feedback Collection:

Questions to ask family members monthly:

- "What do you notice that's different about our family lately?"

- "What do you appreciate about how I'm parenting now?"

- "What would you like to see more of?"

- "How are you feeling about our relationship?"

Child 1 Responses:

_____

_____

Child 2 Responses:

_____

_____

Partner Responses:

_____

_____

Celebration Planning:

Ways Our Family Celebrates Progress:

- Small daily celebrations:

  _____

- Weekly family celebrations:

  _____

- Monthly bigger celebrations:

  _____

- Special recognition methods:

  _____

This Month's Celebration Plan:

- Date: _____
- Activity: _____
- Who's involved: _____
- What we're celebrating:

  _____

Looking Forward:

Goals for Next Month:

1. _____
2. _____
3. _____

Support I'll Need:

- From family: _____
- From friends: _____
- From professionals: _____
- From myself: _____

Affirmation for Continued Growth: *"This month I'm proud of myself for..."*

_____

_____

_____

Appendix C: Emergency Cards

Crisis moments test every OCPD parent's commitment to change. These wallet-sized cards provide immediate support when triggers threaten to overwhelm your progress and damage family relationships.

Wallet Cards for High-Stress Moments

These cards fit in your wallet, purse, or phone case for instant access during overwhelming situations. Print them on cardstock and keep them readily available.

Card 1: The STOP Technique

EMERGENCY PAUSE PROTOCOL

S - STOP what you're doing immediately

Put down everything. Step back.

T - TAKE three deep breaths

Feel your feet on the ground.

O - OBSERVE what's really happening

What am I feeling? What does my child need?

P - PROCEED with intention

Choose your response. Ask: "What kind of

parent do I want to be right now?"

Remember: This moment doesn't define you.

Card 2: Crisis Self-Talk

EMERGENCY SELF-COMPASSION

"I'm having a human reaction to stress."

"This feeling is temporary and will pass."

"My worth isn't determined by this moment."

"I can be imperfect and still be good enough."

"I can repair any damage I cause."

Breathe. You've got this.

Recovery is always possible.

Card 3: Perspective Reset

REALITY CHECK QUESTIONS

• Will this matter in 5 years?

• Is my child safe right now?

• What would I tell a friend in this situation?

• What does my child actually need from me?

• Am I responding to the situation or my fear?

Focus on connection before correction.

Your calm creates their calm.

Card 4: Child-Focused Response

WHAT MY CHILD NEEDS RIGHT NOW

Instead of control, they need:

• Safety and security

• Understanding and empathy

• Space to be imperfect

• Help learning and growing

• Unconditional love

Ask: "How can I help?" not "Why did you...?"

Card 5: Quick Exit Strategy

WHEN TO TAKE A PARENT TIMEOUT

Signs I need a break:

• Raising my voice repeatedly

• Making threats I won't follow through

• Heart racing, jaw clenched

• Focused on being right vs. being helpful

Say: "I need a few minutes to calm down

so I can be the parent you deserve."

Return ready to connect, not battle.

Quick Regulation Techniques

Physical regulation techniques that can be used anywhere, anytime, to manage overwhelming emotions and return to a responsive state.

Technique 1: 5-4-3-2-1 Grounding

Use this when feeling disconnected or overwhelmed:

5 things you can see: Look around and name them silently or aloud

- The blue cup on the counter
- My child's backpack by the door
- Sunlight coming through the window
- The dog lying on the rug
- My child's artwork on the refrigerator

4 things you can touch: Actually make contact

- The smooth surface of the kitchen table
- The soft fabric of your shirt
- The cool metal of the doorknob
- The rough texture of the brick wall

3 things you can hear: Listen carefully

- The hum of the refrigerator
- Traffic outside the window
- My child's voice in the next room

2 things you can smell: Take a gentle sniff

- Coffee brewing

- Fresh air from an open window

1 thing you can taste: Notice what's in your mouth

- The lingering taste of toothpaste

- A sip of water

This technique works because it engages your prefrontal cortex and reduces activation in your emotional centers.

Technique 2: Physiological Sigh

This is the fastest way to calm your nervous system:

1. **Double inhale through your nose:**

   o Take a normal inhale

   o Immediately take a second, shorter inhale on top of the first

   o This reopens collapsed alveoli in your lungs

2. **Long exhale through your mouth:**

   o Make the exhale longer than the inhale

   o Allow your shoulders to drop

3. **Repeat 2-3 times:**

   o Each cycle should take about 6-8 seconds total

   o Focus only on the breathing, nothing else

Why it works: This technique is based on neuroscience research showing it's the fastest way to shift from sympathetic (stress) to parasympathetic (calm) nervous system activation.

Technique 3: Box Breathing

Use when you need sustained calm and focus:

1. **Inhale for 4 counts** (through your nose)

2. **Hold for 4 counts**

3. **Exhale for 4 counts** (through your mouth)

4. **Hold empty for 4 counts**

5. **Repeat 4-8 cycles**

Visualize drawing a box as you breathe: up the left side (inhale), across the top (hold), down the right side (exhale), across the bottom (hold).

Technique 4: Progressive Muscle Release

Quick version for acute stress:

1. **Tense your fists** for 5 seconds, then release

2. **Scrunch your face** (eyes, forehead, jaw) for 5 seconds, then release

3. **Lift your shoulders** to your ears for 5 seconds, then drop them

4. **Clench your stomach** muscles for 5 seconds, then relax

5. **Notice the contrast** between tension and relaxation

This helps release physical holding patterns that maintain emotional activation.

Technique 5: Cold Water Reset

For intense emotional activation:

- **Splash cold water on your wrists** (cooling pulse points calms the nervous system)

- **Hold an ice cube** for 30 seconds

- **Drink ice water slowly**

- **Run cold water over the back of your neck**

Cold temperature activates the vagus nerve, which triggers the relaxation response.

Technique 6: Movement Release

When you can't sit still:

- **Shake your hands** vigorously for 10 seconds
- **Roll your shoulders** backward 5 times
- **March in place** for 30 seconds
- **Do 5 jumping jacks** if space allows
- **Stretch your arms over your head** and take a deep breath

Movement helps metabolize stress chemicals like cortisol and adrenaline.

Self-Compassion Phrases

OCPD parents are typically their own harshest critics. These phrases help interrupt the cycle of self-judgment that often makes parenting situations worse.

For Perfectionist Self-Criticism:

- "I'm learning to parent differently, and learning takes time."
- "Making mistakes doesn't make me a bad parent."
- "I can be imperfect and still be good enough."
- "My worth isn't determined by my children's behavior."
- "I'm doing the best I can with the tools I currently have."
- "Growth requires making mistakes - that's how learning works."
- "I can feel frustrated and still choose love."

- "This is hard for me, and that's okay."

For Overwhelming Emotions:

- "This feeling is temporary and will pass."

- "I'm having a human reaction to a challenging situation."

- "It's normal to feel overwhelmed sometimes."

- "My emotions are information, not instructions."

- "I can feel this way and still make good choices."

- "Strong feelings don't make me a bad person."

- "I'm allowed to have big emotions too."

- "This intensity will decrease if I don't feed it with self-judgment."

For Parenting Mistakes:

- "I can repair any damage I cause with harsh words or actions."

- "My children need me to be human, not perfect."

- "Apologizing to my children teaches them it's safe to make mistakes."

- "One bad moment doesn't erase all the good moments."

- "I'm modeling that people can change and grow."

- "My children will remember how I handled my mistakes."

- "Recovery and repair are always possible."

- "I'm teaching my children that love isn't conditional on perfection."

For OCPD Shame:

- "Having OCPD traits doesn't make me a bad person."

- "I'm working to change patterns that no longer serve my family."
- "My desire for excellence comes from caring deeply."
- "I can honor my values without being rigid about methods."
- "Many OCPD traits have positive aspects when balanced with flexibility."
- "I'm not broken - I'm learning to expand my comfort zone."
- "My family loves me even with my struggles."
- "Healing is possible, and I'm already taking steps."

For Setbacks and Relapses:

- "Setbacks are normal parts of change, not signs of failure."
- "I've made progress before, and I can make progress again."
- "Every time I catch myself and redirect, I'm building new pathways."
- "Change isn't linear - there will be ups and downs."
- "I don't have to be perfect at changing to be making progress."
- "Tomorrow is a new chance to practice what I've learned."
- "My family sees my efforts even when I can't."
- "Small steps forward still count as forward movement."

For Daily Encouragement:

- "I'm exactly where I need to be in my growth journey."
- "My love for my family motivates my willingness to change."
- "Each day I practice flexibility, I get a little bit better."
- "I'm creating a new legacy for my family."

- "My efforts to change are already benefiting my children."
- "I have the strength and resources to keep growing."
- "I'm grateful for my awareness and commitment to change."
- "Every moment is a new opportunity to respond with love."

Crisis Hotlines and Immediate Support

When OCPD patterns escalate to crisis levels or when family relationships become severely strained, professional support may be needed immediately.

National Crisis Resources:

National Suicide Prevention Lifeline

- Phone: 988
- Available 24/7, free and confidential
- Online chat: suicidepreventionlifeline.org
- Text: Text HOME to 741741

Crisis Text Line

- Text: 741741
- Available 24/7, free crisis support
- Trained counselors respond to texts
- Website: crisistextline.org

National Child Abuse Hotline

- Phone: 1-800-4-A-CHILD (1-800-422-4453)
- Available 24/7
- For parents who fear they might harm their children
- Confidential support and local resources

SAMHSA National Helpline

- Phone: 1-800-662-HELP (4357)
- Substance Abuse and Mental Health Services Administration
- 24/7 treatment referral service
- Information about local treatment facilities and support groups

Specialized Mental Health Resources:

International OCD Foundation

- Website: iocdf.org
- Phone: (617) 973-5801
- Therapist directory for OCPD specialists
- Support groups and educational resources

Anxiety and Depression Association of America

- Website: adaa.org
- Therapist directory
- Online support groups
- Educational resources about perfectionism and anxiety

Psychology Today Therapist Directory

- Website: psychologytoday.com
- Filter for OCPD, perfectionism, and family therapy
- Read therapist profiles and approaches
- Contact information and insurance verification

When to Use Crisis Resources:

Immediate Crisis (Call 911 or Go to Emergency Room):

- Thoughts of harming yourself or your children
- Inability to control violent impulses
- Complete breakdown in functioning
- Substance abuse to cope with OCPD stress
- Child expressing suicidal thoughts

Urgent but Not Immediate (Use Crisis Hotlines):

- Feeling overwhelmed and unable to cope
- Constant thoughts of being a terrible parent
- Family relationships completely deteriorated
- Isolation and hopelessness about change
- Panic attacks related to perfectionist failures

Professional Support Needed (Schedule Appointment):

- OCPD patterns consistently interfering with daily life
- Children showing signs of anxiety or depression
- Unable to implement changes despite multiple attempts
- Partner or family expressing serious concerns
- Desire for structured support and guidance

Creating Your Personal Crisis Plan:

My Warning Signs:

1. _____

2. _____

3. _____

My Support People:

- Primary contact: _____ Phone: _____

- Secondary contact: _____ Phone: _____

- Therapist: _____ Phone: _____

- Doctor: _____ Phone: _____

My Coping Strategies:

1. _____
2. _____
3. _____

Safe People for My Children:

- Contact 1: _____ Phone: _____

- Contact 2: _____ Phone: _____

My Commitment Statement: *"When I'm in crisis, I commit to:"*

- Reaching out for help before making permanent decisions

- Using my support network

- Following my crisis plan

- Remembering that feelings are temporary

- Prioritizing safety for myself and my family

Appendix D: Family Agreements and Contracts

Moving from OCPD's rigid rule-making to collaborative family agreements requires new approaches to setting boundaries and expectations. These templates help create structure that supports rather than suffocates family members.

Sample Family Flexibility Agreement

This agreement helps OCPD families establish guidelines for practicing flexibility while maintaining necessary structure. It's designed to be revisited and revised regularly as the family grows and changes.

Our Family Flexibility Agreement

Date Created: _____

Family Members: _____

Next Review Date: _____

Our Family's Commitment to Flexibility

We, the _____ family, agree that flexibility and adaptability strengthen our relationships and help each family member grow. We recognize that perfection is not the goal - connection, growth, and mutual respect are.

Core Principles We Agree To:

1. **Mistakes Are Learning Opportunities**

    o   We will respond to mistakes with curiosity rather than criticism

    o   We will focus on problem-solving rather than blame

- o We will celebrate effort and progress over perfect outcomes
- o We will share our own mistakes to model that everyone is learning

2. **Individual Differences Are Valued**

- o We acknowledge that family members have different strengths, interests, and ways of doing things
- o We will not require everyone to approach tasks the same way
- o We will celebrate unique perspectives and contributions
- o We will avoid comparisons between family members

3. **Flexibility Within Structure**

- o We will maintain routines that support our family's wellbeing
- o We will allow variations within routines when circumstances require it
- o We will discuss and adjust expectations when they're not working
- o We will prioritize relationships over rigid adherence to rules

4. **Open Communication**

- o We will share feelings and concerns respectfully
- o We will listen to understand, not just to respond
- o We will ask for clarification when we don't understand
- o We will address conflicts directly and kindly

Specific Agreements:

Morning Routines:

- Essential elements that always happen:

  _____

- Areas where flexibility is allowed:

  _____

- What to do when running late:

  _____

- How to handle morning conflicts:

  _____

Homework and School:

- Parent's role: _____

- Child's responsibility:

  _____

- When struggling is acceptable:

  _____

- How to ask for help: _____

Household Responsibilities:

- Non-negotiable expectations:

  _____

- Areas for negotiation:

  _____

- Consequences for not meeting agreements:

  _____

- How to request changes:

  _____

Social and Activity Time:

- Balance between structured and free time:

  _____

- Rules about friend visits:

  _____

- Screen time agreements:

  _____

- Family time expectations:

  _____

Conflict Resolution Process:

When disagreements arise, we agree to:

1. **Pause and breathe** before responding in anger
2. **State the problem** from each person's perspective
3. **Listen** to understand each viewpoint
4. **Brainstorm solutions** together
5. **Choose an approach** to try
6. **Evaluate** how it's working after trying it

Parent's Specific Commitments:

As the parent(s), I/we commit to:

- Catching myself when perfectionist urges arise
- Taking breaks when I feel overwhelmed rather than taking it out on the family
- Apologizing when I respond harshly or unfairly
- Asking for the family's input on rules and expectations
- Celebrating progress and effort, not just perfect outcomes
- Modeling flexibility and adaptability

- Seeking support when I'm struggling with OCPD patterns

Children's Specific Commitments:

Each child agrees to:

- Communicating needs and concerns respectfully

- Taking responsibility for age-appropriate tasks

- Being patient when parents are learning new ways of responding

- Contributing to family problem-solving discussions

- Showing appreciation for family efforts to be more flexible

Special Circumstances:

High-Stress Times (illness, major transitions, etc.):

- Lower expectations and increase support

- Focus on essentials only

- Extra patience and grace for everyone

- Simplified routines and increased flexibility

When Someone Is Struggling:

- Offer support without taking over

- Adjust expectations temporarily

- Focus on emotional connection over task completion

- Seek outside help if needed

Review and Revision Process:

We will review this agreement:

- Monthly during family meetings

- Whenever someone requests a change

- After major life transitions

- When agreements aren't working

Signature Section:

By signing below, each family member commits to working toward these agreements while recognizing that none of us will be perfect:

Parent 1: _____ Date: _____

Parent 2: _____ Date: _____

Child 1: _____ Date: _____

Child 2: _____ Date: _____

Child 3: _____ Date: _____

Screen Time Collaborative Contract

Screen time battles are common in OCPD families, where parents often want complete control while children need age-appropriate autonomy. This contract creates collaborative guidelines.

Family Screen Time Agreement

Effective Date: _____ Review Date: _____ Family Members Involved: _____

Our Screen Time Philosophy:

We believe technology should enhance our lives and relationships, not replace them. We want to use screens intentionally while maintaining balance with other activities, family time, sleep, and physical activity.

Collaborative Decision-Making Process:

This agreement was created through:

- Family discussion about everyone's needs and concerns

- Research about healthy screen time guidelines for each age

- Input from each family member about their preferences
- Agreement on trial periods and regular reviews

Daily Screen Time Allowances:

These were agreed upon based on age, family schedule, and individual needs:

Child 1 (Name: _____ Age: _____):

- School days: _____ hours
- Weekend/holidays: _____ hours
- Special circumstances:

  _____

Child 2 (Name: _____ Age: _____):

- School days: _____ hours
- Weekend/holidays: _____ hours
- Special circumstances:

  _____

Screen-Free Times and Zones:

We all agree that screens will not be used:

- During family meals
- In bedrooms after _____ PM
- During homework time (except for assignments)
- During family activities or conversations
- First _____ minutes after coming home
- Last _____ minutes before bed

Screen-Free Zones:

- Dining room/kitchen during meals
- Family car (except long trips over _____ hours)
- Other   agreed-upon   spaces: _____

Types of Screen Content:

Always Acceptable:

- Educational content related to school or interests
- Creative applications (art, music, coding)
- Video calls with family and friends
- Physical activity apps or videos

Requires Permission:

- New apps or games
- Social media platforms
- Content with mature ratings
- In-app purchases
- Online interactions with strangers

Not Allowed:

- Content with violence/inappropriate material for age
- Apps or games that promote addictive behaviors
- Cyberbullying or mean online behavior
- Sharing personal information online

Earning Extra Screen Time:

Screen time can be extended by:

- Completing responsibilities without reminders

- Extra household help
- Physical activity or outdoor time
- Reading or educational activities
- Creative projects or hobbies
- Special family circumstances

Extra time earned this way:

- Maximum additional: _____ minutes per day
- Must be requested and approved in advance
- Doesn't roll over to the next day

When Screen Time Rules Are Broken:

First violation:

- Discussion about what happened and why
- Problem-solving about preventing it next time
- No loss of screen time if child is honest and collaborative

Repeated violations:

- Loss of _____ minutes from next day's allowance
- Additional family discussion about underlying issues
- Possible revision of agreement if rules aren't working

Serious violations (lying, inappropriate content, etc.):

- Loss of screen time for _____ day(s)
- Parent-child conversation about trust and safety
- Possible counseling or outside support if pattern continues

Parent Responsibilities:

As parents, we commit to:

- Modeling healthy screen use ourselves
- Being available for questions about content or online experiences
- Helping problem-solve when screen time limits feel difficult
- Recognizing when limits may need adjustment for special circumstances
- Not using screen time removal as punishment for unrelated behaviors
- Providing engaging alternatives to screen time

Child Responsibilities:

Each child commits to:

- Keeping track of my own screen time honestly
- Stopping screen time when the agreed-upon limit is reached
- Asking permission for new content or apps
- Reporting any uncomfortable or inappropriate online experiences
- Participating in screen-free family activities willingly
- Being honest if I accidentally exceed limits or see inappropriate content

Special Circumstances:

Sick Days:

- Limits may be relaxed for genuine illness
- Must still maintain screen-free meals and sleep schedules
- Educational content encouraged over pure entertainment

Travel Days:

- Extended limits for long car rides or flights
- Family movie time doesn't count against individual limits
- Regular limits resume upon arrival at destination

School Holidays/Summer:

- Slightly extended limits may be negotiated
- Must maintain balance with other activities
- Cannot exceed _____ total hours per day

Friend Visits:

- Host child's screen time limits apply to activities with friends
- Group screen activities (movies, games) don't count against individual time
- Friends must follow our family's content guidelines while visiting

Conflict Resolution:

When disagreements about screen time arise:

1. **Pause** and discuss the specific issue
2. **Listen** to each person's perspective
3. **Review** this agreement together
4. **Problem-solve** adjustments if needed
5. **Try** new approach for agreed-upon time period
6. **Evaluate** if changes are working

Monthly Review Questions:

During our monthly family meetings, we'll discuss:

- Is everyone following the agreement?

- Are the time limits working for each person?

- Are there any new concerns about content or behavior?

- Do any circumstances require adjustments?

- What's working well that we want to continue?

Agreement Signatures:

We agree to follow this contract and to discuss any needed changes as a family:

Parent 1: _____ Date: _____

 Parent 2: _____ Date: _____

Child 1: _____ Date: _____

Child 2: _____ Date: _____

Next review scheduled for: _____

Homework Support Boundaries

OCPD parents often struggle with homework, either taking over completely or becoming frustrated with their child's approach. This template creates clear boundaries and expectations.

Family Homework Support Agreement

Student Name: _____ Grade: _____ School Year: _____ Created Date: _____ Review Date: _____

Our Homework Philosophy:

Homework is the student's responsibility and opportunity to practice and demonstrate learning. Parents provide support and structure, but the work and learning belong to the student. We value effort, progress, and learning from mistakes over perfect completion.

Student's Primary Responsibilities:

- Record assignments accurately in planner/app
- Bring home necessary materials
- Allocate appropriate time for homework completion
- Attempt work independently before asking for help
- Communicate with teachers about difficulties or confusion
- Take ownership of grades and consequences
- Use mistakes as learning opportunities

Parent's Support Role:

What Parents WILL Do:

- Provide a consistent, quiet homework space
- Ensure basic needs are met (snack, water, bathroom break)
- Be available for specific questions when asked
- Help break large projects into manageable steps
- Assist with organization and time management strategies
- Communicate with teachers if patterns of difficulty emerge
- Celebrate effort and progress

What Parents WILL NOT Do:

- Complete assignments for the student
- Correct every mistake before submission
- Stay up late to finish forgotten projects
- Do research or writing that should be the student's work
- Take responsibility for remembering assignments
- Make excuses to teachers for incomplete work

- Redo work to make it "perfect"

Daily Homework Routine:

After School:

- _____ minutes of downtime/snack
- Review planner and organize materials
- Create daily homework plan with time estimates
- Begin work in designated homework space

During Homework Time:

- Student works independently for _____ minutes before asking questions
- Parent checks in every _____ minutes without taking over
- Breaks taken every _____ minutes for _____ minutes
- Student decides when work is complete

Parent Help Guidelines:

When Student Asks for Help:

1. **Ask clarifying questions:** "What part is confusing?" "What have you tried so far?"
2. **Guide thinking:** "What strategy might work here?" "Where could you find that information?"
3. **Provide hints, not answers:** "Try looking at the example" "Remember what we learned about..."
4. **Encourage persistence:** "This is challenging - that's how learning happens"

When NOT to Help:

- Student hasn't attempted the work independently

- Student wants parent to provide answers rather than understanding

- Helping would prevent natural consequences that teach responsibility

- Student is capable but wants shortcuts

- Assignment is assessing what student has learned independently

Difficult Homework Situations:

When Student Says "I Don't Know How":

- Parent response: "What part do you understand? Let's start there."

- Help identify specific confusion rather than taking over

- Guide student to use resources (textbook, notes, teacher handouts)

- Encourage contacting classmates or teacher for clarification

When Student Is Frustrated:

- Acknowledge feelings: "This is really challenging for you"

- Take a 10-minute break if needed

- Help identify what's causing frustration

- Problem-solve strategies together without doing the work

When Work Seems Too Difficult:

- Allow student to attempt independently first

- Help identify what they do know

- Encourage student to communicate with teacher about difficulty

- Focus on effort rather than perfect understanding

Long-Term Projects:

Parent's Role:

- Help create timeline with student input
- Check in on progress at agreed intervals
- Support with organization and planning strategies
- Resist urge to take over when time gets short

Student's Role:

- Break project into smaller tasks
- Work consistently rather than waiting until last minute
- Communicate with parent about progress and challenges
- Accept natural consequences of poor planning

Quality Standards:

"Good Enough" Homework:

- Student's own work and understanding
- Honest effort has been made
- Instructions have been followed
- Work is legible and complete
- Student can explain what they did

When to Redo Work:

- Student recognizes significant errors and wants to improve
- Teacher requests revision
- Work doesn't reflect student's actual capability

- Student didn't follow instructions

Communication with Teachers:

Parent Will Contact Teacher When:

- Student consistently struggles despite good effort
- Homework is taking excessive time (more than _____ minutes per night)
- Student reports confusion about expectations
- Pattern of missing assignments despite organizational support

Student Will Contact Teacher When:

- Confused about assignment requirements
- Unable to complete work despite honest effort
- Need extension due to illness or family circumstances
- Want extra help or clarification

Consequences and Natural Learning:

For Forgotten Assignments:

- Student experiences natural school consequences
- Parent doesn't rescue with emergency deliveries
- Family discusses organization strategies
- Student problem-solves prevention methods

For Incomplete Work:

- Student explains to teacher and accepts consequences
- Parent doesn't make excuses or blame teacher
- Family reviews time management and priorities
- Focus on learning from experience

Technology and Homework:

Acceptable Technology Use:

- Research for assignments
- Educational apps or programs assigned by teacher
- Word processing for typed assignments
- Communication with classmates about assignments

Technology Boundaries:

- No social media or entertainment during homework time
- Parent may monitor internet use for homework purposes
- Gaming/entertainment apps not accessible during homework
- Phone in separate location unless needed for assignment

Emergency Situations:

When Student Is Overwhelmed:

- Take a break and reassess
- Contact teacher if workload seems excessive
- Focus on most important assignments first
- Consider whether student needs additional support

When Parent Is Getting Frustrated:

- Take a parent timeout
- Remember: homework belongs to the student
- Focus on effort rather than perfection
- Seek support from school counselor or family therapist if patterns persist

Monthly Review Questions:

- Is the current system working for everyone?

- Are homework battles decreasing?

- Is student taking more ownership of their work?

- Do time limits need adjustment?

- Are there new challenges to address?

Agreement Signatures:

We commit to following these guidelines and communicating openly about how it's working:

Student: _____ Date: _____ Parent 1:
_____ Date: _____ Parent 2:
_____ Date: _____

Teen Autonomy Agreement Template

The teenage years present the greatest challenge for OCPD parents as their children naturally seek independence. This agreement helps navigate the transition from control to collaboration.

Teen Independence Agreement

Teen Name: _____ Age: _____ Date: _____ Next Review: _____

Purpose of This Agreement:

This contract recognizes that [Teen Name] is developing independence and decision-making skills while parents maintain their responsibility for guidance and safety. We aim to balance increasing freedom with appropriate boundaries and mutual respect.

Core Principles:

1. **Trust is earned and maintained through honest communication**

2. **Freedom increases as responsibility is demonstrated**

3. **Safety is non-negotiable**

4. **Mistakes are learning opportunities, not reasons to remove all privileges**

5. **Both parent and teen voices matter in family decisions**

Current Privileges and Responsibilities:

Social Freedom:

- Friend visits: _____

- Going to friends' houses:
  _____

- Group activities: _____

- Dating/romantic relationships:
  _____

- Social media and communication:
  _____

Transportation:

- Walking/biking boundaries:
  _____

- Public transportation:
  _____

- Rides from friends/friends' parents:
  _____

- Driving privileges (if applicable):
  _____

Academic Autonomy:

- Homework

- management: _____

- Grade expectations: _____
- Communication with teachers:

  _____
- Extracurricular activity choices:

  _____

Personal Choices:

- Clothing and appearance:

  _____
- Room organization and decoration:

  _____
- Personal schedule and time management:

  _____
- Money management and spending:

  _____

Curfew and Check-In Requirements:

School Nights:

- Home by: _____
- Check-in requirements:

  _____
- Study/homework time:

  _____
- Screen time limits: _____

Weekend Nights:

- Home by: _____
- Check-in requirements:

  _____

- Special event exceptions:

  _____

Special Circumstances:

- Late events (concerts, games, etc.):

  _____

- Overnight activities: _____

- Out-of-town trips: _____

Communication Expectations:

Teen Commits To:

- Informing parents of plans, including where, when, who, and what

- Responding to parent texts/calls within _____ minutes

- Being honest about activities and any problems that arise

- Coming to parents with questions or concerns

- Giving advance notice of plan changes when possible

Parents Commit To:

- Listening without immediate judgment

- Asking questions to understand, not interrogate

- Respecting teen's privacy within safety boundaries

- Not using shared information against teen unless safety is concerned

- Responding calmly to problems and mistakes

Decision-Making Process:

Decisions Teen Makes Independently:

- Daily clothing choices

- Friendship decisions (unless safety concerns)
- Extracurricular participation
- Personal room organization
- How to spend personal money
- Study methods and homework approach

Decisions That Require Discussion:

- Social activities involving new people or places
- Significant purchases
- Changes to academic course load
- Dating relationships
- Activities that conflict with family commitments

Decisions Parents Make:

- Major safety rules
- Family vacation plans
- Medical and dental care
- Legal and financial matters
- Household rules that affect everyone

Consequences and Problem-Solving:

When Agreements Are Followed:

- Increased privileges and freedoms
- More input in family decisions
- Recognition and appreciation
- Expanded boundaries

When Minor Rules Are Broken:

- Discussion about what happened and why
- Problem-solving about prevention
- Possible temporary restriction of related privilege
- Focus on learning and trust rebuilding

When Major Rules Are Broken (safety, honesty, legal issues):

- Immediate loss of privileges related to the violation
- Family meeting to discuss underlying issues
- Clear plan for earning back trust and privileges
- Possible involvement of outside support

Building Independence Gradually:

Current Goal Areas:

1. _____

Goal: Increase responsibility/independence Steps to achieve:
_____
_____ *Timeline:*
How we'll measure success:
_____

2. _____

Goal: Increase responsibility/independence Steps to achieve:
_____
_____ *Timeline:*
How we'll measure success:
_____

3. _____

Goal: Increase responsibility/independence Steps to achieve:

_____

Timeline:

_____ *How we'll measure success:*

_____

Future Privileges to Work Toward:

Short-term (next 3 months):

- Later curfew on weekends
- More flexible check-in requirements
- Increased spending money/budget control
- Greater input in family decisions

Medium-term (6 months to 1 year):

- Overnight trips with friends
- Part-time job (if desired)
- Driving privileges or expanded transportation
- More autonomy in academic choices

Long-term (preparing for adulthood):

- College preparation decisions
- Career exploration independence
- Financial management skills
- Complete autonomy in personal choices

Safety Non-Negotiables:

These rules cannot be negotiated and violations result in immediate consequences:

- No illegal substance use
- No getting in cars with impaired drivers

- Always have a safe way to get home

- No illegal activities

- Respect for others' boundaries and consent

- Honest communication about emergencies or safety concerns

Family Relationship Commitments:

Teen Agrees To:

- Participate in family meals/activities _____ times per week

- Show respect for all family members

- Contribute to household responsibilities

- Communicate needs and concerns respectfully

- Be patient as parents learn to let go gradually

Parents Agree To:

- Respect teen's growing need for independence

- Listen to teen's perspective before making decisions

- Acknowledge when we're being overly controlling

- Apologize when we respond poorly to teen's normal development

- Support teen's individual interests and goals

Money and Financial Responsibility:

Current Allowance/Earnings: $_____ per _____

What This Covers: _____
Additional Money Available For:

_____

What Teen Pays For Independently:

_____

Financial Independence Plan:

- Age ___: Begin managing clothing budget
- Age ___: Take over entertainment/social expenses
- Age ___: Manage all personal expenses
- Age ___: Begin contributing to family expenses (if working)

Technology and Privacy:

Teen's Privacy Rights:

- Personal diary, journal, or creative writing
- Private conversations with friends (unless safety concerns)
- Personal social media accounts (with safety monitoring)
- Personal space in bedroom
- Some independence in social media posting

Parent's Safety Responsibilities:

- Monitoring for cyberbullying or predatory behavior
- Ensuring technology use doesn't interfere with sleep, school, or family
- Access to accounts/devices if safety concerns arise
- Teaching digital citizenship and online safety

Conflict Resolution:

When We Disagree:

1. **Both parties take time to calm down** if emotions are high
2. **Each person states their perspective** without interruption
3. **We identify the underlying needs** (safety, independence, respect, etc.)

4. **We brainstorm solutions** that address both perspectives

5. **We agree on a trial period** for new approaches

6. **We evaluate** how it's working and adjust if needed

If We Can't Resolve Issues:

- Request mediation from neutral family member or friend
- Seek family counseling support
- Use school counselor or teen support resources
- Remember that perfect agreement isn't always necessary

Emergency Procedures:

If Teen Is in Trouble:

- Call parents immediately, no matter what time
- Parents will prioritize safety over consequences
- Discussion about choices happens after everyone is safe
- Parents will provide transportation without lecturing in the moment

If Teen Feels Unsafe:

- Call parents, police, or other trusted adult immediately
- Use code word system for discreet help requests
- Always have backup transportation plan
- Trust instincts about unsafe situations

Parent Emergency Contacts:

- Parent 1 Cell: _____
- Parent 2 Cell: _____
- Other trusted adult: _____

- Emergency services: 911

Regular Review Process:

Monthly Check-ins:

- What's working well in our agreement?

- What needs adjustment?

- Are there new privileges to consider?

- Any new concerns to address?

Quarterly Formal Review:

- Assess progress toward independence goals

- Update privileges and responsibilities

- Revise timeline for future freedoms

- Celebrate growth and positive changes

Special Circumstances:

Academic Struggles:

- Increased check-ins with teachers and parents

- Possible temporary restriction of social activities

- Additional support resources

- Focus on effort rather than perfect grades

Social Difficulties:

- Parent availability for consultation

- Respect for teen's social learning process

- Intervention only if safety or wellbeing threatened

- Support in developing healthy relationship skills

Mental Health Concerns:

- Immediate professional support
- Possible temporary adjustment of expectations
- Family therapy to support everyone
- Continued love and acceptance during difficult times

Substance Abuse Concerns:

- Immediate honest conversation
- Professional assessment and support
- Natural consequences while maintaining relationship
- Focus on health and safety over punishment

Legal Issues:

- Parents will provide support while allowing natural consequences
- Legal counsel if needed
- Focus on learning and making amends
- Family will work together toward positive change

Preparing for Post-High School Transition:

College/Career Preparation:

- Teen takes lead on research and applications
- Parents provide guidance and support when requested
- Financial planning discussions
- Independence skill development

Moving Toward Full Autonomy:

- Gradual transfer of all responsibilities

- Continued family relationship and support

- Respect for teen's adult choices and values

- Celebration of successful launch into independence

Agreement Acknowledgment:

By signing below, we commit to working together toward healthy independence while maintaining our loving family relationship:

Teen: I understand that increased freedom comes with increased responsibility. I commit to honest communication, safe choices, and gradual demonstration of adult decision-making skills.

Teen Signature: _____ Date: _____

Parents: We commit to supporting our teen's healthy development toward independence while maintaining necessary safety boundaries. We will work to respond with guidance rather than control and trust rather than fear.

Parent 1 Signature: _____ Date: _____
Parent 2 Signature: _____ Date: _____

This agreement will be reviewed and revised on: _____

Appendix E: Additional Resources

The journey of healing OCPD patterns and creating healthier family dynamics requires ongoing learning and support. These resources provide continued education, practical tools, and community connections for long-term success.

Recommended Books for Further Reading

Core OCPD and Perfectionism Resources:

"Too Perfect: When Being in Control Gets Out of Control" by Allan Mallinger and Jeanette DeWyze This foundational book explains OCPD traits and their impact on relationships. The authors provide practical strategies for developing flexibility while maintaining high standards. Particularly helpful for understanding the difference between healthy striving and destructive perfectionism.

"The Gifts of Imperfection" by Brené Brown Brown's research on vulnerability and shame provides crucial insights for OCPD parents. Her work on wholehearted living offers practical strategies for embracing imperfection while maintaining values and connection.

"Mindset: The New Psychology of Success" by Carol Dweck Essential reading for understanding how fixed mindset thinking perpetuates OCPD patterns. Dweck's research provides concrete strategies for fostering growth mindset in both parents and children.

"Radical Acceptance" by Tara Brach This book combines Buddhist psychology with Western therapy approaches to help readers accept themselves and their circumstances without giving up efforts to grow and change. Particularly valuable for OCPD parents struggling with self-compassion.

Parenting-Specific Resources:

"The Self-Driven Child" by William Stixrud and Ned Johnson Neuroscientist and academic tutor collaborate to show how children develop motivation and resilience when given appropriate autonomy. Challenges perfectionist parenting approaches with research-based alternatives.

"Hunt, Gather, Parent" by Michaeleen Doucleff Anthropologist examines parenting practices across cultures, revealing how many Western approaches increase anxiety and reduce cooperation. Provides practical alternatives to controlling parenting.

"The Explosive Child" by Ross Greene While focused on challenging behavior, Greene's collaborative problem-solving approach is particularly valuable for OCPD parents who tend to impose solutions rather than working with their children.

"Unconditional Parenting" by Alfie Kohn Challenges reward-and-punishment approaches that appeal to OCPD parents. Offers alternatives based on connection and intrinsic motivation.

"The Danish Way" by Jessica Alexander and Iben Sandahl Explores why Danish children consistently rank among the happiest in the world. Emphasizes authenticity, reframing, empathy, and play - all areas where OCPD parents often struggle.

Therapeutic Approach Books:

"Radically Open Dialectical Behavior Therapy" by Thomas Lynch The definitive guide to RO-DBT, specifically designed for overcontrolled personalities. Provides detailed strategies for increasing flexibility, emotional expression, and social connection.

"The Happiness Trap" by Russ Harris Clear, practical introduction to Acceptance and Commitment Therapy (ACT). Helps readers identify when control strategies become problematic and develop psychological flexibility.

"Mind Over Mood" by Dennis Greenberger and Christine Padesky Comprehensive cognitive behavioral therapy workbook. Helps readers identify and change thought patterns that maintain perfectionist behaviors.

"The Mindful Way Through Depression" by Mark Williams, John Teasdale, Zindel Segal, and Jon Kabat-Zinn While focused on depression, this book's mindfulness-based approach is particularly helpful for OCPD patterns of rumination and self-criticism.

Child Development and Understanding:

"The Whole-Brain Child" by Daniel Siegel and Tina Payne Bryson Neuroscience-based guide to understanding children's emotional development. Helps parents respond to behaviors with understanding rather than control.

"Your Child's Growing Mind" by Jane Healy Developmental psychologist explains how children's brains develop and what this means for learning and behavior. Helps parents adjust expectations appropriately.

"The Power of Showing Up" by Daniel Siegel and Tina Payne Bryson Focuses on four building blocks of secure attachment. Particularly valuable for OCPD parents who struggle with emotional availability.

For Teens and Young Adults:

"The Anxiety and Worry Workbook" by David Clark and Aaron Beck Cognitive behavioral strategies specifically for young people dealing with perfectionism and anxiety.

"Mind Over Mood for Adolescents" by Dennis Greenberger, Christine Padesky, and Aaron Beck Teen-friendly version of CBT strategies for managing perfectionist thinking and emotional regulation.

Apps for Mindfulness and Emotion Regulation

Mindfulness and Meditation Apps:

Headspace

- Beginner-friendly guided meditations
- Specific programs for parents and stress management
- Short sessions that fit busy schedules
- Kids' content for family mindfulness practice
- Sleep stories and focus music

Calm

- Daily meditations and mindful moments
- Anxiety and stress-specific programs
- Sleep stories and relaxation content
- Masterclasses on mindfulness topics
- Nature sounds for background focus

Insight Timer

- Largest free library of guided meditations
- Live meditation sessions and talks
- Timer for silent meditation practice
- Community features and discussion groups
- Courses from meditation teachers worldwide

Ten Percent Happier

- Practical approach to meditation for skeptics
- Courses specifically for parents and busy professionals
- Real-world application focus
- Expert teachers and varied approaches
- Sleep content and SOS sessions for acute stress

Emotion Regulation and DBT Skills:

DBT Coach

- Digital version of DBT diary card
- Distress tolerance and emotion regulation skills
- Crisis survival strategies
- Progress tracking and skill practice reminders
- Developed by mental health professionals

MindShift

- Anxiety management app based on CBT principles
- Exposure therapy tools for perfectionist fears
- Mood and anxiety tracking
- Relaxation exercises and coping strategies
- Developed by anxiety specialists

Sanvello (formerly Pacifica)

- Mood tracking and pattern identification
- CBT-based tools for anxious thoughts
- Progress tracking and goal setting
- Community support features
- Audio lessons and coping techniques

PTSD Coach

- While designed for PTSD, many tools apply to OCPD
- Grounding techniques and flashback management
- Symptom tracking and coping strategies

- Crisis contact information storage
- Self-assessment tools

Parenting and Family Communication:

Cozi

- Family calendar and schedule coordination
- Reduces anxiety about forgetting appointments
- Shared shopping lists and meal planning
- Photo sharing and family journaling
- Multiple family member access

ChoreMonster

- Gamifies household responsibilities
- Reduces battles over chores and expectations
- Rewards effort rather than perfection
- Family collaboration tools
- Customizable for different ages

Family Organizer

- Centralizes family schedules and information
- Reduces control battles through transparency
- Shared goal setting and tracking
- Emergency contact information
- Family communication hub

Sleep and Relaxation:

Sleep Cycle

- Natural wake-up during light sleep phases
- Sleep quality tracking without obsessing
- Relaxing sleep aid sounds
- Trend analysis for sleep patterns
- Gentle wake-up options

Noisli

- Background sounds for focus and relaxation
- Customizable sound combinations
- Timer for work and break sessions
- Helps with sensory regulation
- No social features to reduce distraction

Websites and Online Resources

OCPD-Specific Resources:

International OCD Foundation (iocdf.org)

- OCPD section with articles and research
- Therapist directory with OCPD specialists
- Annual conference with OCPD presentations
- Support group information and resources
- Educational webinars and workshops

OCPD Foundation (ocpdfoundation.org)

- Dedicated to OCPD awareness and support
- Research updates and treatment information
- Personal stories and recovery experiences

- Resource lists and treatment provider directory
- Advocacy for OCPD recognition and understanding

Psych Central OCPD Section

- Articles on OCPD symptoms and treatment
- Self-assessment tools and questionnaires
- Treatment option comparisons
- Personal stories and expert interviews
- Regular updates on OCPD research

General Mental Health and Therapy:

Psychology Today (psychologytoday.com)

- Comprehensive therapist directory
- Filter by specialty, location, and insurance
- Articles on parenting and mental health
- Blog posts by mental health professionals
- Treatment center and support group listings

National Alliance on Mental Illness (nami.org)

- Educational resources about personality disorders
- Family support programs and groups
- Crisis intervention resources
- Advocacy and awareness information
- Local chapter connections

Mental Health America (mhanational.org)

- Mental health screening tools

- Educational materials about various conditions
- Advocacy and policy information
- Local resource connections
- Crisis support information

Parenting and Child Development:

Zero to Three (zerotothree.org)

- Early childhood development information
- Parenting strategies based on research
- Social-emotional development resources
- Policy and advocacy information
- Professional development for educators

Child Mind Institute (childmind.org)

- Evidence-based parenting information
- Mental health resources for children and teens
- Symptom checker and assessment tools
- Treatment provider directory
- Educational articles and guides

Understood.org

- Learning and attention issues resource
- Accommodations and support strategies
- School advocacy information
- Community support and connections
- Expert advice and guidance

Mindfulness and Stress Reduction:

Mindful.org

- Articles on mindful parenting
- Research on mindfulness benefits
- Guided practices and exercises
- Expert interviews and advice
- Course and retreat information

Center for Mindful Self-Compassion

- Self-compassion exercises and practices
- Research on self-compassion benefits
- Teacher training and certification information
- Guided meditations and resources
- Workshop and retreat listings

Crisis and Emergency Support:

Crisis Text Line (crisistextline.org)

- 24/7 crisis support via text
- Training information for volunteers
- Research and data about mental health crises
- Resources for specific populations
- Safety planning tools

National Suicide Prevention Lifeline

- 24/7 crisis support by phone
- Chat and text options available

- Resources for loss survivors
- Warning signs and prevention information
- Professional and community resources

Professional Organizations and Support Groups

Professional Mental Health Organizations:

American Psychological Association (APA)

- Division 12: Clinical Psychology
- Division 53: Society of Clinical Child and Adolescent Psychology
- Continuing education opportunities
- Research publications and journals
- Professional development resources

Association for Behavioral and Cognitive Therapies (ABCT)

- CBT and evidence-based treatment focus
- Therapist directory and certification
- Annual convention and workshops
- Professional training opportunities
- Research and practice guidelines

International Association for RO-DBT

- Radically Open DBT training and certification
- Research and treatment development
- Provider directory and resources
- Annual conference and workshops
- Community of practice support

Support Group Organizations:

SMART Recovery

- Self-management and recovery training
- Online meetings and support groups
- Family and friends programs
- Cognitive behavioral approach
- Local meeting directories

Al-Anon Family Groups

- Support for families affected by addiction
- Many OCPD patterns overlap with codependency
- Local meetings and online support
- Literature and educational materials
- Sponsorship and mentorship programs

NAMI Family Support Groups

- Local support groups for mental health families
- Education programs for family members
- Peer-led support and understanding
- Advocacy training and opportunities
- Crisis support and resources

Online Support Communities:

Reddit Communities

- r/OCPD: Discussion and support for OCPD individuals
- r/raisedbynarcissists: Often relevant for OCPD family dynamics

- r/Parenting: General parenting support and advice

- r/mindfulness: Mindfulness practice and discussion

- Various mental health and therapy communities

Facebook Support Groups

- OCPD Support and Awareness Groups

- Perfectionist Parents Support

- Mindful Parenting Communities

- RO-DBT Practice Groups

- Local parenting support groups

7 Cups (7cups.com)

- Free emotional support through trained listeners

- Professional counseling options

- Group support rooms and discussions

- Self-help resources and guides

- Crisis support and intervention

Creating Local Support:

Starting an OCPD Parent Support Group:

1. **Partner with local mental health professionals**

   o Contact therapists who treat OCPD

   o Ask about facilitation or referral support

   o Ensure group has professional backup for crises

2. **Find meeting space**

   o Libraries often provide free meeting rooms

- o Churches and community centers may donate space
- o Mental health centers sometimes host groups
- o Consider online meetings to start

3. **Establish group guidelines**
   - o Confidentiality agreements
   - o No advice-giving unless requested
   - o Focus on personal experience sharing
   - o Regular meeting schedule and format

4. **Promote the group**
   - o Contact local therapists and treatment centers
   - o Post in community mental health resources
   - o Use social media and community boards
   - o Word of mouth through existing participants

Support Group Meeting Structure:

Opening (10 minutes):

- Welcome and introductions
- Review guidelines and confidentiality
- Brief check-in on current challenges

Main Discussion (40 minutes):

- Topic-based discussion or open sharing
- Focus on personal experiences, not advice
- Facilitate balanced participation
- Address group dynamics as needed

Closing (10 minutes):

- Summarize insights and commitments
- Plan next meeting topic
- Exchange contact information if desired
- Brief mindfulness or grounding exercise

Ongoing Professional Development:

Continuing Education for Helping Professionals:

- OCPD-specific training workshops
- DBT and RO-DBT certification programs
- Family therapy and systems approaches
- Mindfulness-based intervention training
- Trauma-informed care for perfectionist families

Self-Education for Parents:

- Annual reading goals in relevant areas
- Podcast subscriptions on mental health and parenting
- Webinar attendance and virtual conferences
- Online course completion in therapeutic approaches
- Regular consultation with mental health professionals

Reference

- American Psychiatric Association. (2022). *Diagnostic and statistical manual of mental disorders* (5th ed., text rev.; DSM-5-TR). American Psychiatric Publishing.

- Association for Behavioral and Cognitive Therapies. (n.d.). *Radically Open Dialectical Behavior Therapy (RO-DBT)* [Fact sheet].

- Bandura, A. (2001). *Social cognitive theory: An agentic perspective. Annual Review of Psychology, 52,* 1–26.

- Center on the Developing Child at Harvard University. (n.d.). *A guide to resilience: Building young children's capacity for resilience.*

- Child Mind Institute. (n.d.). *How can we help kids with emotional self-regulation?*

- Counseling Center Group. (n.d.). *Acceptance and Commitment Therapy for OCD.*

- Creating a Family. (n.d.). *Parenting a challenging child: A collaborative approach.*

- Curran, T., & Hill, A. P. (2019). Perfectionism is increasing over time: A meta-analysis of birth cohort differences from 1989 to 2016. *Psychological Bulletin, 145*(4), 410–429.

- Flett, G. L., Hewitt, P. L., Oliver, J. M., & Macdonald, S. (2002). Perfectionism in children and their parents: A developmental analysis. In G. L. Flett & P. L. Hewitt (Eds.), *Perfectionism: Theory, research, and treatment* (pp. 89–132). American Psychological Association.

375

- Gilbert, K., Hall, K., & Codd, R. T. (2020). Radically Open Dialectical Behavior Therapy: Social signaling, transdiagnostic utility and current evidence. *Psychology Research and Behavior Management, 13,* 19–28.

- Grant, K. W. (2023, August 20). Obsessive-Compulsive Disorder Unpacked: A Quick Guide. Retrieved from https://www.kevinwgrant.com/blog/item/obsessive-compulsive-disorder-a-quick-guide

- Grant, B. F., Chou, S. P., Goldstein, R. B., Huang, B., Stinson, F. S., Saha, T. D., … Ruan, W. J. (2008). Prevalence, correlates, disability, and comorbidity of DSM-IV borderline personality disorder: Results from the Wave 2 National Epidemiologic Survey on Alcohol and Related Conditions. *Journal of Clinical Psychiatry, 69*(4), 533–545.

- HealthyChildren.org (American Academy of Pediatrics). (n.d.). *Perfectionism: How to help your child avoid the pitfalls.*

- Hewitt, P. L., & Flett, G. L. (1991). Perfectionism in the self and social contexts: Conceptualization, assessment, and association with psychopathology. *Journal of Personality and Social Psychology, 60*(3), 456–470.

- Illinois Early Learning Project. (n.d.). *Self-regulation: Emotional regulation.*

- International OCPD Foundation. (2023). *Self-compassion: The evidence-based antidote to maladaptive perfectionism.*

- Lerner Child Development. (n.d.). *Highly sensitive children: Perfectionists.*

- Masten, A. S. (2001). *Ordinary magic: Resilience processes in development. American Psychologist, 56*(3), 227–238.

- Marincowitz, C., Mahomedy, Z., Ndlovu, R., & Fineberg, N. A. (2022). The neurobiology of obsessive–compulsive personality disorder: A systematic review. *CNS Spectrums, 27*(6), 781–797.

- NAMI (National Alliance on Mental Illness). (n.d.). *How can I get help/support for obsessive-compulsive disorder (OCD)?*

- Pinto, A., Teller, J. L., & Wheaton, M. G. (2022). Obsessive–compulsive personality disorder: A review of symptomatology, impact on functioning, and treatment. *Focus, 20*(4), 389–396.

- PositivePsychology.com. (n.d.). *How to overcome perfectionism: 15 worksheets and resources.*

- Raising Children Network. (n.d.). *Building resilience in children 3–8 years.*

- Rodgers, A. B., Morgan, C. P., Bronson, S. L., Revello, S., & Bale, T. L. (2013). *Paternal stress exposure alters sperm microRNA content and reprograms offspring HPA stress axis regulation. Journal of Neuroscience, 33*(21), 9003–9012.

- Rizvi, A., & colleagues. (2023). Obsessive–Compulsive Personality Disorder. In *StatPearls*. StatPearls Publishing.

- The Healthy Compulsive Project (Trosclair, G.). (2018). *A review of RO-DBT (Radically Open Dialectical Behavior Therapy).*

- Tara M Chaplin, Turpyn CC, Fischer S, Martelli AM, Ross CE, Leichtweis RN, Miller AB, Sinha R. Parenting-focused mindfulness intervention reduces stress and improves parenting in highly-stressed mothers of adolescents. *Mindfulness (N Y).* 2021 Feb;12(2):450-462. doi: 10.1007/s12671-018-1026-9. Epub 2018 Sep 21

- The Recovery Village. (n.d.). *Obsessive–compulsive personality disorder (OCPD) treatment options.*

- Torgersen, S., Czajkowski, N., Jacobson, K., Reichborn-Kjennerud, T., Røysamb, E., Neale, M. C., & Kendler, K. S. (2008). *Dimensional representations of DSM-IV cluster B personality disorders in a population-based sample of Norwegian twins: A multivariate study. Psychological Medicine, 38*(11), 1617–1625.

- Van Grootheest, D. S., Cath, D. C., Beekman, A. T., & Boomsma, D. I. (2007). Genetic and environmental influences on obsessive–compulsive symptoms in adults: A population-based twin-family study. *Psychological Medicine, 37*(11), 1635–1644.

- Washington University School of Medicine in St. Louis. (2020). *Perfectionism in young children may indicate OCD risk.*

- WebMD. (n.d.). *Emotional development in preschoolers: From age 3 to 5.*

www.ingramcontent.com/pod-product-compliance
Lightning Source LLC
Chambersburg PA
CBHW062358090426
42740CB00010B/1327